FOOD ALLERGY ADVOCACY

FOOD ALLERGY ADVOCACY

PARENTING AND THE POLITICS OF CARE

Danya Glabau

University of Minnesota Press
Minneapolis
London

The University of Minnesota Press gratefully acknowledges the generous assistance provided for the publication of this book by the Margaret S. Harding Memorial Endowment, honoring the first director of the University of Minnesota Press.

Portions of chapter 1 are adapted from "The Moral Life of Epinephrine in the United States," *Medicine Anthropology Theory* 3, no. 3 (2016), https://doi.org/10.17157/mat .3.3.301. Portions of chapter 3 are adapted from "Food Allergies and the Hygienic Sublime," *Catalyst: Feminism, Theory, Technoscience* 5, no. 2 (2019): 1–26, https://doi .org/10.28968/cftt.v5i2.32070.

Published by the University of Minnesota Press
111 Third Avenue South, Suite 290
Minneapolis, MN 55401-2520
http://www.upress.umn.edu

ISBN 978-1-5179-1055-6 (hc)
ISBN 978-1-5179-1056-3 (pb)
Library of Congress record available at https://lccn.loc.gov/2021061581.

Printed in the United States of America on acid-free paper

The University of Minnesota is an equal-opportunity educator and employer.

31 30 29 28 27 26 25 24 23 22   10 9 8 7 6 5 4 3 2 1

CONTENTS

PREFACE

I am finishing this book in April 2021 against the backdrop of the second spring of the Covid-19 pandemic. I also stand at the brink of my own entry into motherhood, and much of this book is about the politics of mothers and motherhood. The pandemic death toll in the United States increases by nearly one thousand lives per day and nears six hundred thousand in total. The crocuses and daffodils are blooming again in my Brooklyn neighborhood. This year, they do not bring hope or excitement because I am thirteen months into working at home and going out in fear. My fear is less than this time last year, but so is my hope that this whole pandemic situation will blow over soon. I have had only one casual, in-person conversation with someone other than my partner and mother since returning to New York six months ago after briefly living with my in-laws for a change of pace. When my partner and I returned, cases were rapidly rising in the Midwest; this week, they are rapidly rising again in Michigan and Minnesota. As my stomach grows larger, friends and family members jostle to get in line to meet the future baby. I tell them, over and over, that I hope for August but more likely around Thanksgiving, if we're lucky.

Isolation, a search for safety, turning inward to rely only on closest family for sociality and care, the impulse to protect one's children—

the pandemic has generalized many of the conditions of life with food allergies that this book documents. My experience of this past year is just one of hundreds of millions. For those who could previously ignore these sorts of things, it brings into relief the contradictions that inhere in life under capitalism: the constant push and pull between life and loss, the forward motion that provides little time to heal or grieve, and the felt—and for all but the richest individuals, the actual—reality that families and individuals are on their own when illness strikes while living in a country with some of the most advanced health care facilities in the world. Individuals alone cannot protect themselves from the disease. For an individual to be protected, a person's neighbors and colleagues must wear their own masks on the street, in the grocery store, and all day at work. Employers and business owners must invest in enhanced ventilation, and many must make do with temporarily lower profit margins because fewer people ought to be packed into shared breathing spaces. Self-reliance is out the window in a country where health is typically treated as a technical and moral achievement of discrete individuals. Members of communities must care for each other or the death count will continue to rise.

The pandemic has also sharpened the political stakes of caring for family during these unusual times. While the idea that care is political is not new in feminist thought, it has suddenly become mainstream common sense during the Covid-19 pandemic. The United States has been forced to confront its inadequate childcare system and the inflexibility of that system in a time of emergency. As a consequence, opening schools is a hot-button political topic. Wealthy, largely white liberals face off against teachers unions. In New York City, the teachers union represents a large number of working-class Black women who are resisting blanket reopenings simply to protect their own households and communities. Their households are also more likely to include disabled and elderly members than those of white families who are clamoring to reopen, because of racism in health care, employment, workplace safety, and housing policy. Still, opening schools over the safety objections of educators is positioned by the upper middle class as a way to save poor Black and brown children with no other options for care when their families must go to work in low-wage jobs with high risk of exposure to the virus. Poorer families would like this too, but they also know what neglect has done to their schools over the decades. In and around New York City, they have little faith that temporary patches like portable air filters will be adequate in schools already flaking toxic lead paint and with no hot water or soap in the bathrooms for basic hand hygiene.

In many ways, then, this moment is ideal for finishing this book. Politicians suddenly care about how public schools organize childcare, for example. Hygiene and food supply chains are on everyone's mind. Conflicts between different forms of biomedical knowledge, and between biomedical and lay experts, play out in public forums like television, newspapers, and social media. I hope the message this book carries about how care is political, and more specifically how the well-being of children is often invoked as a reason for political action that largely reproduces the conditions that created the care crisis in the first place, will find fertile ground. At the same time, it is deeply frustrating as an author and feminist to watch the United States, and other countries like the United Kingdom, Sweden, and Brazil, get care infrastructure in a period of crisis terribly, terribly wrong. While the coincidence of book and crisis may be fortuitous, the gap between what is and what could be in these times is also psychologically distressing.

Editing a book about the politics of care for allergic children as a food allergic adult gestating my own first child in a world that feels marked by ever-present threats of illness has shifted my relationship to this material. It has not changed my argument or strategy for writing the book. It has, however, changed how passionately I identify with the mothers and other family members of allergic people I encountered in the course of my research. I sympathize deeper than ever with the desire to protect one's children, to give them a good start in life, to replicate the best parts of my own childhood, and to improve on those areas where I felt my own parents fell short. Having clawed my way up from poverty to the professorate in an unlikely fashion, I both experience and resent my own desire to provide for my child's upward social mobility. However, as a full-time education worker, I also identify with the rights of teachers, school nurses, and other care workers to refuse more work, or riskier work, without training, compensation, or increased staffing. Now that I am a member of both camps, I imagine better futures for health activism. In line with both disability justice advocates and with the handful of nurses unions that have gone on strike during the Covid-19 pandemic, I see the struggle with and for care workers to be linked with the struggle for better care for the young, old, ill, and disabled.

This book is not straightforwardly about that solidaristic future. Because it is an ethnography, this book is about the real state of the world, about what happened in the recent past as documented by my ethnographic data. As a result of my choice of topic and sites, it is about what happens when activism occurs mainly within the frames of benefits, rewards, and political representation that constitute the norms of engagement in existing political systems. This strategy has led to wins that are significant to the people directly involved, as well as to many other people managing the specific condition of food allergy. Provisioning epinephrine auto-injectors in schools and some public spaces provides a potentially lifesaving backup for food allergic people who may be caught unawares by a reaction, for example. Greater awareness in the general public prompts transparency from day cares and schools around classroom food policies and prepares other parents to be on board with restricting their children's diets during the school day to protect the one or two allergic children present in the average classroom. However, the strategy behind these wins depends on well-off mothers performing white, feminine norms of socially appropriate American motherhood for lawmakers. Making small advances on targeted policies tailored specifically for the needs of food allergic children means simultaneously reproducing norms of gender, sexuality, family, class, and whiteness that harm many other families, children, and adults by maintaining existing systems of difference and exclusion and cementing them as prerequisites to political representation.

INTRODUCTION

THE REPRODUCTIVE POLITICS OF FOOD ALLERGY

On January 31, 2020, the U.S. Food and Drug Administration (FDA) announced its approval of Aimmune Therapeutics' Biologics License Application for the active ingredient in a new product called Palforzia. The product, according to the approval letter, was now "approved for use in patients with a confirmed diagnosis of peanut allergy . . . in patients 4 years of age and older." It wasn't an instant fix or suitable for treating acute allergic reactions to peanuts. Rather, it was "to be used in conjunction with a peanut-avoidant diet" in people four years of age and older to gradually desensitize people with an allergy to peanut.[1] This approval was a significant win for food allergy advocates in the United States, the people whom this book is about. Palforzia was the first treatment intended to fix the underlying immune dysfunction behind peanut allergy, which, it was hoped, would lead to a permanent cure for the condition. Aimmune had tackled peanut allergy, the most common food allergy in North America, first of all common food allergies. They had plans to expand to others, like milk and egg, which their competitor, DBV Technologies, was already working on. Because allergies to different foods share the same underlying mechanism, the FDA's approval of Palforzia was a sign that not just peanut allergy but food allergy in general was about to become a treatable disease rather than a lifelong condition or disability.

Food allergy advocates and the press expressed enthusiasm about this approval. Fierce Pharma, a pharmaceutical industry online news outlet, gushed about its market potential: "According to Evaluate Pharma . . . Palforzia could hit an estimated $1.28 billion in sales by 2024."[2] *Allergic Living* magazine emphasized that it was the "first-ever FDA approval of a therapy for any food allergy." Food allergy advocate and Facebook allergy support group founder Stacey Sturner, interviewed for the story, said it "represent[ed] a tremendous paradigm shift" and would "significantly increase nationwide access—and relatively quickly."[3] Kids with Food Allergies, a leading U.S. food allergy advocacy organization, highlighted the impact on food allergic families, noting that "food allergies put a significant mental, social and financial burden on families. . . . Palforzia may give many families managing peanut allergies more freedom and greater quality of life."[4] Leading allergists like Jonathan Spergel and Terri F. Brown-Whitehorn at the nationally renowned Children's Hospital of Philadelphia went on a media blitz in the week after the approval announcement, speaking about the benefits of the product to at least seven industry and general-interest news outlets.[5] The news, it seemed, was all good. Families and children would soon have relief from a life-threatening condition, and the company would do well by doing good for food allergic people.

It seemed to me, however, that an important aspect of the drug was overlooked in the public excitement about its approval. This was a product that would take significant skill and care work to use correctly, especially in children. Informed by nearly three years of prior ethnographic fieldwork with parents of allergic children, allergic adults, scientists, and others involved in food allergy advocacy, I wondered what new forms of care and responsibility its use would bring into being, and who would be charged with these obligations. These questions seemed particularly salient because late-stage trials for the product had specifically focused on children, suggesting that they were a prime target market. With children's health at stake, questions of care and responsibility necessarily involved others. These questions implicated feminized caretakers like mothers and teachers most of all.

According to the company's press release, "PALFORZIA is a complex biologic drug used with a structured dosing approach that builds on a century of oral immunotherapy (OIT) research. With OIT, the specific allergenic proteins are ingested initially in very small quantities, followed by incrementally increasing amounts, resulting in the ability to mitigate allergic reactions to the allergen over time."[6] Unlike a daily pill, the product's OIT approach involved eating a small amount of the food each day in escalating doses. Because the person using the product would already be allergic to the peanut protein it contained by design, the individual or their caretakers would have to remain vigilant for signs of an allergic reaction each day after taking the dose. The risk of reaction would also periodically change throughout the early period of therapy when doses were increased. In recognition of this unique risk, the FDA had required the company to submit a risk evaluation and mitigation strategy in addition to the ordinary documentation of safety, efficacy, and manufacturing capabilities that the agency typically required. The risk evaluation and mitigation strategy specified additional training, certification, patient monitoring, and conditions for administration to ensure that the risks of reactions did not outweigh the long-term benefits of treatment. The plan also required the company to provide guidance to prescribers and their facilities and to carefully document the product's sale and use.[7]

This supposed cure, then, was far from simple, even if it was still expected to be lucrative and popular. It created new responsibilities on the part of those prescribed the medication, their caretakers, and Aimmune—responsibilities that went above and beyond a typical pill, cream, or injection product. This was a familiar story to me from my many months of engagement with food allergic people, parents, and advocates. Food allergy is a difficult condition to manage alone, especially for parents of young children, who are the focus of several chapters of this book. Avoiding potentially dangerous allergic reactions means having access to reliably manufactured food that has not been cross-contaminated with a person's allergens and eating that food in an environment where surfaces, other people, and other people's food do not accidentally contaminate it during mealtime. Ensuring safety in the event of a reaction often means relying on others as well;

teachers or babysitters might be needed to administer epinephrine using an auto-injector in a timely fashion, call 911, monitor an allergic person's breathing, and formulate and communicate plans for future emergency responses. The mastermind coordinating this network of care for an allergic child is typically a mother, and her role as lead caretaker is typically treated not as an active choice but as a matter of common sense. When I read the details of the Palforzia approval, I wondered if mom would once again be the one in the hot seat, expected to do the everyday work of ensuring the safe and efficacious rollout of a drug made by a faraway pharmaceutical company.

As this book will show, the politics of care are central to contemporary food allergy advocacy. The private experiences of food allergy management tend to be shaped by the differentiating structures of power that scholars call gender, race, and class. Gendered and classed norms that are enacted in everyday life, such as the norms of good mothering, spill over into public advocacy about the urgency of food allergy care and treatment as political and scientific issues. Food allergy advocates now have audiences and allies in the halls of state houses and Capitol Hill in the United States as well as throughout the global pharmaceutical economy. Food allergy mothers are regular guests on local and national news outlets, where they speak about their efforts to raise awareness about the challenges and dangers of managing the condition. Social media backlash is swift when latenight comedians poke fun at parents' demands for peanut-free flights and lunchroom tables. At the local level, school districts regularly work with parents to institute policies to ensure the safety of food allergic children at school. As a result of these different forms of action, in the United States, food allergy has been enshrined as a priority for public health research, research funding, and food safety regulation. At the core of these advocacy activities lies a persistent set of debates about what constitutes good care for people, especially children, with food allergies; who is an appropriate caretaker; and what can be done to expand the circle of capable participants in care work.

This book argues that this multifaceted story of care and responsibility concerning food allergy is an emblematic story about the reproductive politics of health advocacy in the contemporary United

States. Food allergic living throws into relief the cultural expectations about individual and family responsibility for sick and disabled people, particularly children, and the gendering of care work in the home. These expectations are inflected by the way that race and class have been entwined with public health, child-rearing, food preparation, and hygiene since at least the early twentieth century. The safety measures taken in the private space of the home shape food allergy advocacy efforts in community and public contexts, and inform the politics of science and technology that shape treatment of the condition. The reproductive politics of food allergy that emerge from these activities, examined here through a feminist science and technology studies (STS) and medical anthropology lens, exemplifies Melinda Cooper's contention that the family has been a kind of invisible linchpin holding together public policy and institutions in the United States since the first stirrings of neoliberalism in the mid-twentieth century.[8] Food allergy activism, as well as the everyday dramas that drive it, provide an apt prism through which to view these unfolding politics of family, economy, and reproduction.

REPRODUCTIVE POLITICS AND FEMINIST CRITIQUE

Food allergy advocacy is a stage for reproducing the culturally dominant—that is, white, middle class, and heteronormative— politics of personhood and responsibility in the contemporary United States. These are the core concerns of the type of highly interdisciplinary feminist analysis often referred to as social reproduction theory: analysis of who cares for others, and how, and with the intent of bringing up what sort of people to carry on the activities of society and the economy in future generations. Feminist theorization of social reproduction now weaves through a half century's work in the U.S. feminist canon. Inspired by Marx's and Engels's glancing concern with the problem of how capitalism is sustained through generations, one tradition of white feminist theorists like Shulamith Firestone, Arlie Russell Hochschild, and Sylvia Federici initiated trenchant critiques of the assignment of care work to women in Western societies.[9] The Wages for Housework Committee, a movement with a strong presence in Brooklyn, New York, in the 1970s, even went so far as to argue that care work should be assigned a wage so that it might be made legible as valuable in contemporary capitalist societies.[10]

Black U.S. feminists like Angela Davis, bell hooks, and Patricia Hill Collins complicate white feminist critiques by demonstrating the social and personal value of caring across the generations under the conditions of oppression frequently experienced by Black women.[11] In the lives of many Black women, reproductive work is accomplished through collaboration across households and generations. In Black feminist writing, reproductive work within one's own biological and chosen family is often positioned as gratifying and necessary for the sustenance of Black communities. It is not perceived as a form of gendered oppression, as many white feminists have seen it. As Dorothy Roberts documents, for example, when familial and caretaking bonds are violently broken, whether by white slaveholders in the early nineteenth century or by agents of the racist child welfare system today, they interrupt community stability as well as intergenerational care and knowledge transfer.[12] The work of caring hits differently for Black women and Black feminist scholars, whose family and community histories have been shaped by legalized theft of their children and the children of their ancestors, than it does for white women seeking liberation from childbearing and household chores in order to take on paid employment outside the home.

The contention that food allergy advocacy is a form of reproductive politics relevant to these feminist traditions requires some terminological unpacking. In particular, what does my use of "reproductive" refer to? I use it in two ways. First, I often use it to reference immediate biological concerns, often voiced in urgent terms by food allergy mothers: keeping food allergic children healthy and alive so they can grow to adulthood. Yet although biological survival may be the goal of keeping peanut butter away from a peanut-allergic child, succeeding at this effort is made possible by the social arrangements, such as family relationships or student–teacher communication, through which provision of biological comfort, health, and safety are ensured. For humans who rely on each other to ensure collective well-being, biological reproduction is necessarily social reproduction as well. At other times, and in keeping with how it is sometimes mobilized by

Black feminists,[13] it refers to the maintenance of relations of domination along the axes of race, class, and gender. Food allergy advocacy and immunological science reproduce patriarchal gender relations, for example, by positioning mothers as the ideal caretakers of children. In practice, these two senses of the term "reproduction" are not easily separated. For that reason, I offer up the capacious analytic of "reproductive politics" to capture the multiple ways in which reproduction is embedded in the politics of food allergy advocacy.

The current book brings feminist critiques of reproductive politics into conversation with literature on health advocacy and the politics of biomedicine in STS and medical anthropology. I seek to make three feminist interventions in these conversations. First, I aim to show how whiteness, heteronormativity, and middle-class values are reproduced through the activities of health advocacy. Prior scholarship in STS has examined the institutional and epistemological interventions made by groups of patient activists,[14] such as the work done by European patient activist groups to introduce new research priorities into professional biomedical science. Comparatively fewer accounts have focused on how these movements do or do not reproduce class, race, and heteronormativity. Some feminist STS scholars like Michelle Murphy and Helen Hester have investigated the ways that feminist and trans medical activists seize the means of reproduction.[15] That is, they design, manufacture, and distribute medical technologies like hormones and menstrual extractors on the margins of or entirely outside official circuits of biomedical knowledge and product sales. Other work that does investigate how class, race, gender, and sexuality inflect health activism, such as Steven Epstein's classic work on AIDS activists in the 1980s and 1990s, does not firmly position health activism as an issue of social reproduction.[16] The current work offers a pointed feminist intervention in STS that builds on these various strands of (in)attention paid to how health activism plays a socially reproductive social role.

Second, I aim to demonstrate how the activities of health activists reflect and extend the socially reproductive functions of biomedicine. For example, in the case of food allergy management, the intensive focus on nuclear families, schools, and mother–child relationships is mirrored by what is studied and considered as fact in immunological research. To make this point, I draw on Black feminist ethnography, policy, and theoretical research on the history and ideology of the family in the United States. These analyses direct my attention toward the specific pieces of biomedical advice and scientific theories about food allergy that support the social reproduction of raced, gendered, and classed hierarchies of care and concern in this country.

Third, I aim to show the close connections between private reproductive activities, like parents feeding young children and overseeing the education of adolescents, and the public politics of food allergies, like large-scale messaging campaigns and legislative advocacy. Here my ethnographic content leads the way. Comparing multiple forms of evidence, like one-on-one interviews and information provided on the websites of nonprofit advocacy groups, shows how closely private considerations are linked to public activities, like awareness campaigns and lobbying. This book's project, in sum, is to reposition health activism as an activity that is socially reproductive and to insist on the importance of social reproduction to STS and medical anthropology.

This book is a work of both ethnography and theory. It is the culmination of nearly three years of multisited ethnographic fieldwork. To my knowledge, this is the first book-length ethnography to document life with food allergies in the United States. As such, it covers a great deal of ground as it explains how food allergy works; how information about the condition is transmitted among providers, patients, and caretakers; and how everyday, private experiences with the condition inform public discourse and advocacy. At the same time, this book aims to make a theoretical intervention in international and interdisciplinary scholarly conversations about health activism: to demonstrate the relevance of social reproduction analysis to this topic of study. To do so, it draws on secondary literature from a variety of fields, principally feminist theory, anthropology, STS, and disability studies. Audiences in STS and medical anthropology may have the most to learn from the book's theoretical interventions, while readers in feminist and disability studies may find the empirical content useful as a case study that demonstrates another site in which care, bodily norms, and reproductive politics are worked through in real life.

The deep tensions around who benefits from socially reproductive work has serious implications for how inclusive and wide ranging the social reconfigurations promoted by food allergy advocates might finally turn out to be. On the one hand, advocates are fundamentally rethinking what it means to be a normal, healthy person. By positioning food allergy as a disability and broadening the circle of potential caretakers for allergic children, advocates challenge the individualizing tendencies of biomedicine and the privatization of the nuclear family and domestic space. On the other hand, to do this work successfully means leveraging the power and privilege afforded by affiliation with white, heteronormative, upper-middle-class identities and networks—networks that are often mediated through family. When many of the solutions offered by food allergy advocates neglect questions about cost and access to health, reinforce gendered responsibility for care, and reify the heteronormative nuclear family as the basic social unit, how radical can the calls to redistribute responsibility and reposition bodily difference as ordinary really be? Much like other contemporary "mothers' movements,"[17] apparently radical claims lead to retrenchment into patriarchal ordering of the family and individualized decision making that impedes collective progress. In short, activism can reproduce some parts of the status quo while changing others. This is the ongoing dilemma of food allergy advocacy in the United States today, and a primary concern of this book.

FOOD ALLERGY ADVOCACY IN THE UNITED STATES

Allergy is a confounding condition that has long resisted biomedical attempts to cure it, whether through direct intervention in symptoms or through alteration of the underlying immunological mechanisms. In the battle at the boundaries of the self, immunity has been a key biological and metaphorical defense system.[18] In 1906, Clemens von Pirquet defined allergy as "the general concept of changed reactivity," encompassing "the vaccinated, the tuberculous, the individual injected with serum" who displayed changed reactivity, as well as those who became ill in response to insect stings, strawberries, and crabs (a phenomenon called "idiosyncrasy" by his contemporaries).[19] Allergy confounded medical scientists in this relatively early moment in the reign of germ theory and the rise of the field of immunology because the body appeared to be attacking itself rather than an outside invader. This kind of immunity was by definition disordered, going against the principle that immunity was meant to divide and protect the self of the individual's body from the outside influences that threatened to overtake it.[20] Allergy seemed to be a perversion of this protective mechanism.

Food allergy turned out to be an even odder phenomenon than other forms of allergy. In food allergy, the body harms itself after misidentifying life-sustaining foodstuffs as foreign invaders to be isolated and destroyed. It was so mysterious and difficult to treat that the study of food allergy effectively fractured the field of allergy and immunology in the second half of the twentieth century.[21] As allergy became a popular metaphor for defense of the modern self, scientists and doctors concerned with allergy in general and food allergy in particular became isolated from colleagues engaged in the more prestigious study of basic immunology and autoimmune diseases.[22] Perhaps as a consequence, few reliable remedies existed for food allergy by the 1990s, when rates of the condition among children began a rapid and sustained rise.[23] The ubiquitous epinephrine auto-injector device, available in branded versions like the EpiPen and Auvi-Q in the United States, is the current best defense against complications and death from an allergic reaction to food. However, it only controls the acute symptoms of an allergic reaction already under way. Basic theoretical understanding of the mechanism of food allergy had not, by the time a crisis was declared in the early 2000s,[24] yielded reliable immunity-altering or preventive measures beyond simple avoidance of the substances, like common proteins found in foods like peanuts, eggs, and milk, that trigger allergic reactions for sensitized individuals.

This sudden rise in the rates of food allergy in the 1990s is the historical moment at which this book begins. Among the participants in my research, several core activists and physician-scientists became engaged in the field through managing their children's or patients' food allergies beginning in the 1990s, when awareness and knowledge about disease management were both scarce. Through in-person, and later online, support groups, mothers of allergic children shared practical tips and fears about the health and lives of their children. Nonprofit organizations like the Food Allergy Action Network (FAAN) and the Food Allergy Initiative (FAI) sprung up to consolidate community knowledge, raise public awareness, and collect funds for research toward cures. Physicians resurrected earlier, abandoned treatment protocols—some dating as far back as 1908[25]—to treat the immunological dysfunction that causes food allergy using desensitization therapies called immunotherapy. By the late 1990s, researchers were again adapting sublingual immunotherapy techniques used for respiratory allergies for food allergy, with oral, skin-based, and other new therapies developed in the early 2000s.[26] The convergence of these various interests in food allergy from physicians and parents of food allergic children in the 1990s and early 2000s forms the basis for awareness campaigns, political lobbying, and research priorities today.

The current U.S. food allergy or food allergy activist community emerges from these multiple interests and activities and is not a unitary or natural entity. I understand this community to be a network of complex and partial connections of which I have a situated perspective. It is a diverse coalition united by shared concerns about the safety of people with food allergies that includes adults and teens with food allergies, many mothers and a few fathers of food allergic children, entrepreneurs, physicians, researchers, food manufacturers, philanthropists, pharmaceutical companies and their employees, and workers at nonprofit organizations.[27] But the perspective that most strongly informs this book is that of mothers of food allergic children.[28] This focus is a result of the nature of ethnographic research sampling and ethics, both of which shape access to different participant groups and individuals. I chose to focus on research with adults for ethical reasons and to use a snowball sampling method—that is, to follow the networks of advocacy by reaching new participants through referrals of previous ones. There is also always an element of chance in ethnography. Whom you meet at an in-person mealtime event with a group of people you have never met before, for example, may depend on something as contingent as what table you choose to sit at to eat your dinner.

These diverse actors bring an assortment of motivations to advocating as or on behalf of people with food allergies. There are many moments in this book when actors prioritize the many problems faced by people with food allergies differently, or address them at different scales. Actors in the community advocated differently according to their interests, resources, and the knowledge afforded by their standpoints,[29] yet were materially and socially connected in multiple ways. For example, in 2015, when I was deeply engaged in interviews and ethnographic participant observation, many of the mothers of allergic children whom I spoke to were highly instrumental in their efforts and focused on their own family's social and health needs. Several participants expressed to me that they were happy just to win disability accommodations for their child from a local school. Their efforts were supported, however, by mothers with organizing and legal expertise who led national webinars organized by Food Allergy Research and Education (FARE) and Kids with Food Allergies (KFA) that taught viewers about the legal rights and procedures for accommodation outlined by the Americans with Disabilities Act and the Rehabilitation Act of 1973. Their presentations, in turn, were supported in part by multinational pharmaceutical companies, like Mylan and Sanofi, who were also sending company-supported lobbyists to state capitals to lobby for passage of bills relaxing the prescribing requirements for epinephrine auto-injectors—devices such companies happened to manufacture and sell at that time.

During my intensive period of ethnographic research, from late 2013 to early 2016, food allergy advocacy had three interlocking aims. The first two will make up the focus of this book; the third is a topic less concerned with the politics of the contemporary U.S. family and thus will be dealt with elsewhere. These aims, I argue throughout this book, were shaped by raced, classed, and gendered understandings of what it means to live a good life, what levels and forms of risk are acceptable for individuals and families, and the gendered arrangements of care work that persist in U.S. households despite decades of feminist activation against patriarchal family norms. Seen through the lens of reproductive politics, these aims often sustained normative systems of identity, economics, and power. But this does not mean such efforts should be dismissed or villainized. At the same time, using the social status, knowledge, financial, and other resources at hand made life with food allergy more livable for mothers, families, and individuals managing the condition.

First, the food allergy community worked hard to raise awareness about the condition in the public sphere to better ensure safety for people with food allergy. Efforts often focused on explaining what food allergies are, describing how they pose threats to life and health, and disseminating information about what research is being done to treat them. These appeals were typically specifically tied to the everyday, personal experience of life with food allergy, especially caretaking practices and the individual experience of managing allergic reactions. Educating audiences about the importance of epinephrine auto-injectors such as the EpiPen figured high up in their messaging. Community members were active on every platform they could find, including blogging on their own websites, posting to social media sites including Twitter, Facebook, and Instagram, writing editorials for nationally recognized news platforms, organizing and speaking at patient- and parent-focused conferences, sitting on the advisory boards of private companies and nonprofit organizations, and initiating and contributing to official National Institutes of Health and Centers for Disease Control and Prevention reports. These efforts connected networks of actors through family ties, financial ties, expert networks, and institutional ties to turn a matter of private worry into a public matter of concern.[30]

Second, and built on the rhetoric offered in public awareness messaging, advocates launched state legislative campaigns to ensure more food allergic people had access to epinephrine auto-injectors. Bills to encourage the availability of epinephrine auto-injectors in public schools and other public spaces were coordinated nationwide by nonprofit organizations, pharmaceutical company lobbyists, and networks of individual mother-advocates and tailored to local conditions to ensure passage. These laws typically relaxed prescribing regulations and Good Samaritan laws specifically in relation to these devices to allow nonprescribed, or stock, devices to be held by entities like schools for use on anyone who had an allergic reaction on the premises. By the close of 2016, every state in the United States had one of these laws on the books—a testament to the organizational capacity of food allergy advocates. At the same time, these campaigns, as I discuss in chapters 4 and 5, raise significant questions about the interests of the pharmaceutical industry in public health measures.

Finally, and outside the main scope of this book, advocates sought to reform U.S. food safety regulations. They did so through formal advocacy for and involvement in food labeling rulemaking within the FDA and by putting pressure on food manufacturers to exceed the legally mandated minimum requirements for allergen labeling. Advocates and people with allergic family members started their own food companies, including nationally distributed ones like Enjoy Life Foods, and pledged that their products would exceed mandated or scientifically recognized thresholds for allergen contamination. Major manufacturers slowly acquired these independent companies and began to follow their lead once they recognized that claims to moral and technical superiority were important marketing tools in specialty food markets. While regulatory solutions around allergen labeling are difficult to enforce, market-based solutions have become widespread. In some cases, company promises form the basis for alliances between food allergy advocates and caretakers, people with celiac disease, and people with interests in other specialty diets.

Despite an overall orderly and cordial tenor to their work, those closest to food allergies—patients and parents of allergic children—sometimes find themselves moving in a direction they did not intend. Activist priorities and strategies are not fixed across time and space; rather, they respond to other stakeholders and events. No clearer example of this exists than the panicked blog posts written by food allergy moms in the summer of 2016. Upon going out to refill their children's epinephrine auto-injector prescriptions in advance of the coming school year, many realized that the broader access to epinephrine they had been advocating for did not equate to easier access in the everyday sense of the ability to financially afford filling their prescriptions. Civic participation in that effort thus did little to assuage an important aspect of the daily struggle of managing food allergies: scraping together the funds to pay for increasingly expensive medications understood to be lifesaving and necessary. How did patients and caretakers end up here? Who was to blame? Who was supposed to be looking out for their interests? And what comes next? These are the questions this book will ultimately seek to answer by tracing the networks[31] that structure the formation and transmission of knowledge and power in food allergy worlds.

THEORIZING HEALTH ACTIVISM

We live in an age where an individual's health status provides standing for making claims on the nation-state. Medical anthropologists have extensively examined this phenomenon, a dynamic dubbed "biological citizenship" by Adriana Petryna and "therapeutic citizenship" by Vinh-Kim Nguyen.[32] The recognition of patient advocacy as a legitimate form of political action is often hard won, requiring that activists become well versed in navigating extensive, even global, networks of power, and demonstrate and defend the credibility of their expertise.[33] While these efforts are often heroic and make life safer and better for thousands of individuals, what concerns me in observing patient activism in the twenty-first century is that the formation and recognition of these kinds of expertise threatens to further entrench established social hierarchies. Emily Martin expresses similar concerns in her work on the immune system in the midst of the AIDS crisis: "By the terms of the new ideal flexible body, certain categories of people (women, gays) may yet again be found wanting. What is at stake is which of us is thought fit to be part of an emerging stratum of elite worker-citizens."[34] For those who master these moves, pressing claims based on health conditions can be a powerful way to ensure that one's interests are attended to on political stages at the local, state, and national level.

Living with a nonnormative body—one that is disabled, diseased, fat, female, nonwhite, transgender, queer, or nonbinary—makes one an outlier to the liberal project in the United States, and makes such health-based claims on the state both much harder and much more necessary for daily life. Individuals who fall into these and other categories, or combinations of categories, are figured as deviant, damaged, incomplete—as having a kind of "failed subjectivity," in Sara Ahmed's evocative phrase.[35] With a historically thin and currently eroding health care safety net, needing acute or ongoing access to specialty medical care constitutes a particularly costly and dangerous form of personal failure in the contemporary United States. The case- or disease-specific judgments of medical experts concerning how to manage such unruly bodies typically stand in for serious policy change concerning how best to foster social and political inclusion. Extreme examples often occur near the end of life when physicians are often forced to ask whether patients are able to represent their interests in their own care. At what point is their autonomy too wounded to count? Who can then count as an appropriate representative?[36] While end-of-life discussions are not a primary focus of food allergy advocates in my research, similar questions arise when debating appropriate care for children, who are typically not assumed to have the capacity to make decisions about their own health.

In light of these limitations to liberal inclusion for people who fall outside the bounds of what is considered normal, health activism in the United States is often tangled up with contestations about who is a fully fledged social actor and political subject. Critiques of normative assumptions about what a human body ought to be able to do appeared with increasing frequency in the talk and work of the food allergy community over the period of my ethnographic research. Yet while activists attack the archetype of a narrowly defined normative body, their arguments draw strength from the naturalization of racialized and gendered divisions of caretaking labor. Mothers, especially when they are white and middle class, are understood as the natural caretakers of allergic children, so they are the ones who have the "natural" authority to represent the cause of food allergy in the public sphere. In other words, while denaturalizing the normatively able body demanded by liberal political institutions, gendered roles concerning caretaking are simultaneously publicly represented as the natural order of things.

Those who serve as the public faces of food allergy advocacy rarely question other aspects of normative American personhood. In my research interviews, participants generally did not question the structural arrangements that make access to fee-for-service and fee-for-product health care, quality schools staffed by well-resourced educators, and high-quality childcare available only to families and individuals with deep pockets and white-collar jobs. Instead, starting and supporting for-profit specialty food companies, medical device startups, and pharmaceutical giants that are developing new and improved products are often the vanguard of the movement. Participating in such ventures is couched in the language of expanding choice in marketplaces like the grocery store and pharmacy by both individuals and advocacy organizations. Expanding choice is seen as an unquestionable moral good. Yet this orientation overlooks the considerable work it takes to be free to have meaningful choice. Solving the problems posed by food allergy in this way offers safety and convenience to those with wealth to spare, thereby reproducing the capitalist core of family life in the United States.[37]

The Body Political

An important part of the story about food allergy advocacy in the United States is how activists challenge take-for-granted assumptions about what a "sick" body looks like and how it ought to be protected. The U.S. food allergy advocacy community, as I encountered it in 2013, formed around a shared desire to protect people with food allergies—especially children—from threats to health and life. These threats emerge, in their view, from the social agency of people, like unthinking neighbors, teachers, and friends, who share allergy-triggering foods with allergic individuals. They can also arise from the unruly agency of nonhuman materials, especially potential impurities in the foods that people with food allergies want to eat.[38] The central task for most food allergy advocates is therefore to convince their communities and the public that food allergies truly are dangerous and that sufferers can only stay safe when their families, friends, and communities participate in clearly delineated care practices.

These claims can be best understood by putting their work in conversation with that of disability theorists.[39] Only a handful of parents and activists I interacted with explicitly identified disability activism as an umbrella category that also includes food allergy advocacy. But like many disability activists, food allergy advocates are often motivated by their social and embodied experiences with a somatic condition that differs from the profile of the normal, able-bodied human of contemporary biomedicine. In resonance with the work of disability scholars like Tom Shakespeare and Rosemary Garland-Thompson,[40] food allergy advocates often trouble the assumption that disability is a biological fact that can be exclusively located in the bodies of individuals. That view—known as the medical model of disability—implies that an individual is damaged, and that medical or social interventions ought to be focused on repairing their individual deficiencies. By contrast, disability activists and disability studies scholars have worked to resituate the locus of disability in society, including in social interactions and in the built environment, a perspective often called the social model of disability. In resonance with disability scholarship and activism, mothers of allergic children often push back against the medical model by arguing that their children are not sick or even disabled, just that rigorous attention must be paid by everyone in the child's life—parents, grandparents, friends, teachers, babysitters, and coaches—to prevent them from eating food contaminated with their allergens.

Like other disability and health activists before them, food allergy advocates displace the locus of disruption caused by the condition in question in order to demonstrate that social exclusion stems from societal responses to bodily difference rather than proceeding as a natural consequence from a biomedical diagnosis. To enact this inversion of responsibility, much of the food allergy community's awareness efforts center around educating restaurateurs, loved ones, caretakers, teachers, and the public about what small steps can be taken to make most foods safe for people with food allergies to eat and how to administer emergency medications if someone does experience an allergic reaction. The focus, in other words, is on distributing responsibility for care beyond the individual, and that individual's parents in the case of allergic children. Only when that fails, or when they believe there is a high chance that it will fail, do people typically turn to legal enforcement, like strengthening disability legislation in anticipation of injury or pursuing damages via tort law in retribution when a restaurant does not take proper food safety precautions. This is not a new kind of claim to make in the United States or in disability theory, but it continues to be contested ground for people with many kinds of illness and disability, including people with food allergies, their representatives, and their caretakers.

Recent scholarship at the interface of design studies, STS, and disability studies illustrates how the expectations in place today for managing disability in domestic spaces are deeply gendered. Bess Williamson, for example, describes disabled men and women in the post–World War II United States as "tinkerers" who find ways to make domestic spaces work for them and their particular capacities.[41] Yet the ways that spaces were altered and who was recognized as innovators reflected the gendered expectations for the postwar home. Williamson, for example, highlights contributions to the *Toomey J Gazette*, a magazine for polio survivors with an all-woman editorial team. Women traded tips for constructing faucet turners to help them clean the house. In one issue, mouth sticks for tasks like dialing the phone or writing were arrayed around a feminine pair of lips, demonstrating the variety of devices readers and writers had come up with to solve similar problems. Meanwhile, disabled veteran men were coached on how to resume life outside the home. They were trained to drive modified cars and trucks and expected to accept the sometimes significant discomfort of wearing artificial limbs to fit into public life. Such practices were elaborated and shared among disabled people contemporaneously with the general expansion of rehabilitation services for veterans after the war.[42]

These kinds of practices and support services coalesce as what Aimi Hamraie calls the normate template in industrial design—that is, the building codes and design standards that embody normative assumptions about the capacities of the average body.[43] As Hamraie discusses at length, the modern form of the normate template codified, and continues to reflect, these kinds of deeply gendered postwar assumptions about who is responsible for everyday tasks in family life. The construction of disability in the home and the perception of what "problems" it poses (and which of those can be solved) remain inextricably linked with the gendering of care work in the contemporary U.S. home. These historical examples demonstrate how disability is an axis of difference that is constructed with and through other forms of difference, such as gender and class. In this book's focus on the reproductive politics of food allergy, normative expectations concerning gender, race, and class all intersect with ideas about how to characterize the social consequences of food allergy for people who live with it, including whether or not it counts as a disability.

From an anthropological perspective, these discussions about the social construction of disability are also questions about how bodies come to matter in social worlds. The body has long been a topic of interest in anthropology. The body has even been said to figure as the "existential ground of culture" and thus foundational to any study of social life.[44] From this view, ill and disabled bodies might trigger concern for members of a community, culture, or society because they threaten to break down patterns of reciprocity, ritual, and support that hold them together. In other words, living with a body that can't fulfill its social functions seems to pose a challenge to social personhood. Medical anthropology's response to this problem is often to suggest that the circuits of care and expertise that sustain people in need of aid are themselves important aspects of social life.[45] Care work that pivots around moral obligations based on professional capabilities and social ties can produce new kinds of reciprocal relations, or what Faye Ginsburg and Rayna Rapp call "disability worlds."[46] It may even provide the impetus for remaking entrenched networks and ways of being in relation to others in the world, as it does in key ways for the food allergy activists documented in this book. The question this book asks: What worlds are being made, and for whom?

The Politics of Mothers' Movements

Food allergy advocacy is one example of an important genre of health activism today, what Heather Hewett refers to as a "mothers' movement."[47] In the contemporary moment, mothers' movements make claims on the state and to the public in ways that have distinctive, and at times contradictory, relationships with medical authority. One model of mothers' movement is that of U.S. antivaccination activists, a movement that many scholars have drawn comparisons to on hearing about this project on food allergy advocacy. This movement tends to have an antagonistic relationship with medical authority. Rather than trust medical experts or epidemiological techniques that portray childhood vaccinations as low risk, mothers trust themselves—their own observations of their children, their own judgments about cause and effect, and their own solutions, such as natural diets and vaccine rejection.[48] Legal suits against vaccine makers are a primary tool by which this antagonism is registered in the public record,[49] although private expressions of mistrust happen every day behind the closed doors of the clinic. This type of mothers' movement seeks to supplant technoscientific expertise with motherly expertise as a result of distrust of the experts and of the modern systems of population governance that their work embodies.

A contrasting model of a mothers' movement from Japan are the "radiation brain mom" activists that organized in light of ongoing environmental contamination after the Fukushima nuclear disaster in 2011.[50] In this instance, documented in a 2015 ethnography by Aya Hirata Kimura, mothers did not distrust the techniques or epistemology of science. They distrusted the government experts who were leading the formal investigations into the status and effects of nuclear contamination. In response, they developed their own expertise in scientific methods and generated their own evidence of and responses to environmental contamination. Their approach is evocative of other environmental justice movements, such as the community advocacy work after the Union Carbide chemical spill in Bhopal, India, in 1984 and the activism of women employees in the FDA in bringing to light so-called sick building syndrome.[51] This type of mothers' movement does not seek to replace the epistemic authority of technoscientific expertise but to improve it—what might be seen as enacting a "feminist science" along the lines of what Helen Longino suggests in "Can There Be a Feminist Science?"[52] It seeks answers to situated questions that are specific to children and women and their everyday lives as part of nuclear families. Importantly, this type of movement emphasizes strategic collaboration with scientists and the construction of mother-advocates as technoscientific experts in their own right.

Food allergy advocacy, the mothers' movement of concern in this book, has a slightly different relationship to biomedical expertise. In general, food allergy advocates have a friendly relationship with doctors, scientists, and pharmaceutical company executives and workers, and they largely trust the advice of doctors and public health experts. This is perhaps because biomedical solutions are only part of the set of activities one must engage in to manage food allergy day to day. Many food allergy mothers felt a responsibility, as it was described to me time and time again in my research, to provide their children with a "normal" childhood, full of social events like birthday parties with decadent cakes and after-school sports, despite any complications or dangers introduced by their condition. Stories about successfully creating the conditions for a normal childhood against tough odds are central to the claims parents and other activists make concerning biological citizenship in political testimony and popular writing. The ideal childhood hoped for, and sometimes reached, in these stories is highly nostalgic, an enaction of an illusory, simpler time in the past that was devoid of social conflict. In these narratives, and in contrast especially to environmental justice movements, there is little acknowledgment of the highly variable access to health care, food, and financial resources that people with food allergies in the United States actually have. The ideal version of a food allergic childhood draws on raced, classed, and gendered aspirations of the "good life" in arrangements that prescribe social roles for mothers, fathers, children, and other caretakers while minimizing the ways in which these categories act as justifications for myriad forms of domination.

Although food allergy affects all racialized groups in the United States,[53] white, middle-class women are most often at the core of food allergy activism. They leverage their gendered position as mothers to tell authoritative stories to the press, to local, state, and national legislative bodies, and to the general public. These stories blend lessons about the responsibility to protect biological human life and an acute desire for the normative lifeways and milestones that their families expect to participate in as part of U.S. family life. The middle-class imaginary that their testimony draws from foregrounds strong bodies and stable communities as the basis for perpetuating intergenerational reproduction of class position, gender roles, race-linked aspirations, and memories. Further, the most effective activists are taken seriously because they are also armed with training in technoscientific language through access to good education and professional training. They also have access to the cultural and financial capital to seek out experts and resources to fill in any gaps in their technoscientific expertise.

The persona presented by many food allergy mothers and activists in their work is notable not only for the emphasis placed on a class-linked kind of feminine virtue and expertise but also for its whiteness. Food allergy advocates succeed when they activate a nonthreateningly "nice" femininity. As anthropologist Setha Low points out, "niceness" is code for "white" for white, middle-class Americans.[54] The self-described niceness of food allergy activists, as I will argue in later chapters, is an expression of a racialized orientation to the American political process. Black women and other women of color risk being labeled sexually deviant, subservient, or overly aggressive—or some combination of the three—when they undertake similar work on behalf of their children, in health care as well as in other domains.[55] Black women in the United States are seen as too aggressive, too fecund, and too subservient to be considered ideal mothers in the American imaginary.

Furthermore, the stories food allergy advocates tell depict a particular vision of what constitutes the good life that is inflected by the racialized history of the American family.[56] The vision of family life they describe is typically characterized by stable nuclear families under no significant threat from police or other agents of the state, filled with wholesome after-school activities held at good public schools, and located in the kinds cohesive, stable communities that were long off-limits to people of color thanks to redlining. As scholarship on Black motherhood and the education of Black children reveal, however, this is not a universally accessible dream. Savannah Shange's examination of how Black children traverse the education system provides a prime example. The education of Black children is over-whelmingly inadequate in the United States, does not serve young people well when transitioning to college or job markets, and is closely integrated with the criminal justice system. Overcrowding and lack of supplies due to systematic underfunding of public schools, micro-aggressions in the classroom, and outright violence in schools and in the surrounding communities are part of the everyday experience of Black schoolchildren. These trends hold even in supposedly progressive schools like the Robeson Justice Academy in San Francisco.[57]

To add STS flavor to these conversations, I further contend that these dynamics of race, class, and gender in food allergy activism are not only about history and identity but are also about epistemology. Feminist STS scholars, for example, have laid out the stakes of "seeing like a woman" in modern societies that are suffused through and through with technoscience.[58] With women largely excluded from the production of scientific knowledge since the birth of Enlightenment scientific epistemology, the very content of scientific knowledge excludes women's experiences in the world.[59] Instead, it reencodes human social norms as "natural," including systems of gender-based domination that provide post hoc justifications for the oppression and exclusion of women from the scientific enterprise.[60]

In parallel to these critiques, critical race theorists have written extensively about the epistemic authority of whiteness.[61] Whiteness grants access to a wide variety of kinds of power in the United States, including ensuring the basic right to bodily safety and integrity, allowing a person to be regarded as someone worth listening to, and shaping one's political aspirations, strategies, and tactics. George Yancy articulates it clearly when he explains, "Marking whiteness is about exposing the ways in which whites have created a form of 'humanism' that obfuscates their hegemonic efforts to treat their experiences as universal and representative."[62] Whiteness, these scholars contend, goes deeper than identity. It is a way of seeing the world that allows certain relations and hierarchies to be seen and others to remain beneath notice. In other words, whiteness can be understood to be a social position with epistemological consequences, analogous to how feminist STS scholars have positioned feminist objectivity and women's identity as modes of seeing the nature of reality via science and technology.

In food allergy activism, gender and whiteness shape not only the stories people tell but also their political imaginations and aspirations. As Sara Ahmed puts it, "Whiteness is an orientation that puts certain things within reach."[63] White epistemology, particularly in the United States, presumes that it is already a social fact that political claims are equally heard and responded to, regardless of differences based on racial categories or one's status as descended from colonized people, enslaved people, a descendant of white European colonizers, or a mix. In my particular ethnographic context, I observed how the epistemological positions of whiteness and femininity structured food allergy activists' awareness of their own political agency and their assumption that existing political tools were adequate for their cause. For this reason, I contend, things like alliances with otherwise predatory pharmaceutical companies seem logical because they are technically and socially possible from a position of whiteness. More imaginative challenges to the social structures that make chronic illness disabling, including challenges to the emphasis on nuclear families and the assumption that individuals ought to take care of themselves without assistance from the state, remain uncontested.

The kind of political clout that food allergy advocates acquire—even that which they imagine to be possible to acquire, and therefore worth going after in the first place—is not equally available to everyone. It is available to people with the right social connections, the right education, the right way of speaking, and the right way of dressing: culturally white and nonthreateningly feminine relationships, education, and ways of being. Importantly, though, my articulation of the connection between whiteness, normative femininity, and political power does not mean that I seek to undermine their efforts. Rather, it requires that we reflect on whether the demands made by white, well-off women reflect the specific, niche anxieties of that group or whether the ideals they fight for are articulated capaciously enough to include women in other financial situations, to queer and lesbian and trans women, to complicated, extended families or families with only one adult in the household, and to Black, brown, mixed-race, Indigenous, and undocumented women and their families.

It may not be comfortable to think about how racial histories inflect political epistemology, expectations, and strategy in food allergy activism, especially when the actors involved advance the admirable goal of fostering greater inclusion for a wider array of human bodies in society. But food allergy advocacy, like all forms of activism, is ultimately about imagining new worlds to make the future more inhabitable for more people. It is thus necessary to think about how power operates through the tools activists use to press their claims. These tools for making futures may contain assumptions about power and visibility that grow out of highly unequal, contentious, and hierarchical histories and presents concerning the management of health and childhood in the United States.

THIS BOOK

This book argues that food allergy advocacy is a form of reproductive politics. Activists' efforts reproduce the centrality of the normative, white, heterosexual, middle-class family to health and well-being in the United States. It tells a situated, empirically based story about food allergy activism that has broad implications for the relationship between individuals and collectives, between institutions of medicine and the state, and between gender, race, and capitalism. These claims are grounded in extended multisited ethnographic research[64] conducted between 2013 and 2016. Additional analysis of food allergy publications, publicly available records of food allergy organizations, and mainstream news about food allergies related to the stories and themes that emerged from ethnographic investigation continued from 2016 to 2020.

Like many contemporary ethnographies, this one began with an interest in people and a topic, with understanding of the theoretical importance of what I had observed and participated in emerging later during the analysis and writing processes. My initial introduction to allergy was facilitated by my alumni and institutional networks, with key introductions made in late 2013. These introductions led to five months of participant observation in two academic allergy clinics in the northeastern United States in 2014. I shadowed two physicians in two offices each, for a total of four clinic locations. Because there is a strong tradition of junior doctors and scientists shadowing more senior medical professionals, and senior professionals see this mentorship as part of their professional responsibility, this participation was enthusiastically granted, and I was treated as a respected junior colleague. At times I was a fly on the wall, listening and taking deidentified notes about doctor–patient interactions with pen and paper. Other times, I shuttled blank papers and vials from room to room at the request of physicians, nurses, or technicians. I also conducted qualitative, semidirected oral history interviews with dozens of patients as they waited for appointments or readings of allergy skin tests about how they experienced the condition called allergy, inclusive of both food and respiratory allergy. During the period of shadowing, I also attended a series of monthly seminars for medical residents to learn the basics of clinical approaches to allergy, both theoretical and practical. For example, I learned to fill vials using medical-grade needles with mock allergy-testing solution.

While getting acquainted with allergy medicine, I reached out to food allergy support group leaders and physicians and researchers at more institutions throughout the United States. This led to the second phase of research, which ultimately lasted from mid-2014 to early 2016, and was more narrowly focused on food allergy than allergy as a whole. It consisted of interviews with leaders and participants in food allergy activism and travel to food allergy events throughout the country. Supported by institutional grants and fellowships, I attended two small conferences near my home; three national, patient-focused conferences; and one international medical conference. Through intercepts at conferences and subsequent snowball sampling, I was able to conduct interviews with some of the leading voices in food allergy research and activism as well as many other participants in advocacy efforts. During this time, I also began following a number of publicly available social media feeds of leading food allergy writers, artists, and entrepreneurs on Twitter. I interviewed some of the prominent social media voices as well. I also truly became a participant during this phase, taking on small roles in the community such as coleading a support group for food allergic adults[65] and writing blog posts. By spring 2016, I had conducted over seventy interviews and filled several notebooks with ethnographic field notes and interview notes.

The content of my interviews and observations gave me a multidimensional view into how life with food allergy shaped individuals' and families' engagements in activism, advocacy, and scientific knowledge production and their relationships with others in their familial and social networks. For example, interviews often gave me a narrative perspective on how individuals became enroled[66] in the allergy medical specialty or in activist efforts concerning the condition. Even for biomedical experts, an interest in specializing in allergy frequently grew out of personal or family experiences adapting to an individual's new allergies. I framed one-on-one interviews with activists, parents, support group leaders, physicians, entrepreneurs, and scientists as open-ended, life history–style interviews in order to learn the stories behind how people become involved in food allergy activism as well as to learn more about how the content and aims of activism changed over time. Observations in the clinic allowed me to observe how physicians communicate information about allergy (including food allergy) to patients, including what information they see as essential for patients to understand.

In the later months of research, attending events like conferences and half-day workshops organized by and for activists and nonexperts allowed me to learn about the multiple, often contradictory priorities and attitudes about food allergy. It also gave me insight into the power dynamics that existed between and within different individuals, groups, and professions involved in advocacy. These events provided opportunities to make sure I was conducting interviews and media analyses that captured a wide variety of views about food allergy and food allergy activism, not just an expert, biomedical view. These experiences informed the questions I then asked in interviews with activists who were interested in raising awareness about food allergy. It also shed light on why some people did not trust their doctors, whom they viewed, for example, as using imprecise metaphors or withholding information about allergy and immunology from them.

What results from these varied ethnographic techniques is a

text focused on contemporary issues in food allergy activism and research—especially the period 2010 to 2020—but one that is situated in a deeper recent history of activism and research from the late 1990s onward, as viewed from the perspective of study participants and secondary research. Some chapters lean more heavily on ethnographic interviews and observations, while others rely more on media and textual analysis and the work of medical historians. Some chapters dwell primarily with key events of the last eight years, while others situate their claims in the century-long history of allergy and immunology science, or in the nineteenth-century roots of modern biomedicine. In the interest of making a focused argument about how food allergy activism reproduces race, class, and gender—only one of many arguments that could be made on the basis of the aforementioned methods and materials—I follow and remix sources and forms of evidence to tell stories that are both faithful to reality and situated in their claims.

Some readers may find this book to be a nontraditional ethnography because it is a hybrid of both empirical reporting of a style familiar across qualitative fields in the humanities and social sciences and theoretical development rooted in feminist and STS questions. This book's main theoretical intervention is the contention that health activism is a form of reproductive politics. It is targeted primarily at the fields of STS, feminist studies, and medical anthropology, and secondarily at disability studies and nonscholarly activist readers. Empirically, I strive to provide an accurate snapshot, recounted in the ethnographic present, of my situated experience of food allergy activism in the United States from the years 2013 to 2016. This snapshot may be equally useful to scholarly and nonscholarly readers as documentation of some of the major events and issues in food allergy advocacy during the period of research. Three years of ethnographic research yielded a wealth of disparate, often conflicting data. Not all of that data speaks to the central concerns of the present book. I have taken up some of them in other settings,[67] but as with any ethnographic project, the full scope of material may not ultimately be published in full in any form. At the end of the day, my aim is to make both a theoretical intervention in relevant literatures and to introduce food allergy advocacy into the ethnographic social science literature as a compelling topic and site of analysis of health activism.

The five chapters of this book each take up different crosscutting themes and key events in food allergy advocacy that demonstrate how it operates as a form of reproductive politics. The first three chapters focus on the private space of the home and describe three major aspects of getting and adapting to a food allergy diagnosis to show how children, mothers, and families are the focal points of food allergy interventions. They outline the typical trajectory of individuals and families, from receiving a diagnosis and learning about the importance of epinephrine auto-injectors, to encountering, challenging, and integrating biomedical knowledge about food allergy into one's own biographical story, to taking targeted steps toward creating an allergy-friendly, hygienic home. The next two chapters examine the arguments that advocates and advocacy organizations make when taking their case to the public and to legislators, which continue to center children, families, and mothers as key constituents in need of services and protection. Basing public policy on claims about the special status of domestic life, children, and families maintains the nuclear family as well as the race, class, and gender norms it encodes as a cultural and political ideal. By beginning the book in the home and moving to an analysis of public advocacy and messaging, I show how reproductive labor in the home is not separate from public activism. Rather, it informs and shapes it in important ways. Finally, the book ends with a reflection on the efficacy of this mode of health advocacy. What gets overlooked when progress toward equity relies so heavily on positioning mothers, children, and nuclear families as the primary objects of concern?

Chapter 1, "The Moral Life of Epinephrine," provides an introduction to two key concerns of families managing food allergies, specifically access to epinephrine auto-injectors and fear of children dying from allergic reactions. These issues set the stage for subsequent discussion in later chapters about the distribution of responsibility and the selection of advocacy priorities. It also introduces many of the actors and interests that the book examines in more detail later on. The food allergy community is heterogeneous in its interests. However, it is brought together by an affective economy[68] of shared hopes and fears concerning life with food allergies and shared experiences with feeling and witnessing allergic reactions. The hopes and fears of many parents of food allergic children are informed by a shared U.S. middle-class conception of the role mothers ought to play in caring for children. Gendered assumptions about care work, child-rearing, safety, and family decision making are deeply intertwined with notions of what counts as the good life.

The following chapter, "Who Is to Blame? Navigating the Causes and Cures for Food Allergy," offers a survey of how the food allergy community interfaces with ongoing efforts to discover root causes and cures for what some have described as a food allergy epidemic. Efforts to date have focused on children as a result of a combination of social, biological, and financial reasons. Activists, parents, and adults with food allergies negotiate what nondeterministic models of immune system development and plasticity mean for their own lives as they get involved in clinical trials for new immunotherapeutic treatments and follow emerging research on the etiology of the condition. With many biomedical theories and interventions focused on fetal development and very young children, responsibility for the condition often falls squarely on pregnant women and new mothers. Allergy science, in short, figures as a kind of reproductive politics. It reinforces cultural attitudes about the mother's "natural" role in child-rearing while provoking additional motherly anxiety above and beyond that prompted by everyday food allergy management and undermining trust in expert explanations.

In light of biological realities, what is then to be done to live safely with food allergy? The third chapter, "The Hygienic Sublime: Making Food Safe for People with Food Allergies," examines what food allergy mothers and allergic individuals consider safe for people with food allergies to eat and how safety is made and managed in the home. The logic of food safety that informs many of these activities draws from twentieth-century domestic hygiene ideals in which a clean home signifies a happy and healthy home. This ideal—which I dub the hygienic sublime—depends on and reproduces a highly gendered division of labor. Because a gendered division of home work is a culturally available solution, and because it often works to keep allergic children safe, it often serves as a template for how to order care work and responsibility outside of the home as well. In other words, what works in the home is often translated to inform public hygienic and caretaking expectations, thereby elevating and replicating the assumptions that underlie domestic labor arrangements in the public sphere. Making food safe for people with food allergies in both settings draws on and reproduces gendered relations in the home while opening up new opportunities for the (re)production of class status and gendered responsibility within the family.

The next two chapters examine how reproductive politics cross into the public sphere, specifically in legislative advocacy strategies and advocacy organizations' positioning. The fourth chapter, "Activist Politics: Disability Law, Legislative Advocacy, and Public Motherhood," analyzes several important moments illustrating how public policy affects the everyday lives of children with food allergy and how their representatives in turn aim to shift policy through legislative advocacy. During my active ethnographic research, policy and advocacy were largely focused on advocating for state-level bills allowing doctors to prescribe stock epinephrine to public and private facilities, especially schools, where such policies affected the safety of allergic children on a daily basis. This chapter reports the background of how policy and legislation affect allergic schoolchildren and the key tactics and rhetoric activists and advocacy organizations used to move new legislative bills forward. Local and individual activism around disability access in schools provided important templates for the national effort and positioned children as the prime beneficiaries of stock epinephrine campaigns. But when local and individual efforts were translated into state and national campaigns, tensions began to arise between advocates, pharmaceutical industry actors, and labor organizations. These tensions demonstrate the reproductive politics at stake in legislation and public policy concerning health.

The final body chapter is motivated by the question of what happens to an advocacy movement when a major piece of its platform is achieved. "The EpiPen Pricing Scandal and the Future of Food Allergy Advocacy" considers some of the new tensions and entanglements that formed after the successful passage of stock epinephrine legislation in all fifty U.S. states in 2016. Food allergy advocacy organizations had to respond to public controversy about the price of epinephrine auto-injectors like the EpiPen, made by pharmaceutical giant Mylan, which had been an accomplice to advocates in pushing for stock epinephrine legislation. This moment, and what has come since, shows food allergy advocacy organizations remaining largely friendly to and aligned with the ambitions of for-profit pharmaceutical companies even though company policies effectively restrict access to epinephrine to those who can afford its rising price. These events and choices raise serious questions about whose interests had previously been served by food allergy advocacy, even though public discussion tended to focus on the needs of families and children. What logics of domination and liberation were in fact being advanced alongside the more obvious reproductive politics of food allergy advocacy?

The book concludes with a meditation on what sorts of worlds health activism in the United States can make. Is health activism doomed merely to reproduce normative hierarchies of race, class, and gender, or are other outcomes possible? By zooming out from the particular case of food allergy to consider the demands of disability justice activists, Black feminist scholarship on the family, and the potential changes initiated by widespread racial justice activism in the United States today, this book considers what other sources of inspiration health activists might draw on in the future to shape their demands and movement priorities.

Donna Haraway argues, "It matters what stories tell worlds, what worlds make stories."[69] Projects of making the future, such as the work of food allergy advocates, simultaneously make politics and reproduce certain kinds of kin relations. The work of food allergy parents, advocates, and organizations structure how we imagine ourselves to be related in both intimate and public spheres, and when relations in one setting ought to inform those in the other. Feminist epistemology is uniquely positioned to understand and critique how science and technology reproduce societal scripts about difference and domination in the natural world. This move provides justification for sexism, classism, racism, colonialism, and other forms of oppression by claiming that they are rooted in irrepressible natural urges. It produces a politics of technoscience that reinforces the ills of the past and present by building exclusionary politics into technologies and infrastructural systems that are, if they succeed, hailed as creating the future. Critiquing, rewriting stories, and imagining otherwise are key resources for making better worlds.

1

THE MORAL LIFE OF EPINEPHRINE

On Saint Patrick's Day in 2014, I rode a commuter train from my home in a major East Coast city to a suburban county synonymous with white flight and white privilege. I was going to attend an evening workshop on managing food allergy in schools hosted by a regional chapter of a national food allergy advocacy organization. It was a sunny day, but barely above freezing. More than half of the seats on the train were occupied with early revelers, even in the middle of the afternoon. Six stops out from the city's major train hub, I disembarked into a bedroom community and walked for a mile through a gently hilly suburb toward a three-story, dark brick middle school building. Inside, I joined a few women in early middle age who had also come for the event, and we walked down the hall together to take our seats for the evening in the school auditorium.

This ordinary, even boring, suburban scene was the site of one of my first forays into attending food allergy awareness events. But it is significant for this book because it remained a linchpin for piecing together how gendered ideas about responsibility and morality were mobilized by food allergy parents, doctors, and advocates. Surrounded by markers of white, middle-class security, parents, educators, and medical professionals discussed their sense of vulnerability in light of living with and caring for people with food allergy. The juxtaposition of security and vulnerability was striking to me. I am a mixed-race Black Caribbean and white Eastern European woman who grew up poor on a rural organic farm. My parents could rarely afford to take me to the doctor, even when I began to develop what I later learned were allergies in my early teens. When I visit my white family in these types of towns to this day, I am often profiled, treated rudely, and followed in stores and other public places by white people—and conversely, greeted with warm welcomes of solidarity by other Black and brown people. When I heard in the speakers' voices that a medical condition could be a source of fear and threat in a place that struck me as comfortable and insular, it drew my attention to the layers of reproductive politics on display throughout the evening.

The evening unfolded in what I would come to see as a typical fashion for these types of events. An audience of mostly white, middle-aged women with vibrant regional accents filed in and scattered throughout the well-maintained stadium seating. One woman, the organizer of the evening, introduced the event by talking about her family's personal experience adapting to her children's severe food allergies while managing the food allergies of her brother and husband. Then a prominent medical expert, a man, stepped onstage to deliver a two-part talk about current medical research and best practices for managing food allergy in schools. PowerPoint slides were projected onto a screen behind him while he talked to highlight his current research and writing. The audience consisted of mostly women, including many school nurses, a few local parents, both men and women, and me.

Echoing then-current medical consensus,[1] the expert allergist explained that epinephrine auto-injectors were the one and only effective treatment for anaphylaxis. Food allergy could be an anxiety-provoking condition, yet deciding to use the device also triggered fear in nurses, parents, and children. Knowing the facts about epinephrine was the answer for overcoming fear to respond correctly in an emergency. To drive home the point that epinephrine should always be used, the allergist repeated the phrase "anaphylaxis is epinephrine" many times during his talk. The form of epinephrine he was specifically referencing was epinephrine delivered via an epinephrine auto-injector device, like Mylan Pharmaceuticals' market-leading EpiPen or Sanofi's Auvi-Q competitor device. These devices are designed to be quickly and easily used by the person needing the medication in an emergency. Food allergic individuals are supposed to carry epinephrine auto-injectors on their person at all times. The person (or their caretakers, in the case of young children) should prepare to use it without hesitation at the first sign of an allergic reaction.

A woman sitting a few seats away from me raised her hand at the end of the talk. She explained that she cared deeply about the kids at her school. The responsibility for keeping kids with food allergies safe and healthy weighed heavily on her. As she spoke, other people in the audience nodded and murmured in sympathy. The school nurses among them, like care workers throughout the country, cared for a growing number of children with food allergies. The incidence of food allergies among children had nearly doubled from 1999 to 2011 in the United States, to an estimated 5.1 percent of children.[2] Keeping kids with this potentially fatal condition safe in the presence of triggering foods was an increasingly significant part of a school nurse's job.

This book's examination of food allergy advocacy begins with this auditorium scene because it contains crucial threads of the story of how health advocacy work is a form of reproductive politics. A medical professional, a man, delivered a talk based on scientific principles and know-how to an audience of mostly women. Those women were directly in charge of taking care of people with food allergies in their everyday lives and jobs. The allergist delivered his message as a prescription for both biomedically and morally correct action. Furthermore, he emphasized an individualized, pharmaceutical-dependent approach to managing food allergy. Individual patients, or the people directly responsible for them in the case of children, were to use a prescription drug delivery device to respond to individual medical emergencies in the moment. The majority of the women on the receiving end of the expert's message occupied a doubly feminized caretaking role as both nurses and primary or secondary school staff. Nurses shared how they felt acutely responsible for helping to bring up the next generation of their community. Finally, the whole event took place in a coastal suburban county whose name is synonymous with the intergenerational transfer of white wealth and status.

This chapter starts disentangling the reproductive politics of food allergy by closely examining the device highlighted in the physician's comments, the epinephrine auto-injector. The coming pages follow the device from the market to the clinic to the online spaces where parents of allergic children share and discuss stories about it. Following what I call the moral life of epinephrine sets the stage for the chapters to come, where epinephrine auto-injectors figure at different moments as practical, lifesaving tools, as a political cause, and as the focal point of a health care cost scandal that raises questions about food allergy advocacy strategies. This chapter follows these devices through four sites with relevance to reproductive politics: the market, the clinic, the home, and online discourse.

THE MORAL LIFE OF EPINEPHRINE

Food allergists and food allergy parents and patients see epinephrine auto-injectors as necessary, lifesaving biomedical tools, yet their moral significance remains largely unexamined in the social science literature on allergy. Understanding their moral significance in the context of everyday life with food allergy is important for grasping why they have become a high-priority cause in food allergy advocacy. Previous research on allergy in Europe and North America has examined how patients and researchers interpret the condition to be an effect of toxic modernity, the controversies surrounding the disease category and its effects on patient identity, and the public imaginary surrounding the peanut allergy "epidemic."[3] However, to my knowledge, no one has yet closely examined how the ever-present technological artifact of the epinephrine auto-injector shapes the experience of the disease. Key moments in a food allergic person's life revolve around epinephrine: preparing for allergic reactions by learning to use the device, reorienting family and social life around food allergy preparedness, and going online to find support from others who have made it through life-threatening reactions. Following the device as it is used and discussed in these contexts illustrates how a technological artifact can take on contextually specific moral significance, and as later chapters will further elaborate, become an anchor for reproductive politics in public food allergy advocacy.

Arjun Appadurai's Introduction to the edited volume *The Social Life of Things* (1986) provides some guidance for understanding how a medical object can take on a more-than-economic importance through socially embedded use. Appadurai argues for a shift from asking what economic value commodities have at an abstract level after the fact of their value is established to understanding how commodities take on economic value in the first place, through the historical fact of being exchanged by people in a society. The "formal truth" in Marxian theory, that exchange creates value, is not enough for anthropologists to accept at face value, according to Appadurai. The methodological challenge for anthropologists, he argues, is to "follow the things themselves, for their meanings are inscribed in their forms, their uses, their trajectories . . . [in order to] interpret the human transactions and calculations that enliven things."[4] In this chapter, I modify Appadurai's approach to more specifically focus on one aspect of the social life of things: the moral importance of lifesaving objects. For my analysis of epinephrine auto-injectors, I call this the moral life of epinephrine.

Medical devices are by nature morally significant because their use sustains the well-being of the human body. It is a truism among anthropologists that the body is intimately linked to subjective being, social life, and political belonging.[5] In diagnosing and curing what ails us physically, biomedical interventions have the potential to change how individuals experience the world, understand themselves, and relate to others. Medical diagnosis in particular shapes the contours of kinship, nonkin social affiliations, self-identity, and political orientations.[6] If bodily experience is, as Csordas argues, "the existential ground of culture,"[7] providing the baseline experience of the world and the means by which individuals in a society relate to one another, then technologies that enable, prolong, or end human lives are exceptionally potent social objects. Medical anthropology teaches that medical technologies have the capacity to make and modify subjects and social worlds.

Work on ethics and morality by anthropologists offers another necessary entry point for understanding how responsible use of epinephrine auto-injectors is organized within families and communities. Some anthropologists have emphasized documenting and analyzing the varied experience of morality in action through ethnographic methods. For Jarret Zigon and C. Jason Throop, for example, focusing on the moral dimensions of experience shifts the working definition of morality from the register of the normative and obligatory to an "attuned concern for the relationality that constitutes our very existence."[8] A study of moral experience, according to them, is a study of "our experiences of the world and how we might struggle to transform these experiences, to rethink them, to interpret them, to reinhabit them, and to reposition ourselves variously as sufferers or actors on the differing scenes that in part constitute our social existence."[9] James Laidlaw, by contrast, seeks a middle ground between ethnographic concern for the practices of embodied life and moral philosophy's interest in seeking to understand how "virtue" and "the good" are defined.[10] He argues that anthropologists should bring together the practice-oriented dimension of morality suggested by Bourdieu's concept of habitus—the idea that what is morally correct is what one learns to do as part of one's culture- and class-specific embodied training about how to live—with moral philosophical interest in discovering what counts as virtue and the good.

My approach in this chapter, and at points elsewhere in this book, tries to integrate these views by using ethnographic data to understand how practices and ideals concerning virtue and the good mutually constitute each other. This chapter begins with an analytic strategy that is closer to Zigon and Throop's emphasis on how moral experience and action play a role in (re)shaping the world. This perspective is again central in later chapters, such as chapter 4, because advocacy and activism are always aimed at effecting change. Laidlaw's insistence on paying attention to situated meanings of virtue and the good is instructive for guiding analysis of the fears and aspirations of caretakers toward the end of this chapter and in chapter 3. Teasing out such moral orientations from interview and social media data guided my investigations into histories of whiteness in medical and food history—contexts that lay the groundwork for arguments in the next two chapters about the reproductive politics of biomedical and technocratic remedies for food allergy.

As I do throughout this book, I view the moral stakes primarily from the perspective of food allergy moms, who comprised the most robustly represented group in my ethnographic research. I also draw on the analysis of their actions and attitudes as offered by a food allergic woman toward the end of this chapter. This allows me to include a moment of reflexive, emic critique from the field. Her reading of the actions of those around her indicates that while there was a majority opinion on epinephrine auto-injectors, it was not universally held within the food allergy community.

Cheryl Mattingly's work on moral laboratories similarly synthesizes aspects of these two anthropological perspectives on morality. Moral laboratories are those moments in which different meanings of a good life must be negotiated and brought into at least temporary alignment to enable action. In Mattingly's analysis of such "experimental" moments within the clinic among lower-income, urban, Black women in the United States shows how mundane encounters between individuals in settings characterized by medical crisis and material need can shape the meaning and practices of care, duty, and hope. Medical therapies intervene and interact with ordinary, nonexpert understandings of what is right and good, as well as with systems of anti-Black and gender oppression.[11] Mattingly demonstrates that Black mothers dealing with medical crises must frequently make calls about how best to live, as well as how to make a better life for their children in the future.

I extend this line of inquiry into the socially differentiated moral content of health care in the United States into my own topic and sites. In the rest of this chapter, I consider how biomedical discourse about food allergies and epinephrine, as it is conveyed to and by patients and caretakers of allergic patients, carries with it moral prescriptions about how to be a good caretaker of one's own body or the body of one's child. A major difference between my study and Mattingly's is the economic, geographic, and racial context of my participants. They are generally middle- to upper-middle-class white women, most living in nuclear families in rural or suburban areas, and mostly content to simply pass on their social status to the next generation. In my field sites, determining appropriate relations of care for children with food allergy often serves to reproduce social life rather than remake it.

This chapter narrates the moral life of epinephrine auto-injectors as they move within and between pharmaceutical markets, the clinic, and online and off-line discussions of how to confront the fear of living with food allergies. This strategy connects the multiple sites of this ethnography to set the stage for the rest of the book in two ways. First, it documents the experiences of fear, trepidation, uncertainty, and risk that people managing food allergies experience—experiences that motivate some individuals to get involved in food allergy advocacy. Second, it shows how centering these devices in food allergy advocacy contributes to the reproduction of raced, gendered, and classed expectations about who can be a responsible caretaker. Understanding the moral life of epinephrine sets the stage for later chapters where epinephrine auto-injectors figure at the center of many personal and political debates about how best to manage food allergy, who should do it, and how best to advocate for the changes necessary to enable such care work. That is, it situates the debates about reproductive politics that will come in later chapters of this book.

SCENE 1: THE MARKET FOR EPINEPHRINE

I begin following the moral life of epinephrine at a large scale: in the difficult-to-locate marketplace for auto-injectors. The rapidly rising price of the device on a supposedly free market is a moral issue that sets the stage for certain reproductive politics on advocacy stages that are discussed in subsequent chapters. The price of epinephrine auto-injectors is a moral issue because pricing a medical intervention assigns a dollar amount to what a society is willing to pay to keep people healthy. It equates moral status as a person with the financial means to purchase a material object. It is also a mechanism of reproductive politics because the supposedly free market for U.S. health care ends up assigning final responsibility for care to nuclear families, within which gendered norms tend to designate women as caretakers.

In the costly and largely privatized U.S. health care system, medical devices circulate freely—that is, with limited government oversight of price or distribution. Individuals are largely responsible for paying for lifesaving treatments through privately purchased or employment-linked health insurance. The well-being, and indeed the very life, of individuals are private matters to be privately managed and generally are not matters of public interest or concern. Such privatization, as Melinda Cooper argues, is designed to return the responsibility for caretaking, and even for life itself, to the nuclear family.[12] What appears to be a public matter—the capitalist market for the device—in fact drives reliance on gendered norms of the family as the default template for care. The nuclear, middle-class family is the site of care; this is treated like the natural order of things.

Product "Choice": Trust versus Novelty

When I initiated my ethnographic research in late 2013, there were two epinephrine auto-injectors that dominated the market, Mylan's EpiPen (relaunched in its current form by Mylan in 2007) and Sanofi's Auvi-Q (launched in January 2013 and removed from the market in October 2015). Both work in roughly the same way. The device is removed from a protective case, a piece of plastic is removed from one end that activates the device and exposes the needle, and the patient quickly swings the needle end into the large muscles on the outer side of the upper thigh. The device strikes the thigh and clicks, injecting the medication while it is held in place for five to ten seconds. The needle retracts to protect the patient from unnecessary sticks when the device is removed from the surface of the body. The devices come in two doses, a 0.3 mg dose intended for children and adults weighing over sixty-six pounds, and the 0.15 mg version intended for children weighing fifteen to sixty-six pounds.

Epinephrine (also known as adrenaline) is a hormone and neurotransmitter produced by the human body in the adrenal glands. It acts on the circulatory system by stimulating the heart muscle and constricting blood vessels, and it acts on the nervous system by producing the fight or flight response. When administered during the severe, multisystem allergic reaction known as anaphylaxis, epinephrine stops the blood vessel leakage that causes the symptoms of anaphylaxis, like hives, redness, and swelling of the airways. Outside of the hospital setting, epinephrine is most often delivered for an allergic reaction using an epinephrine auto-injector. These devices are about the size of a marker and consist of a needle, a dose of medication, and a protective plastic case that covers the medication and the needle before and after use.

Both global and country-specific medical guidelines tell physicians that prompt use of epinephrine is the primary method for reducing the risk of serious injury or death resulting from anaphylaxis.[13] Food allergy physicians in the United States now counsel their patients to keep two auto-injector devices on their person at all times, and the market-leading EpiPen brand devices are sold in packs of two. The second injector can be used if the first fails, if there is a delay in getting the person to the hospital and the reaction returns, or if the reaction is so severe that the person continues to react after the first injection.

When it was available, Sanofi's Auvi-Q also spoke to users in a prerecorded, slightly mechanical woman's voice, guiding the user through the process of using the device. The feature was intended to make the device easier to use. It also seemed to deepen the connection between the user and the device for some of the users I spoke to. It spoke in measured, clearly articulated standard American English, conveying a sense of calm and competence through the careful, unhurried diction of a white woman. The voice began automatically when the device was removed from its case but paused when it was time for the user to take each action. The voice was there to help and guide, but not to command. The choice of a woman's voice suggested a mother or nurse patiently and willingly caring for the user. Its style of speech clearly indicated a white woman. The human voice of the Auvi-Q conveyed the message that the user was not alone and would be taken care of in the event of an anaphylactic emergency. The device invited users to entrust it with their life.

The voice feature, and the caring posture of the device that it implied, inspired mixed feelings among my research participants. One allergist with a peanut allergy explained that the product was simply a much more practical shape to carry in his pocket and had no opinion on the voice. Perhaps the physical design will encourage more people to keep it consistently on their person, he mused when we discussed it. His nurse, on the other hand, was a rare dissenter to the general enthusiasm I heard for the product. She expressed discomfort and annoyance with the automated voice, preferring to teach patients to use a different, voiceless device. One parent explained to me that her seven-year-old son is proud to carry his Auvi-Q with him. He kept it in a pocket of his cargo pants. His attachment to this object centered on its technological novelty. For him, it was not just medicine; it was his very own gadget that sets him apart from his peers. Because he liked the device, he was never without it, making him a responsible food allergy patient.

Many food allergy bloggers appreciated this device because they believed it could widen the social horizons for food allergic children. For others, the longer, trustworthy history of the EpiPen brand, personal and community familiarity with its use, or inertia around changing prescriptions when the newer device was released precluded adoption of the Auvi-Q. Those who preferred the Auvi-Q noted how it enlarged the circle of people who could be responsible for stepping in to help care for someone with serious food allergies in a moment of allergic crisis. Because it guided users through the injection process, it removed the need for an adult trained to use the device to be present if a small child needed to use the device. A talking epinephrine auto-injector thus made it possible for children to more safely participate in childhood activities like sports and summer camps. The voice feature even gave the Auvi-Q an edge over the EpiPen for some people.

Auto-injectors as a Business Opportunity

Epinephrine auto-injectors also were, and continue to be, big business for the pharmaceutical companies who make them. The price U.S. users pay for epinephrine auto-injectors is the result of a complicated calculation involving multiple middlemen, payers, and a complex supply chain. For those with private insurance in the United States, it is common to pay $10 to $40 for every doctor's visit, service, or filled prescription that is covered, with potentially many charges being incurred from a single visit to the doctor's office or pharmacy. Prescriptions can commonly range into the hundreds of dollars per month. Many people only access such benefits after paying the first several thousand dollars of care out of pocket each calendar year, especially those employed by smaller companies or those who purchase insurance outside of an employer benefits plan. Not all prescriptions and services are covered, and some carry higher fees, often when they are brand-name or specialty products. In this context, food allergy alone has been estimated by one pediatrician to cost U.S. families more than $25 billion per year—more than $4,000 per food allergy family in special food, emergency medical costs, and doctor's visit and drug copayments.[14] Out-of-pocket costs translate into profits throughout the health care payment landscape—profits for insurance companies, testing companies, health care providers, and drug and device makers.

Epinephrine auto-injectors are not unique in the financial burden they produce for users, and they are likely not unique in how they prompt families to default to gendered norms in providing care in resource-limited situations. Throughout the U.S. health care system, the presumed care orientation of biomedicine is increasingly subsumed to the market logic of health care economics. What is used in medical practice is determined both by what works according to expensive, strategically designed, controlled studies and what can be justified by financial modeling.[15] Food allergy is no exception to this story. In some ways, it exemplifies these trends. In the second half of 2015, for example, two news reports shook the food allergy community by revealing the commodity status of epinephrine auto-injectors. This coverage forced reflection on the fact that epinephrine auto-injectors have different kinds of value to different actors with an interest in food allergy: morally potent, lifesaving, but expensive companions for people with food allergies and profit-generating commodities for the companies who produce them. While I will discuss the fallout of the rising price of the EpiPen on food allergy activism in more depth in chapter 5, I will briefly mention the episode here to provide the necessary context for understanding the moral life of epinephrine.

The first of two widely read reports about the rising price of the EpiPen epinephrine auto-injector was an investigative piece released by the news outlet Bloomberg News on September 23, 2015. The piece put concrete numbers on the high—and rising—cost of Mylan's epinephrine auto-injector, the EpiPen, that advocates and parents had already been feeling for some time.[16] Their research confirmed what I had been hearing from food allergy advocates for months: the price of EpiPens had increased significantly. It had risen from $57 per device in 2007, when Mylan acquired the device, to a typical price of $415 for a two-pack in 2015. The rise in prices, according to the Bloomberg report, contributed to a jump in revenue generated by the product, from $200 million in 2007 to over $1 billion with a 55 percent profit margin in 2015. At the time the article came out, it made up 40 percent of Mylan's profits. Its brand equity—a term of marketing art that refers to a product's reputation and the loyalty it inspires in customers—made it impervious to competition from a less expensive generic version, according to Mylan CEO Heather Bresch. At the time, this was not an outrageous claim; in the first half of 2015, the device had an 85 percent claim on the market. For the company, the EpiPen epinephrine auto-injector was a hot commodity whose profitability was ensured in part by its image as a trustworthy and lifesaving device.

A second news item added to the worries of people with food allergies when, on October 28, 2015, Sanofi announced an enormous recall of all Auvi-Q devices on the market.[17] The recall underscored that these devices are potentially fallible and that access to them is subject to the exigencies of corporate strategy and regulatory oversight. A blog post on one food allergy activist's website, Oh Mah Deehness!, is representative of the reactions among food allergy bloggers. In a blog post entitled "All Auvi-Q Epinephrine Autoinjectors Recalled," the activist wrote, "You could view the recall as being in an abundance of caution and therefore showing how sensitive Sanofi is being to consumers or you can wonder about the timing and the lack of actual clear instructions for how to handle the issue." She also reported that the recall came less than a week after she received an e-mail from the company encouraging her to purchase more of their devices before the end of a promotional pricing program, making her suspicious of their motives.

The high price of replacing both Auvi-Q and EpiPen auto-injectors at the time of the recall made upcoming decisions about how best to care for her daughter both morally and economically fraught:

> The costs of replacing medication, between new doctor's appointments for prescriptions, potentially missing work or school to sort matters out, and more are factors that Sanofi can't control. I have preferred the Auvi-Q in form and function since it was released but will be sending my daughter to school tomorrow with a set of EpiPens. The sheer expense of a mid-year replacement (ie, replacing the EpiPen with an Auvi-Q if new batches ship) make reverting back to the Auvi-Q another year away for us.[18]

This tension between financial value and the practical, lifesaving usefulness of epinephrine auto-injectors complicates both responsible caretaking and responsible patienthood for people living with food allergies. For example, how can patients or caretakers comply with medical advice to have two auto-injectors with the allergic person at all times (which often means buying duplicate pairs for school and home or home and work) and still have the personal financial resources to live the good life that maintaining their health is intended to enable? What are the financial stakes of using an auto-injector when a reaction is suspected but not confirmed, a common scenario? Should a user or caretaker risk wasting $200 or more to give an injection if it is a false alarm? Who pays the cost—which can range from hundreds to tens of thousands of dollars—for the doctor-recommended ambulance ride to the hospital and stay in the emergency room?

As they circulate in the market, the moral content of epinephrine auto-injectors and their influence on reproductive politics remain largely potential. Within food allergy families, as I will document, responsibility for providing appropriate care with auto-injectors and other tools tends to fall to women. Outside of families, the responsibility tends to fall to feminized children's caretakers like nurses and teachers. The high price of the device raises other moral questions about the relationship between individuals, families, and the market for medical products. For one, it raises questions about who is responsible for financing appropriate medical care. In the U.S. context, this responsibility is borne to a large and increasing extent by insured individuals and members of their state-recognized nuclear families who are also typically allowed to share in their insurance benefits. As epinephrine auto-injectors move from markets into clinics and the hands and homes of specific allergic individuals, these nascent issues of gendered and private responsibility become clearer. The family, the clinic, and the home become sites where everyday decisions about food, hygiene, and epinephrine auto-injectors strengthen and reproduce gendered norms of care.

SCENE 2: EPINEPHRINE IN THE CLINIC

The second part of this sketch of the moral life of epinephrine takes us to the clinic. This is where devices exit from abstract circulation in the medical products market and find their way into the hands of patients, caretakers, and other potential users. Mismatch between medical practice norms and the everyday needs of food allergic people sets up food allergy patients and caretakers, especially mothers, to feel as though they are constantly on the verge of failing to act responsibly. Patient education rituals led by physicians and nurses establish epinephrine auto-injectors as morally significant objects in the lives and habits of people with food allergies. But these encounters are not necessarily satisfactory or sufficient for people managing food allergy in their day-to-day lives. Epinephrine auto-injector training focuses on responding with pharmaceutical preparedness to an allergic reaction once it starts. By contrast, managing everyday life with food allergy focuses more on preventing contamination and reactions in the first place. Moral conflicts thus arise in the disjuncture between the expectations for responsible epinephrine auto-injector use as articulated by health care providers in clinical encounters and the lived experience of managing food safety on a daily basis.

In an individual's initial appointments with an allergist for a suspected food allergy, medical professionals typically teach patients and caretakers how to use epinephrine auto-injectors to be prepared for the next episode of anaphylaxis. Throughout the dress rehearsal, practitioners emphasize both the device's technical details and moral importance. Once a food allergy is confirmed by medical history, diagnostic tests, or both—typically news delivered definitively in the first or second visit—the allergist (or, more commonly in the clinics I visited, a dedicated allergy nurse) demonstrates how to use an epinephrine auto-injector with a training version of the device. These training devices do not contain medication but have the same mechanism, shape, and size as real auto-injectors.

One day, in the clinic where I spent the most time observing the daily work of allergy medicine, I asked an allergy nurse to walk me through the training ritual as though I were a patient. I sat in a small white interior room with yellowish wood cabinets, counter space, and a sink along one wall. I was seated on a gray synthetic leather chair with wide, flat, upholstered arms where patients could comfortably rest after receiving allergy shots for respiratory allergies. The space was divided into smaller cubicles, each with a chair, by white curtains that hung from the ceiling and could be slid open or closed. I sat down, and we began the exercise. The nurse instructed me to remove the end cap of the EpiPen trainer, which I held in a fist in my right hand. I then quickly swung the device through the air so the functional end firmly struck my outer, upper right thigh hard enough that the needle in a real, working unit could have passed through clothing, skin, and subcutaneous fat into the muscle of the leg.

The user who goes through this type of demonstration is typically the food allergic individual. A caretaker might be in charge of the device in a demo or real-world administration if the allergic person is a child or if, in a real-life emergency, the user is too ill to administer the medication alone. Before and after the rehearsal, the health care provider advises patients on the symptoms that ought to prompt use of an auto-injector, the importance of carrying it on their person at all times, and the need to avoid eating any foods they discover they are allergic to through diagnostic testing and the patient's history. In my demo, it was the allergy nurse, not the attending physician, who walked me through these basics. After such a demo, the patient leaves, prescription in hand or sent electronically to their pharmacy of choice. They are now, in the eyes of some clinicians, prepared for life with food allergy to the extent that biomedical interventions can aid them.

This pharmaceutical approach to food allergy prescribes a technological object as a quick fix to the complex moral, bodily, and social problem of how to live with food allergy. Science studies scholars have found similar approaches to the technological management of risk in a wide variety of contexts, from nuclear preparedness to bioweapons to other areas of biomedicine, including treatments for cancer and high blood pressure.[19] In contemporary technoscientific contexts, especially in the United States, being prepared for disaster is presented as being as good as not facing a risk at all. Technology can clean up the mess, so why worry about prevention? As Stefan Timmermans describes in his history of CPR, it takes a great deal of work among medical researchers, educators, and advocates to make a single, heroic medical intervention seem like the obvious solution to a medical crisis.[20] But once a quick fix is established in professional practice and the popular imagination as the preferred way to avert death, it becomes difficult to dislodge.[21] The moral life of epinephrine, especially as it passes through the clinic, exemplifies this tendency for a quick fix to stand in for a comprehensive response to a medical problem.

Emphasizing the use of epinephrine as a lifesaving intervention in clinical encounters imbues auto-injectors with a high degree of moral significance. Yet it falls short of providing people with food allergy with all of the strategies they will need to manage their new diagnosis. Several of the allergists I observed and interviewed in my research pointed out that they also suggest that new patients (or their caretakers, in the case of children) consult local support groups or websites. In one clinic, a physician even prepared packets of information for newly diagnosed individuals that included brochures for regional food allergy support groups. However, such referrals are the furthest that physicians and nurses go in offering practical advice for mealtimes and social gatherings.

Instead, generations of newly diagnosed children, adults, and parents have taught themselves how to read food labels, what to ask food manufacturers to learn whether allergens came in contact with their preferred foods, and how to assertively refuse allergenic foods offered by friends and family members through trial, error, and discussions in support groups. None of these management techniques are quick technical fixes. They are, in fact, deeply social. They involve disclosing a food allergy diagnosis to someone else, quickly building a rapport, gathering information from one or more other people, and deciding whether it is useful and trustworthy as a basis for action, such as deciding whether it is safe to eat a particular brand of cookie. Yet these nonpharmaceutical, interpersonal negotiations are the primary techniques people rely on to avoid having an allergic reaction to food in the first place. Epinephrine use in everyday life is a sign that these tactics have failed, that the person in charge has failed, and that disaster has arrived. Using epinephrine is something to ward off rather than something to celebrate. In everyday situations, epinephrine remains potentially present as a kind of mild threat—a warning that preventive measure could go wrong, someone could eat their allergen, and, if they responsibly prepared for disaster, they could then return to safety by treating the reaction with an auto-injector.

The limited information most food allergy patients receive about how to live with food allergy feels like an ethical lapse to many on the receiving end of biomedical advice. However, when it comes to treating food allergy, the most robust evidence in the medical literature concerns the administration of epinephrine. There have been few studies of successful techniques for allergen avoidance designed to provide what biomedical practitioners would consider robust evidence for different types of prevention strategies. For an allergist to go out on a limb without evidence to make lifestyle recommendations solely on the basis of patient reports—even if they are the physician's own patients, and even if they have heard similar stories over and over again—would contravene the evidence-based mood of the contemporary biomedical clinic.[22] In effect, for a physician to advise patients extensively on everyday techniques to avoid allergic reactions, without clear medical literature about how best to do that, would constitute a kind of ethical breach according to today's norms of the profession. The literature suggests that timely administration of epinephrine during an allergic reaction results in fewer deaths from anaphylactic reactions and that there are no adverse effects from epinephrine so severe as to prevent its use in any situation where allergic reaction is suspected or likely.[23] Therefore, following the evidence, timely administration of epinephrine during an allergic reaction is the cornerstone of good biomedical practice.

The pharmaceutical-focused clinical encounter stands as an emblem of the different moral expectations of physicians and patients concerning food allergy. Physicians and their staff, bound by evidence and trained to turn toward pharmaceuticals and other technologies as treatments, train newly diagnosed food allergic people how and when to use epinephrine auto-injectors. These same devices operate as reminders of failure and fear for the people who are tasked with being prepared to use them to save their life or the life of a person in their care. The moral life of epinephrine auto-injectors in the clinic is thus deeply fraught. It simultaneously reveals the limits and power of biomedicine to people with food allergies, especially when they are newly diagnosed.[24] For many food allergy families, the limitations of pharmaceutical preparedness opens up a gap between the ideal situation and reality that is filled by an intensification of gendered domestic work. In other words, the shortcomings of clinical solutions to food allergy position epinephrine to get swept up in the reproductive politics of caretaking, specifically the gendering of care work in the home. Normative gender expectations about caretaking come to dominate both preparedness and caretaking measures in real life while setting the stage for the formation of food allergy support, advocacy, and awareness campaigns.

SCENE 3: THE MORAL CAREER OF A FOOD ALLERGY MOM

As epinephrine auto-injectors make their way into the home of newly diagnosed individuals, they often enter into a moral drama about the intensification of women's responsibilities in the home. Care work, including food preparation, enforcing hand hygiene among children, and building relationships with other parents and caretakers, are the everyday tools for responsibly managing food allergy. Epinephrine auto-injectors stand in waiting as everyday life unfolds and serve as reminders about the intensive care needed to make life with food allergy safe and livable. Learning to live safely with food allergies and how epinephrine auto-injectors fit into this life is a process that prompts reflection on personal preparedness and responsibility and reinforces gendered and classed organization of caretaking expectations within the nuclear family. In this section, I follow how one woman navigates this process to become an allergy mom, a term that many of my research participants used to describe themselves and people in food allergy advocacy networks. Her story illustrates a common trajectory, including how auto-injectors are imbricated with other techniques and technologies to sustain a healthy and vibrant life with food allergy. The gendering of care work in this setting also demonstrates how some of the core concerns of food allergy advocacy, like awareness about and access to epinephrine auto-injectors, are also issues of reproductive politics.

Erving Goffman's framework of the moral career helps to parse the life histories of food allergy moms in formation. A moral career narrative foregrounds the changes in social interactions and moral values that occur when learning to live with a chronic condition. Goffman describes what he calls the "moral career of the mental patient" who is committed to an asylum as both a moral and social project.[25] This is a moral transformation because it forces the patient to reinterpret, and potentially rewrite, the story of his life and achievements. He develops a new understanding of the self, the moral qualities of those with whom he interacts, and the character of his relational bonds to others. It is also a social transformation because induction into life as a mental patient requires breaking old social bonds organically formed through the life course. The patient forms new, compulsory bonds with other inmates, with caretakers on the outside, and with orderlies, nurses, and doctors on the inside.

Breaking and building social bonds trigger Goffman's archetypical patient to reevaluate himself and those around him. The hoped-for outcome is to create a new situation for the patient that is more in line with normative expectations for his comportment and behavior, based on his social positioning. The patient must make an appropriate display of his reconfigured moral self to win release from the institution. "Contingencies" like socioeconomic status, "visibility of the offense," the proximity and kind of treatment available, and actions taken on the patient's behalf while he is institutionalized can derail or facilitate the process.[26] The patient learns to see himself differently and to adapt to a new social situation. Ideally, the patient emerges from confinement with new alliances, enmities, standards of conduct, and moral codes that model what will be expected on the outside. These new relationships and attitudes are decidedly prescriptive. Because the whole purpose of confinement in an asylum is to return patients to normal behavior, their new relationships are expected to conform to the most strictly normative parameters of class, race, and gender.

Similarly, a food allergy diagnosis prompts mothers of food allergic children to reevaluate expectations for their own relationships and often reinforces normativity, especially normative ideas about gender roles in the home. Mothers of food allergic children become food allergy moms through this process. Existing social relationships are strained, but new ones are formed as a consequence of managing the disease. The rigid biological limitations on what can and cannot be eaten by a food allergic child delimits the transformation instead of the walls and institutional organization of an asylum. Food allergy moms in the making must rework relationships with members of their nuclear family and extended kin, colleagues, and nonkin caretakers like babysitters and teachers. They also form new bonds over their shared condition with food allergic adults and parents of allergic kids. They often find that a new food allergy diagnosis complicates decisions about whom to trust with caring for their children, puts interactions with school officials on contentious ground, and limits the civic and professional projects to which they can commit themselves. Through it all, many of my participants sought reassurance in normative ideas about motherhood along their journey. They often inhabited and reproduced the normative boundaries of this role as a tool for navigating their new situation.

One of my first contacts in the food allergy world told me her story, which exemplifies the moral career of a food allergy mom. This woman, whom I will call Sarah, had two children with food allergies, both of whom were diagnosed as babies. She suspected there was something wrong with her first son when he began breaking out in "dynamic" rashes and eczema and having bloody, mucousy stools. His symptoms began when he was only four weeks old, while Sarah was nursing and eating her ordinary diet. Sarah's second son exhibited similar symptoms several weeks after birth. Her pediatrician and allergist offered her epinephrine prescriptions for her children and counseled her to avoid feeding them commonly allergenic foods. However, they provided little advice on how to live day to day with kids with food allergies. Medical advice had a lot to say about how to treat anaphylaxis but little to say about food preparation, play dates, and returning to work outside the home. These tasks fell into the box of mothering, not doctoring.

Mealtimes at Sarah's house illustrated the moral precarity of being a food allergy mom. Eating together posed significant challenges because her two sons' allergies did not overlap. For example, one son reacted to dairy and drank soy milk to prevent reactions, and the other reacted to soy and drank cow's milk. Confusing dairy milk and soy milk could result in serious illness for one or both children.[27] No hugging or kissing was allowed during lunch or dinner until everyone washed up. The siblings sometimes used their dirty hands against each other as weapons because even touching allergen residue onto the skin could cause both of them to develop rashes. None of these details were covered by her physician when she was taught the basics of how to use an epinephrine auto-injector. Yet these were the type of challenges that occupied much of her time managing her sons' allergies. Food allergy, in Sarah's experience, was a caretaking challenge just as much as it was a biomedical diagnosis.

Sarah focused her attention on the care work that raising two food allergic children required. At first, she experienced significant stress when her children began attending neighborhood play groups because they could not participate in every activity in typical ways. Off-limit foods were everywhere. Other moms did not seem to care about helping her clean allergens like peanut butter off play surfaces. Upset by what she called a "lack of awareness [and] lack of compassion," Sarah eventually started a support group in her town for parents of food allergic children. The group allowed her to connect and commiserate with other mothers facing similar issues. She and the other mothers in the group found comfort in connecting with like-minded food allergy moms. It was useful for everyone in the group to share ideas about how to deal with school teachers and officials and find allergy-friendly foods. As a leader of the group, she also contacted national food allergy support and advocacy organizations. She linked the local group to national issues. The support group was a space for connecting and building solidarity based on the feminized, care-focused role of food allergy mom.

However, the support group did not turn out to be a panacea for the everyday stresses of living with food allergies. Her younger son, who was seven years old at the time we spoke, had recently begun experiencing new anxieties linked to his allergies. While Sarah explained that increased anxiety is developmentally appropriate for a child of his age, she worried because his anxiety was entirely focused on food and eating. She attributed that to the constant vigilance the both he and she maintained to manage his food allergies. The fact that his anxiety symptoms—a tight, sore throat—mimicked his first symptoms of an allergic reaction made the situation especially distressing. The symptom overlap complicated the ability to recognize when a reaction occurred, and thus when epinephrine ought to be used. An epinephrine injection could save his life if he was experiencing an allergic reaction, but if he was not, it could trigger an unnecessary trip to the emergency room, as well as the potential for medical complications or additional food allergy–related trauma, if he was not. Sarah knew she should use an auto-injector if her son experienced symptoms, given his known food allergies. But she might also have reason to choose not to do so when she considered sudden symptoms in the current context of her family's experience.

Managing two kids with food allergies dramatically changed Sarah's professional aspirations and self-image. She was effectively unable to work while also caring for her two food allergic children. She put her career on hold in order to shuttle the kids to frequent doctors' appointments, cook all meals at home, and advocate for her sons at school. While she had considered returning to work by the time we spoke, the intricacies of mealtime and lack of care concerning allergen contamination from other parents and care workers prevented her from returning to work. She felt that she was constantly trying to "walk a line between seeming crazy and keeping these kids alive." She did not trust that anyone else could do it as well as she had, even though her efforts had not been perfect. Food allergy put her in a position where she felt like she was required to be a stay-at-home mom, whether she wanted to be one or not.

Indeed, many of the food allergy moms I spoke to felt, like Sarah, that they had no choice but to retreat from their careers and focus on being a full-time mom. Over and over again, women told me about how their husbands were unwilling to give up their careers and how extended family and community members were untrustworthy. There was no one else available who could be trusted. The gendered experience of Sarah and other food allergy moms was mirrored by that of one food allergy father I spoke to in depth, whom I will describe in chapter 3. He felt like he had failed in his role as a man when he became the primary caretaker for his allergic child.

In the face of a medical diagnosis with no simple solution, the heteronormative ordering of care work becomes the basis for organizing roles in the family and home. Men work outside the home to provide shelter, money, and health insurance, and women stay home with children to guard them from the dangers of a contaminated world. Mothers like Sarah still felt compelled to follow the cultural script even when they recognized the limits of this paradigm as less than ideal or even oppressive. The moral career of a food allergy mom might start in the clinic with learning to use an epinephrine auto-injector, but it mostly unfolds in the home, at the dinner table, and on the playground. The two-parent, heteronormative nuclear family ideal provides the template for the moral career of the food allergy mom.

Toward the end of our conversation, Sarah shared a pair of stories about the experiences of other families. First, she recounted the story of a sixth grader with a nut allergy who ate a cookie with nuts in it while sitting shiva for a family friend. Her parents treated her ensuing asthma symptoms, but epinephrine wasn't used because she did not tell her parents about eating the cookie. The girl died. Then Sarah told me the story of a fourteen-year-old boy who died in October 2013 after being in a coma for two weeks. His illness had been triggered by a severe reaction to peanuts. This second story was familiar to me already because it had been circulating on food allergy blogs in recent weeks. The boy, Giovanni Cipriani, had eaten a snack mix containing unlabeled peanuts, a food to which he had a severe allergy. According to an essay Giovanni's mother wrote for the Food Allergy and Anaphylaxis Connection Team, a food allergy advocacy organization, she did not inject him with epinephrine and call 911. Instead, she gave him antihistamines and drove him to a nearby emergency room by herself. By the time they arrived, he had stopped breathing. He fell into a coma and never awoke before dying three weeks later.[28]

I understood these stories as a way for Sarah to illustrate how dangerous it is for children to live normal lives with food allergies. Despite her efforts to manage mealtime and build relationships with other mothers to raise community awareness, her kids remained perpetually at risk of a deadly unforeseen reaction. These stories also connected her experience to the public conversations about food allergy and epinephrine auto-injectors that were going on at the time. Mothers, bloggers, and food allergy advocacy nonprofits were sharing both stories on social media and in press releases to encourage the prompt use of epinephrine auto-injectors for food allergy reactions. Epinephrine was front and center in these morality tales designed to illustrate the worst case scenario of what could happen with inadequate preparedness: death. Telling these stories was a way for Sarah to teach me, then a novice in the world of food allergy, about the paramount importance of epinephrine auto-injectors. This too was part of her role as a food allergy mom: educating those around her who still had more to learn about the power of epinephrine auto-injectors to keep people with food allergy safe.

Sarah's moral career as a food allergy mom illustrates a common kind of ambivalence toward epinephrine auto-injectors. These devices are potentially lifesaving, and thus morally potent. But they are also but one of many tools needed to manage food allergy, especially for allergic children. To fill in these gaps between biomedical advice and real life, women often double down on the gendered role of mother to take the lead on cooking, cleaning, and interfacing with other parents and caretakers. Epinephrine auto-injectors are actually a tool of last resort in the context of everyday household management, to be used only in the event of failure on the part of a food allergy mom or other caretaker. They thus serve as a warning, and their use signals a failure of responsibility. The moral career of a food allergy mom is a kind of moral drama in which epinephrine has the power to save the day when all else—including the mother herself—fails. Sarah's story demonstrates the hazards that accompany the role of a food allergy mom and the complicated role that epinephrine auto-injectors play in both allaying and signifying the risks of the job.

SCENE 4: DEATH TALK

The fourth and final scene of the moral life of epinephrine takes us to community and public settings where parents and advocates exchange stories about epinephrine use. Epinephrine anchors the morality of food allergy activism through the circulations of stories about epinephrine auto-injector use that portrays its appropriate use as the mark of responsible patients and caretakers. To consider this final aspect of the moral life of epinephrine, I examine death talk. Death talk consists of storytelling about epinephrine that circulates via social media, blog posts, and in-person conversations between food allergy moms and advocates. The two stories Sarah told me, about two children who died from allergic reactions, are brief examples of this genre.

Death talk stories play two major roles in food allergic advocacy: educating people about the importance of epinephrine auto-injector use and creating common ground among people living with food allergy. The normative morality of food allergic people and caretakers echoes the biomedical wisdom that opened this chapter: epinephrine is a lifesaving medication, and epinephrine auto-injectors ought to be used whenever an allergic reaction occurs. Death talk circulates widely among food allergy advocates, teaching listeners what constitutes responsible caretaking. Most often it looks like members of nuclear families caring for their own in the absence of responsible bystanders and community members.

Death talk is a hallmark of food allergy activist texts and one of the genres of talk that circulates widely when people meet in person. I learned the term from a participant with whom I became close during my research. A trained social worker and food allergy therapist, her life revolved around food allergies, yet she tried to resist the fear many feel while living with the condition. Although food allergies can sometimes lead to the serious, multisystem allergic reaction called anaphylaxis, and although anaphylaxis can sometimes lead to death, death talk makes food allergy, anaphylaxis, and death seem identical in all cases. The dramatization of the danger of food allergies and the power of epinephrine serve explicitly normative roles: to teach the proper role of epinephrine in food allergic life. This reinforces the idea that families are primarily responsible for the health and life of allergic people. Death talk thus speaks to the reproductive politics of food allergy by naturalizing close family as the individuals best able to care for people with the condition.

Death talk is abundant on food allergy blogs. It presents a predictable narrative arc of escalating danger followed by or interspersed with lessons about responsibility. One post that exemplifies the genre appeared on the Allergy Eats! blog during the summer of 2014. Entitled "Our First Experience with the Epi—All the Details and 16 Lessons to Take Away," the piece tells the story of what happened when the writer's teenaged son ate a cookie containing hidden nuts at a party.[29] At first the son and parents do not believe the reaction is severe and treat it with Benadryl. Eventually the son senses that something may be seriously wrong, and the parents call 911 for an ambulance to take him to the hospital. The reaction recurs hours later, to the surprise of both the family and the emergency room staff.

The sixteen lessons of the post's title are written in bold, italic type to grab the reader's attention. Epinephrine features prominently in eight of them. Lesson 2, for example, states, "Teach your teens to carry their autoinjectors. Help them find a way to avoid any embarrassment they may feel. Have them read this story if necessary." Lesson 7 instructs the reader, "When you decide to use the epi, be strong in your conviction—you're doing the right thing. Don't hesitate!" This is echoed by lesson 13: "Did I mention—Don't Fear Using the Epi! Fear NOT using it!" The writer ultimately credits the food allergy community for his family's successful treatment of the reaction. Others in his network had equipped him with the appropriate knowledge about the importance of being prepared to use epinephrine auto-injectors.

A more unsettling example of death talk is a periodically updated blog post on the online support website No Nuts Moms Group. Titled "Remembering Those We Have Lost to Food Allergies," the post consists of a list of names in bold red text, followed by age, cause of death, and a link to a relevant online news article, arranged by year of death. A typical entry reads, "Michael Saffioti, 22, died from dairy allergy after eating oatmeal containing dairy." Another, from 2008, features more dramatic language: "Daniel Sargent, 30, collapsed after taking a bite of a chocolate chip cookie."[30] The news stories they link to describe the events leading up to the death, provide some basic facts about their life, and explain that food allergy is apparently on the rise in the United States. In the comments section, which had one hundred eight posts in September 2021, some readers express their gratitude for the list, while others report that the list drove home for them the seriousness of food allergies. This list of worst-case outcomes provides evidence of what happens when patients do not follow recommendations for epinephrine use. The message is that without vigilance, there is a straight line from food allergy diagnosis, allergen exposure leading to anaphylaxis, and death.

These two popular blog posts share the pedagogical aim of educating readers about appropriate responsibility. They show how preparedness is the best defense against a reaction and subsequent complications; they also show how to step in to help, should a reader later witness someone experiencing an allergic reaction. Among people with food allergies and parents of allergic children, there is a widely shared (and, tragically, sometimes confirmed) fear that food allergies are not taken seriously by people without the condition. Educating the public about food allergy by telling morality tales about epinephrine is one way to teach people unaffected by allergies how serious the condition can be. By making audiences more aware of the dangers of food allergy and of the necessity of the use of epinephrine to reverse adverse reactions, food allergy writers aim to make them more responsible for those around them with food allergy. In the longer term, and like other patient advocacy movements, raising awareness is understood to bring greater attention from researchers and greater representation in political debates about the distribution of limited health care resources.[31]

A second role these stories play is to bring people living with food allergies—especially parents of allergic children—together through narrating their shared food allergy experiences. The closing appeal of the Allergy Eats! blog post alludes to this function:

> I have learned so much over the years reading and hearing about everyone else's experiences—the right decisions and the wrong decisions. We are all in this together! And if I hadn't learned from you that giving an epi too late can be fatal, that epinephrine can't harm your child, that the relief of an epi is virtually instantaneous, that getting an anaphylactic sufferer off his feet is important, that calling 911 after administering an epi is "mandatory," etc., well . . . thank you for teaching me![32]

Sharing these blogged testimonials about epinephrine use—including failures and near misses—via e-mail mailing lists and social media posts provides yet another way for parents to build and maintain a network based on shared fear. For many, that fear gets channeled into advocacy work that reaches beyond their families and local communities. For example, the Allergy Eats! blog is part of a larger platform that helps people with food allergy identify restaurants with appropriate food substitutions and safety protocols for an individual's allergies. Blending business, advocacy, and personal testimonials, the platform's website attempts to simultaneously educate people about food allergic living and facilitate life with food allergies.

Death talk stories are also passed from person to person in private moments. In this context, they help to build a shared understanding of responsible caretaking. Anxiety often comes to the fore in such person-to-person communications. For example, during a phone interview, Shelley, a nursing professional whose son has severe food allergies, told me a detailed story about her son's first anaphylactic reaction as a baby. Rather than administering epinephrine and taking him to the hospital, she gave him an oral antihistamine—a mode of treatment that is no longer recommended for anaphylaxis—and monitored him closely for over a day. Already familiar with the signs and symptoms of medical crises from her training, she managed the superficial symptoms, like facial swelling, but began to worry when too many hours passed without her son producing urine. She knew that could be a sign of kidney failure. At this point, Shelley began to doubt and regret her decision not to give epinephrine. She had made that decision because she wanted to avoid the time and cost of a trip to the emergency room and because she had confidence in her ability to handle a medical emergency if it occurred. Her son's condition soon reversed, but she described it to me as a close call. She would not recommend anyone else make the same decisions she had, even though, in practice, things turned out well for her son.

While Shelley's story happily ended in recovery rather than death, it followed the death talk story arc: escalating danger with a through line of anxiety about using an epinephrine auto-injector, followed by advice for proper action. In Shelley's case, she was navigating a unique added layer of complexity: how to balance her skill as a nurse with her needs as a parent to both sustain her son's life and weather the financial consequences of caretaking decisions like having her son taken to the hospital in an ambulance. As an expert, she is confident, but as a mother, she wonders if she is making the appropriate choice to monitor her son at home. Her need to consider financial dimensions of medical care is unique to the U.S. context and further illustrates how the market circulation of epinephrine auto-injectors is a moral issue that positions responsibility for good care within the nuclear family. In this case, responsibility specifically resides in the person of Shelley, a mother. In the end, this episode of death talk also serves its pedagogical purpose: She addresses me and the imagined future readers of my ethnographic texts to discourage others from making the same decisions she made. Together, Shelley's story and the Allergy Eats! blog post not only exemplify the death talk genre but also demonstrate how death talk often centers the family and mothers as key agents of responsible care. In both cases, death talk is both a morality tale central to following the moral life of epinephrine and an indication of some of the reproductive politics of food allergy management.

The morality presented by food allergy death talk obscures many of the complexities about using auto-injectors, implying that most choices, accidents, and resistance to following the dictates of biomedical authority to the letter are simply negligence. However, as this chapter has shown, the moral life of epinephrine brings together domains and moral quandaries that extend well beyond the level of the individual. Epinephrine auto-injectors bind the market to the clinic and bind the clinic to the home and the nuclear family; they also bind online and off-line discourse. An apparently simple story about how anaphylaxis should be treated with epinephrine is actually a series of complex moral experiences in which (potential) users respond to different pressures and trade-offs, including considerations of finances, gender roles, family politics, expertise, and more. Stories like Shelley's illustrate that the normative morality of food allergy care does not capture the complexity of making real-life decisions about how to responsibly respond to an allergic crisis. Using her own nursing expertise in managing medical crises creates a loophole that allows her to avoid using an auto-injector and going to the hospital. Because everything turns out all right for her son, in hindsight, it appears that she made responsible choices.

MORALITY AND REPRODUCTIVE POLITICS

This chapter has explored how epinephrine auto-injectors structure moral obligations between those with food allergy, those who care for them, and those who play supporting roles in the drama of food allergic living in the United States. Analyzing these devices in their multiple, everyday contexts makes it clear that they are more than just high-tech, quick-fix tools. They have value that is more morally complex than the dollar amount printed in a health insurance plan's price list. Inspired by recent anthropological literature, I have focused in this chapter on the moral dimensions of the device to map out its moral life as it circulates between abstract medical markets, clinical encounters, the home, and public and private discourse. Epinephrine auto-injectors are lively objects, not dead commodities.

These devices make certain individuals, namely mothers of allergic children, more responsible than others. This is one dimension of their relevance to reproductive politics. Because biomedical practitioners have little advice to offer for the everyday management of food allergy outside of using epinephrine auto-injectors in the event of anaphylaxis, responsibility for ordinary preventive measures becomes a private matter to be handled by members of nuclear families. Responsibility is often further channeled to women and mothers in light of default, gendered notions about who is the appropriate family member to be held responsible for children and for the health of the family. Mothers tend to take on this role, with some gladly accepting it but others expressing hesitation. The moral career of Sarah, a food allergy mom, shows how these decisions unfold over time and in response to specific, situated experiences. Yet as the next two chapters will argue, the assignment of caretaking responsibility to mothers does not happen in a vacuum. It is shaped by histories of modern home hygiene in the United States and by recent and ongoing decisions by biomedical researchers about what research questions are worth answering. Further, gender is not the only structural constraint on caretaking; race and class figure prominently in U.S. history and in the present of food allergic living as well.

It is crucial to understand the moral life of epinephrine auto-injectors because they figure prominently in the public and legislative advocacy around food allergy in the United States. As chapters 4 and 5 will demonstrate, public-facing advocacy campaigns to expand epinephrine access are a form of reproductive politics. Many advocacy messages and strategies rely on and reproduce gendered, raced, and classed ideals of caretaking and responsibility. Individual and family experiences with epinephrine auto-injectors, including who is typically responsible for using them, influence the messages and tactics of food allergy advocacy. Specifically, personal experience in the home contributes to the reification of families (especially white and middle-class families) as the appropriate site of care and mothers as the ideal agents of caretaking. While epinephrine auto-injectors do not fully determine the shape of food allergy advocacy, they are ever present and become highly politicized in certain contexts. The moral sensibilities that accrue to this type of device inform the strategies of food allergy advocacy well beyond the boundaries of the nuclear family and the home.

2

WHO IS TO BLAME?

NAVIGATING THE CAUSES AND CURES FOR FOOD ALLERGY

In late 2015, all eyes in the food allergy world were on a peanut-dusted Israeli children's snack called Bamba. This unassuming treat, a puffed corn flour–based tube covered in mildly salty and deliciously fatty peanut powder, was perhaps, a group of U.K.-headquartered researchers hypothesized, the reason why Israel had lower rates of food allergy than other countries in the industrialized world.[1] The treat was already easy to find in major global cities like London, where the research was based, and New York City, another hub of food allergy research in the United States. The news quickly spread that responsible parents worldwide could prevent the development of peanut allergy in their children by proactively offering Bamba as a teething treat, like their Israeli counterparts already did. While the researchers were careful to situate this suggestion as only preliminary, for a time, Bamba was a widely discussed silver bullet for preventing peanut allergy.

The LEAP (Learning Early About Peanut) and LEAP-On (a twelve-month extension of LEAP) studies[2] were the first large-scale interventions to systematically test the hypothesis that the timing of introduction of commonly allergenic foods into the diet could shape allergy outcomes later in childhood. Through a placebo-controlled study, they found that infants introduced to allergens including eggs and peanuts by oral ingestion before four months of age had lower chances of developing allergies to that food until age five. By comparing the results of the study to global trends in allergy incidence, researchers thought they had found a promising answer to reducing the incidence of peanut allergy in Israeli parents' use of Bamba as a snack for teething babies.

This moment was a culmination of several decades of work attempting to uncover the physiological origins of food allergy, and it turned out that important clues were embedded in existing parenting practices. Biomedical scientists had long been asking how hereditary factors, environmental hygiene, maternal diet during pregnancy, development of childhood immunity, and diet interact to make some people food allergic while sparing others with shared kin and similar life histories. Once these complex mechanisms were understood, researchers hoped, early interventions could be designed to prevent the development of allergies in infants and young children, perhaps with lifelong preventive effects. It now seemed that Israeli parents, at least, were already doing some of what needed to be done. The snacks they fed their children, informed not by medical studies but by market availability of Bamba, family tradition, and simple enjoyment, were suddenly scientifically significant.

This chapter argues that solutions to allergy (including but not limited to food allergy) proposed by biomedical researchers, food allergy moms, and activists are an important form of reproductive politics. They shape patterns of care in the family as well as advocacy campaigns about food allergy. Medical research centers the family as crucial to food allergy management, reasserts the social necessity of the nuclear family, and naturalizes gender roles within it. Early twentieth-century allergy interventions for respiratory allergy and asthma focused on altering the home environment and assumed that someone would be available to coordinate purchasing, home design, and caretaking. That unmarked agent more often than not was a woman. Other remedies that focused on the family saw family relationships as potentially pathological and proposed removing children to cure atopic conditions like asthma. More recently, research on the hygiene hypothesis and early food introduction studies focus on the sharing of pathogens and food among family members. Remedies and prevention measures in recent research continue to focus on early childhood health and feeding in the home as the potential keys to tamping down rates of allergy, including food allergy. In all of these ways, allergy research, and particularly food allergy research, looks to the family and to private caretaking practices as the ideal means for preventing and treating allergy. Reproductive work is recruited as a tool for best biomedical practice. The social roles that map onto this work are made to appear natural and inevitable.

Research on early introduction that recommends that parents feed children Bamba is a good example of this. It is a product that lies well outside of the category of prescription drugs and other specialized tools typically associated with biomedicine. It falls squarely in the domain of everyday parenting practices, via the snack aisle of the grocery store. Although parenting has been thoroughly investigated and deeply shaped by expert biomedical knowledge, it is still largely treated as a domain that is ultimately the responsibility of adult parents, organized in nuclear family units, to get right on their own.[3] There are many ways parents can fail, however, and in the United States, this is coupled with a highly variegated array of punishments and very little material help available to correct course when they do. This attitude extends to food allergy households. Beyond a certain point, as the previous chapter discussed, most allergists do not see it as their responsibility to counsel their patients on diet and other lifestyle factors, even though these activities are crucial to maintaining good health with food allergies. The Bamba recommendation implicitly reinforces the expectations that adults within nuclear families[4] will be vigilant caretakers of the health of the next generation.

The incursion of biomedical expertise into caretaking practices is generally embraced by food allergy parents and allergic adults, but the applicability of certain causal mechanisms to individuals' lives is at times contested. Many parents and adults with food allergy follow the scientific literature. Some even work diligently to digest and summarize new findings in blogs, newsletters, and magazine columns for other people managing food allergies in their households without the time, access, or inclination to read medical journals. Yet for women in particular, there is also a critical awareness that emerging recommendations about maternal health, home hygiene, and food preparation often mean more work for mother. While aligning themselves in general with biomedical expertise, I often heard mothers critique certain findings that seemed implausible or potentially harmful to their own families and personal ambitions. In books, public talks, social media posts, and one-on-one conversations, some mothers discuss the finer points of their disagreements with experts and offer alternative theories. Their views are shaped both by their understanding of the science and aspects of their personal experiences that seem to exceed the bounds of biomedical interest or knowledge.

By contesting biomedical delegation of food allergy management and treatment to the nuclear family, the women I write about in this chapter suggest a need for a more expansive understanding of who is responsible for health and illness. Their engagements with biomedical expertise challenge the positioning of mothers and nuclear families as uniquely responsible for ensuring the individual health of allergic children. Viewed as an issue of reproductive politics, such contestations offer a critique the institution of the family as the only location for the reproduction and nurturance of human bodies, future citizens, and future workers. As critical geographer Sophie Lewis suggests in a transnational study of surrogacy clinics, biomedicine's inroads into managing biological and social reproduction within nuclear families is, somewhat paradoxically, opening up new avenues to critique the institution of the family.[5] In the case of food allergy science, critiques of the responsibilization[6] of nuclear families originate with those who are cognizant that they stand the most to gain from improvements in food allergy treatment and prevention. However, they also have much to lose if they fail to enact the ideal homemaker and caretaker on top of their many other ambitions and responsibilities.

ALLERGY SCIENCE AND THE HOME

The home—and by extension the family and caretaking practices—has long been central to food allergy research and management. Since the early days of allergy research, for example, many of the scientifically lauded solutions to allergy have focused on how to control encounters between the body and the home environment. As Carla Keirns writes, allergists in the first half of the twentieth century "established both a medical specialty (clinical allergy) and a distinct mode of medical practice that included a detailed analysis of the patient's home environment and occupation, skin tests for specific allergens, and a new form of desensitization therapy (through vaccinations). If the macroenvironment could not be controlled adequately or easily, then they would attempt to manage the patient's body and its microenvironment—the patient's home."[7] To control the home environment, people managing allergies were often enticed to buy sophisticated new technologies through sales pitches that described hypermodern, clean indoor spaces. Even the expensive undertaking of home renovation was recommended by at least one midcentury physician as a potential remedy to allergies triggered by the home environment (a recommendation that, as the next chapter will detail, remains popular today).[8] These early and mid-twentieth-century legacies have persisted into the present day, with home management and caretaking practices in the home remaining central points of research and intervention for allergy treatment.

The modern history of allergy begins in 1906, when Austrian pediatrician Clemens von Pirquet coined the term in a short paper entitled "Allergie." In von Pirquet's formulation, "allergy" "denote[d] any form of altered biological reactivity," from reactions to foods to reactions to antisera used at the time to prevent the development of communicable diseases like diphtheria. His term joined Charles Richet's 1902 coinage, "anaphylaxis," which referred to an even more expansive set of phenomena, "the absence of protection" against "foreign" substances.[9] Both of these terms represented attempts to deal with an emerging problem in clinical medicine and the growing field of immunology. How could physicians and researchers explain the fact that some individuals responded negatively—sometimes violently so—to external substances that affected others in beneficial or neutral ways? Today, "allergy" is an umbrella disease category that includes food allergies, environmental allergies, eczema, and asthma. Conditions that used to be considered allergy, like serum sickness (the condition that initially sparked both von Pirquet's and Richet's interest in altered reactivity), are still recognized as an aberrant type of immunological response, but they are now categorized as distinct from allergy.

From early in the history of the disease, control of many types of allergy and asthma, including food allergy, extended biomedical rationality to ordinary housework and personal hygiene practices. The home was recognized as a potentially risky place for allergy sufferers—a risk to be managed with help from the latest biomedical protocols and technological innovations. For example, as Gregg Mitman recounts in his history of asthma and environmental allergy, the introduction of air-conditioning in the 1930s was marketed for its ability to reduce symptoms of hay fever in addition to its cooling effects.[10] A focus on the family, and not just the home, truly came onto the scene with the advent of "parentectomies," or the removal of children from their immediate families, in the 1930s.[11] As Matthew Smith explains, mid-twentieth-century physicians sometimes attributed childhood asthma to psychodynamic distress.[12] Parentectomies removed children from their parents and homes, often dropping them across the country to Western lung retreats like Denver's National Jewish Hospital in hopes that lengthy separation would heal their minds and bodies.[13] Both the physical space of the home and the social space of the family were seen as key points of intervention for the treatment of allergy under early and mid-twentieth-century environmental and psychodynamic paradigms.

In recent years, the development of new food allergy safety protocols has drawn inspiration directly from home hygiene techniques. For example, one set of experiments published in the most prestigious U.S. allergy journal, the *Journal of Allergy and Clinical Immunology*, sought to determine the most effective way to remove allergens from school lunch tables. The researchers found that using household cleaning products, including Formula 409, Lysol sanitizing wipes, and Target brand cleaner with bleach, effectively removed peanut proteins that commonly trigger allergies from table surfaces. Dish soap mixed with water was less effective. In the study's second experiment, hand sanitizer and plain water failed to remove peanut allergens from hands, while Tidy Tykes wipes, antibacterial hand sanitizer, Wet Ones antibacterial wipes, liquid soap, and bar soap were effective.[14] This study validates the type of cleaning techniques that an individual or caretaker would use in a private home while providing further specificity about exactly which techniques are demonstrably most effective in laboratory conditions. Bringing simple home techniques into the lab converts everyday habits into scientifically supported, and thus more widely generalizable, best practices.[15]

For much of the modern history of allergy, food allergy was seen as the least interesting, least prestigious, and least credible type of allergic illness to study and treat within the medical establishment. There was seemingly little to be done to treat food allergic patients other than food avoidance because techniques that were helpful for diagnosing or treating respiratory allergies tended to fail when used for food allergy. Skin tests that rose to popularity in the 1930s, for instance, were effective in less than a quarter of cases where food allergy seemed to be present, according to a 1953 study by Will Spain.[16] Early attempts at using allergy immunotherapy protocols to treat food allergies also had underwhelming results. Allergy immunotherapy is a treatment regimen that consists of introducing small and increasing amounts of the food a person is allergic to into his or her body, typically via skin or mouth, over the course of days, weeks, or years, depending on the protocol. But consuming the food a person is allergic to, especially by mouth, presents a high risk of anaphylaxis, unlike injections of respiratory allergens, which can be done with minimal risk. Even placing a person's allergen on the skin can trigger itchy rashes or anaphylaxis. Early food allergy immunotherapy thus had high rates of iatrogenic reactions at the same time that immunotherapy was becoming a staple of allergists' offerings for environmental allergies. Furthermore, when this treatment was first attempted for food allergies, epinephrine auto-injectors were not yet available, meaning that little could be done to stop and reverse a reaction should it occur. Allergy immunotherapy for food allergy was therefore largely abandoned, and research into treating the condition slowed.

By the middle of the twentieth century, food allergists were "stripped of the tools employed by other allergists," treated with suspicion by "orthodox" non–food allergists, and left on their own "to discover other ways to diagnose and treat patients."[17] After abandoning skin testing and immunotherapy, there was little to be done about food allergies—that is, there were few effective technological or pharmaceutical interventions for physicians to prescribe—besides listening to patients. Whereas people with asthma could go to specialized doctors, wards, and even hospitals, people with food allergies were typically told to live as they always had and to try to avoid their allergens. Even more damningly in the eyes of non–food allergists and other medical specialists, theories of food allergy retained echoes of outdated humoral and environmental medicine theories. Smith describes this as an "environmental turn in food allergy" from the 1950s to the 1970s, which other allergists saw as tainting food allergy with environmentalist politics and which provoked backlash from many in the medical establishment.[18] Food allergy treatment, like asthma treatment, also became inflected by psychodynamic theories linking disease to psychological development and family dynamics in the postwar era, justifying the practice of parentectomies.[19] Midcentury orthodox allergists who relied on skin testing and immunotherapy to treat environmental allergies thus considered food allergists a liability to the legitimacy of allergists as a whole.[20]

Food allergy research remained something of a backwater until the 1980s. That decade saw a rapprochement between allergy and immunology, signaled by two things: the expulsion of clinical ecology, a subfield that considered a variety of environmental causes for allergies to which many food allergists had gravitated in the 1960s and 1970s, from orthodox allergy; and the consolidation of allergy science and clinical testing around the immune signaling molecule immunoglobulin E, or IgE. As Smith writes, this nearly simultaneous expulsion and reframing of allergy as detectable only through IgE testing set the stage for a "transform[ation of] food allergy into a very specific, attenuated, and limited phenomenon, adhering to the way orthodox allergists had defined it all along" in the 1990s.[21] Food allergy became more narrowly defined, and allergy diagnosis and treatment could be more closely policed through the use of immunological diagnostic testing. However, it was once again in the sights of immunology clinicians and researchers.

Throughout the 1990s and into the 2000s, amid a perceived rapid rise in rates of food allergy and increased public attention, the topic again became a scientifically interesting and active research field. Subcutaneous immunotherapy (allergy shots) for peanut allergy were tried again, and new forms of treatments delivered by mouth and on the surface of the skin (epicutaneously) were theorized and attempted.[22] Parent-led support organizations founded in the late 1990s and early 2000s, like Food Allergy Initiative, or FAI (part of Food Allergy Research and Education, or FARE, since 2012), formed and began to put pressure on professional organizations and individual scientists to accelerate research in pursuit of an effective food allergy immunotherapy regimen. Allergist physician-researchers like Robert Wood and Wesley Burks established laboratories that led the pack in elucidating the mechanisms of allergic sensitization and conducting a new wave of clinical trials of desensitizing allergy immunotherapy protocols. These laboratories would go on to train and mentor many of the generation of physician-researchers to rise to prominence in the 2010s, seeding the current wave of food allergy research and the development of food allergy immunotherapies that are expected to become commercially viable by the early 2020s.[23] These physicians, and many of those who trained under them, also developed loyal followings among patients and the community of mother-advocates.

Pivotal to this latest wave of food allergy research in the 2000s and 2010s is an understanding of the condition as indelibly shaped by the allergic individual's direct environment, especially the household. The hygiene hypothesis, first proposed by David P. Strachan in 1989, is one important touchpoint for contemporary research on the connection between the environment and individual allergic bodies. His study connected rates of hay fever in English children and young adults to the number of siblings in a family through a retrospective analysis of over seventeen thousand individuals. Strachan interpreted the results to suggest that "allergic diseases [could be explained] by infection in early childhood, transmitted by unhygienic contact with older siblings, or acquired prenatally from a mother infected by contact with her older children [and by l]ater infection or reinfection by younger siblings."[24] It is not the encounter of an individual with microbes per se that is theorized to be important in the development of allergic diseases in many specific instances of this paradigm. Rather, it is the communication (infection and reinfection) of pathogenic disease within a family with multiple children that offers a protective effect. At the core of this important modern immunological paradigm, which now shapes research in many subfields of immunology and beyond, is the home, the mother's prenatal health, and the nuclear family.

The hygiene hypothesis continues to offer a possible explanation for allergy etiology, although the proposed immunological mechanisms that make up the concept have proliferated since 1989.[25] For example, research on Amish farm families supported the idea that microbial exposure early in life protects against the development of allergic diseases, and suggested that a specific mix of household dust may contribute as well.[26] In particular, researchers theorize that exposure to endotoxins (by-products of the breakdown of some kinds of bacteria) triggers immunological mechanisms that reduce rates of allergy.[27] Other research, like the LEAP studies' examination of the impact of peanut dust in homes on the development of infant allergies, shares an interest in understanding how environmental materials shape allergic sensitization.[28] In this study, the materials of interest are not microbes but rather food. In both cases, researchers identify early family life, whether caring for animals or introducing peanut early into the diet, as key to shaping later immunological status.

In emerging paradigms for food allergy immunotherapy, the family remains responsible for food allergy outcomes because treatments are designed to be administered at home to children over a long period of time. In 2015, the food allergy treatment company Aimmune Therapeutics (which at the time had recently been renamed from Allergen Research Corporation, or ARC) announced the first positive results for a phase 2 study of an orally delivered, long-term treatment for peanut allergy, AR101, at the annual America Academy of Allergy, Asthma, and Immunology meeting in Barcelona, Spain.[29] Unlike the typical pharmaceutical intervention, AR101 is a peanut protein powder developed using food-grade peanut flour. The treatment is administered daily for a minimum of three years by mixing carefully measured amounts into food, a treatment called oral immunotherapy (OIT). Their earliest direct competitor, DBV Technologies, also shared positive early results in 2015 from a phase 2b clinical trial.[30] DBV similarly used ingredients derived from edible peanut in their treatment, but their product delivers the dose to the patient via a specially designed skin patch, a treatment called epicutaneous immunotherapy. Both treatments were initially studied for safety in adults, and later children as young as four years old. Allergists suspect that starting treatment in young children and toddlers will increase the long-term efficacy.

If such food-based treatments are widely commercialized and children do end up becoming the prime market for new food allergy immunotherapy products, treating food allergy will mean more work for mother.[31] In the case of Aimmune's edible peanut flour, doses are disguised in a complementary but strong-tasting food, like applesauce. Users must be carefully monitored for potential reactions after every dose and must not exercise before or after the treatment. Family evenings formerly spent relaxing or doing things together must thus accommodate extra food preparation work followed by a time of quiet rest and careful watchfulness for long periods of time. In the case of DBV's product, the skin patch is designed to gently scratch the skin for highest efficacy. Irritated skin is an almost inevitable result, potentially requiring further vigilance and treatment of secondary skin issues caused by the primary food allergy treatment. In the culturally dominant heteronormative family paradigm, it will most likely fall to mother to watch nervously for an allergic reaction, to prepare medicated meals daily, or to apply skin remedies if treatments cause new forms of discomfort. Father, meanwhile, might feel extra pressure to be out working to earn the thousands of dollars a year these treatments are expected to cost or to maintain insurance eligibility for the family. Extrapolating from clinical studies of other forms of allergen immunotherapy, either treatment will require a minimum of three years, and potentially a lifetime, of use. Treating food allergy with this latest generation of products is poised to further involve the home and the family in food allergy treatment—indefinitely.

Domestic labor and family relations have remained pivotal to successful management and treatment of food allergy since the term "allergy" was coined in the early twentieth century. Although this has been true for many forms of allergy, including asthma and environmental allergies, it is especially true for food allergies. Food allergies, the scientific evidence suggests today, are shaped by many different forms of domestic labor: cleaning, maintaining a building, managing exposure to disease, and purchasing and preparing food. Further, household hygiene practices have served as a template for scientific management of allergy outside the home, as in the science of cleaning surfaces. New food allergy prevention measures and treatments, like food allergy immunotherapy and feeding Bamba to young children, will demand new forms of rationalization and biomedical oversight of daily domestic routines. Constant vigilance is needed to mediate the proper relationship between the vulnerable allergic body and its environment, including other people, other species, pollen, microbes, and food residues. In the process, domestic labor is interrogated, rationalized, and incorporated into biomedical protocols as a resource for the management of chronic allergic conditions.

THE MACHINE IN THE GARDEN

While biomedical experts rationalize domestic labor as part of food allergy management, parents of allergic children and adults with food allergy turn to biomedical theories of allergy etiology to craft causal explanations to explain the apparent misfortune of having the condition. Personalized etiological narratives often involve an examination of both biomedical research and the polluting conditions of modern life in the United States to explain an individual's diagnosis of food allergy. These narratives reveal a latent tension in the food allergy world between a commitment to modern, technoscientific modes of food allergy knowledge and management and nostalgia for utopian visions of the healthful, natural past. I regard the latter as "machine in the garden" explanations. Such stories posit that technology-driven aspects of modern life are ultimately responsible for rising rates of suffering in the modern world, and they suffuse the etiological fables of people with food allergy. Machine in the garden stories constitute, in Leo Marx's telling, a distinctly American attitude toward technology that has underwritten national ideals of progress and possibility since the early seventeenth century.[32]

Both allergic adults and parents of allergic children navigate a variety of theories about what aspects of modern life and technology causes food allergies. Their explanations weave together personal experience and the top-line results of biomedical research. In the accounts discussed in this section, the immediate experience of life with food allergies serves as a litmus test for the credibility of biomedical theories of food allergy etiology. Scientific dictums that do not align with personal experience are viewed with suspicion or dismissed. But the interpretations and solutions proposed do not simply fall into striving for a purer, simpler past way of life. An underlying faith in scientific progress is common among food allergy advocates, mothers, and writers and forecloses this easy solution. Instead, people living with food allergy share hybrid theories and issue demands that biomedical experts improve modern science by exercising greater skepticism in validating new research and results. Because many of the scientific claims position early childhood as the key to understanding food allergy etiology, families and households are also implicated in challenging the scientific status quo and responsibly implementing best practices as they improve. The interplay between biomedical knowledge and family responsibility is another knot in the web of the reproductive politics of food allergy.

A Dangerous Food Supply

In the globalized networks of contemporary biomedicine, the attitude that allergy is an artifact of polluted environments is not unique to the United States. For example, Roberta Raffaetà finds in an ethnographic study of Italian allergy clinics that Italians also explain their condition through narratives characterized by nostalgia for a premodern mode of life. Raffaetà argues that "naturalness is a crucial concept in Italian discourses on health" and a positive value for taking care of one's health, personal appearance, and grooming.[33] Raffaetà situates Italian patients' nostalgia in mid-twentieth-century Italian social movements that emphasized a return to natural food in response to the rapid industrialization and centralization of the Italian economy. These movements in turn inspired late twentieth-century American natural food movements, like the American branch of the slow food movement, which, appropriately enough, originated in Italy. Raffaetà finds that several individuals she interviewed assumed that the unnatural, polluted landscapes of the post–World War II–era Italian landscape contributed to the etiology of allergy. She positions the average allergy patient's concerns about "naturalness" as opposed to and ignored by the biomedical establishment, a fact that drives many allergy sufferers to complementary and alternative medicine practitioners. Italian allergy patients who consult such specialists for their allergies are concerned, first and foremost, with the naturalness of treatment options. Furthermore, patients' hesitancy to embrace modern medicine is consonant with a generalized suspicion among many Italian health seekers about whether twentieth-century technoscience is helpful or harmful to contemporary Italian society.

Some figures in U.S. food allergy advocacy pose critiques of modern food systems that echo this Italian perspective. Anxieties about modern life are often linked to concerns about parenting, gender roles, and family life as well. The conference talks and writing of food systems critic Robyn O'Brien stand as a prime example of such machine in the garden critiques. O'Brien was one of the most prominent proponents of a connection between genetically modified organisms (GMOs) in the food system and the increasing rate of food allergies in the United States in 2015 when I encountered her work. According to her 2009 book, *The Unhealthy Truth: One Mother's Shocking Investigation into the Dangers of America's Food Supply—And What Every Family Can Do to Protect Itself,* O'Brien began her professional life as an equities analyst, setting up nine-figure investment deals and directing business strategy decisions. Eventually she left the corporate world to have four children, and she brought the same type A fervor that got her through business school and into a prestigious career to the task of child-rearing. When her youngest, a girl named Tory, had an allergic reaction at family breakfast one day after having her first taste of eggs, O'Brien became determined to discover what initiated her daughter's condition.

Modern food systems quickly caught O'Brien's attention in her search for a culprit. "What had changed," she asked, "in our food to make it suddenly so toxic to our children? . . . When had food—one of the most immediate, personal ways I knew to sustain my kids—become so friggin' dangerous?"[34] Despite her growing suspicion, O'Brien invited her readers to see her as an objective commentator. She explained that pointing the finger at industrial food production was particularly upsetting to her because she considered herself a fellow businessperson. She "believed in our system and its leaders," including their ability to make decisions that are both profitable and beneficial for consumers.[35] Before long, she came across the work of two controversial diet gurus: Kenneth Bock, whose writing and clinical guidance links the "toxic food supply" to a variety of health problems, including asthma, autism, allergies, attention-deficit/hyperactivity disorder, and other behavioral problems, and Joel Fuhrman, who warns parents that "the shift to 'fake food' has actually altered our immune system[s]" and triggered the allergy epidemic.[36]

As she became immersed in food system critiques and food allergy activism, O'Brien was upset to learn about what she saw as the laxity of American food standards. For example, she writes that she was shocked to find that the U.S. FDA allows the use of artificial colors like Yellow Number 5 that are banned in other countries and does not mandate label disclosure of genetically modified ingredients. In O'Brien's view, such modern food products could pose unknown risks to eaters in the United States. In contravention of her earlier work for and faith in corporate America, O'Brien concludes that the entire system—rules and rulemakers alike—was corrupted by food industry actors. As a result of their influence, she argues, consumers are uninformed about the risks of modern food. Research suggesting detrimental health effects of GMO corn and soy, the dangers of growth hormones in milk, and the multifaceted effects that the polluted food system can have on children's bodies and development are all suppressed, O'Brien believes, as a result of industry pressure.

Even the groups that ought to represent the interests of patients aren't immune, she suggests. For example, she traces financial support for the patient-centered nonprofit Food Allergy and Anaphylaxis Network (FAAN, now part of Food Allergy Research and Education [FARE]) back to Kraft and Dura Pharmaceuticals. She also discovers that some funding for academic research on the etiology of peanut allergy comes from the U.S. peanut growers' industry group, the National Peanut Board.[37] The complexity and industry power in the modern American food system, in O'Brien's view, produces biased science and poses a number of undisclosed dangers to children.

Although U.S.-based food allergy activists like O'Brien share the worry that modern life (especially modern food) is implicated in allergy etiology, their attitudes differ in some key ways from the Italian allergy patients Raffaetà writes about. The most vocal participants in the food allergy advocacy world are, like O'Brien, generally well versed in the biomedical explanations of allergy and deeply faithful to the promise that biomedical knowledge and technocratic governance will lead to a cure for allergic illnesses. Skepticism about modernity is less of a blanket assessment of the polluted nature of modern life and more of a forensic project to determine which specific elements of modern life should be blamed for triggering susceptible bodies to become allergic.[38] In some instances, like in O'Brien's work, there is also skepticism of the modern business and advocacy landscape, such as financial relationships between the food industry and patient advocacy organizations. Rather than seeking a return to a lost, preindustrial state of purity, different camps among both experts and patients more specifically blame (singly or in combination) food system features like GMOs, pesticides, and food processing, maternal exposures to commonly allergenic foods, early childhood exposure to antibiotics and vaccines, and environmental exposures to foods and pets during childhood for food allergies.

The link between naturalness and safety is further complicated by the list of foods to which people are commonly allergic in the United States. The most common allergens, the top eight, include peanut, tree nuts, fish, shellfish, milk, soy, eggs, and wheat—basic ingredients used in many simple, "natural" foods. Simply returning to the diets of one's grandparents or great-grandparents would mean, in many cases, eating more of the foods that people are commonly allergic to. Instead, for many food allergic people, eating specialty foods with proprietary nonwheat flour mixes or grain-based egg substitutions that are lab tested for texture and contaminants is the safer and easier option. In other words, a return to innocence fails as a blanket strategy for food allergy. While modern life may set up the conditions under which an allergy epidemic arises, there is no immediate, universal solution to be found by returning to a simpler, more pastoral way of life for many U.S. food allergy sufferers because of the nature of the disease itself. If the machine is present in the garden, it is now too late to displace it.

Hazardous Modernity

The personal history told to me by one of my principal contacts in food allergy advocacy, Jenna, offers a particularly nuanced example of how these tensions between a pastoral, natural past and a polluted present play out in searching for an explanation for a food allergy diagnosis. Jenna's story also offers the relatively unique perspective in my research of an allergic adult raising allergic children. When I spoke to her, Jenna was a woman in her thirties who led several initiatives offering support and training for food allergic adults. Jenna's own food allergies appeared in adulthood, after several bouts of acute autoimmune disease as a young adult. She therefore had an even more complicated set of potential causes to consider than many individuals I spoke to. I first heard of Jenna's work via social media. After an e-mail exchange, she invited me to meet her at a U.S.-based food allergy conference I attended in 2014. After that, I spoke to her and interviewed her several times in 2014 and 2015. At that time, her food allergies numbered in the dozens, severely restricting her diet. Yet you would never suspect her history of serious illness when meeting her in person. She was energetic, active, and always smiling. Her face was framed by long, wavy brown hair, and she was always eager to tell stories about her childhood spent on a farm.

Jenna had an elaborate theory of food allergy etiology that included selective suspicion of many aspects of modern life. She had an encyclopedic knowledge of the various biomedical theories of the etiology of allergic conditions as well as detailed recollections and records of her own medical history. During our first interview, Jenna provided an introduction to her rejection of the idea that modern hygiene plays a pivotal role in allergies. Comparing her personal life history to biomedical theories prompted skepticism of the various hygiene hypothesis–style explanations, which she explained this way:

> One theory is the hygiene hypothesis. People are like, well, people are over clean. But I'm like, OK, time out, let me stop you right there. I grew up on a farm. I grew up in the middle of agriculture. I picked fruits and vegetables. I've eaten dirt. I have had well water, I've had tap water. I lived with cats and dogs and animals and goats and chickens and sheep and horses. I've been in wheat fields and strawberry fields, the whole nine yards. So hygiene, you know. . . . While we cleaned up and washed our hands at the end of every day or when we came inside, I just don't buy into that theory. At all.

Having children changed her attitude toward hygiene in general, but the fact that only one of her children developed food allergy enhanced her skepticism of the hygiene hypothesis. As time went by, the pattern of her children's allergies only added to her list of questions:

> I think I became more hygiene conscientious when my daughter was born, which was twelve years ago, or my son. . . . My son, here's another example, another reason why I don't buy into that. My son was born in the same hospital as I was, one floor apart. He spent the first few months of his life on the same farm, on the same ranch, that I grew up on. And then later on in life we went to live in the city and live the city life. But he just developed food allergies. He just developed food allergies and seasonal and environmental allergies. And he's sixteen. His body changed and he developed them for the first time in his life. So while he's still technically a child, he's an adolescent. Late onset as well.
>
> And my daughter, who was born in Denver, born in the city, not raised on a farm, though she went to the farm later on, but has been a city girl her whole life, has no food allergies. None whatsoever. Not even a little. Not seasonal allergies, not environmental allergies, no food allergies, nothing.
>
> So I totally don't buy that theory.

Finally, comparing her health history to the stories of other food allergic adults supported Jenna's skeptical view of early childhood hygiene as a key factor in the development of food allergy:

> I talk to adults and a lot of the adults that I talk to have very similar experiences. They were raised in rural areas or in farming with dirt and worms. They weren't city kids necessarily, not that they were all farm country kids. And some of them still do! Some of them still live in rural America and don't have . . . they're not living in hospitals. And not that that's very sanitary either.
> But anyway. So that theory is out for me.

After expressing her skepticism of the hygiene hypothesis, Jenna then went on to enumerate and reject other theories of what causes food allergies, including changes in immunizations, pesticide residue on foods, the changing proportion of certain foods in the American food supply, and a lack of breastfeeding. As with her assessment of the hygiene hypothesis, she used evidence from her own life to undermine each one. She had been fully immunized and had immunized both of her children, but they all had different allergy profiles, weakening the case that vaccines cause allergies. She hadn't breastfed consistently, but only one of her children had food allergies. This made her skeptical of the American Academy of Pediatrics' guidance at the time that including common allergens in a mother's diet while breastfeeding could limit the later development of food allergies.[39]

Jenna's theory, rooted in her own experience, was that there was a causal link between allergies and other autoimmune disorders. She believed that biomedical research had a role to play in discovering the truth; more scientific research would uncover further support for this link. Jenna found evidence for this theory in her own experience as an autoimmune patient and food allergic person and as a leader of support groups for allergic adults. In both cases, she had noticed a strong association between the development of autoimmune disorders and allergies. In food allergic adult support group conversations, she told participants facing skepticism about their food allergies from colleagues and friends that their condition was autoimmune in nature, with scientific evidence for this idea to come in the near future.

This theory fit so perfectly with her experience and with the experience of the other adults with allergies that she talked to on a regular basis (mostly women, many with autoimmune conditions as well as allergies) that it seemed to be the most plausible to her. Orthodox or not, if a theory didn't square with her own history and embodied experience of the condition, it was not plausible to her. But if it did fit, then she needed more scientific evidence to support the theory's validity.

In a conversation about a month after our first interview, Jenna shared some new suspicions about potential links between GMOs, the American food system, geography, and allergy. She pointed the finger at changes in food production, such as the shift from traditional agriculture to high-tech production techniques, exemplified by hydroponically grown tomatoes. A particular risk, in her revised view, was the consumption of GMOs. Through reading and reflecting on information available online, Jenna had made an analogical link between the genetic modifications in foods and the potential for genetic instability in human bodies. The novel characteristics of these foods, she explained, meant that human bodies did not "know what to do with foods anymore" and were "genetically modifying themselves" to keep up. Changing the compositions of some foods via genetic modification could, she hypothesized, change how human bodies process all foods. Compounding the effects of these novel foodstuffs was the fact that her own body and the bodies of many food allergic adults were already under stress because of the geographic instability of the contemporary labor market—specifically, the fact that adults must often move from one region to another for work. "We're humans," she told me, "and our bodies adapt, and they change, and they are improvising." These improvisations were not necessarily always good; sometimes they could lead to food allergies.

Geographic instability, genetic novelty, and high-tech food production: According to Jenna, these features of modern life in the United States destabilize the human body, leaving it vulnerable to developing allergic sensitivity. But this is not exactly an issue of policing the natural/unnatural boundary, or of advocating for a more natural lifestyle. Indeed, in this second exchange, Jenna conceded the irony that eating with food allergies often means eating more processed foods and fewer whole or natural foods. Whole food staples like wheat flour, legumes, eggs, milk, and raw nuts were some of the most common allergens, and frequently off-limits for food allergic people. Foods marketed as allergy friendly typically substitute complex mixtures of highly refined flours (often including buckwheat flour, potato flour, rice flour, and tapioca starch, to mimic the stickiness of wheat gluten) for wheat flours. Mixtures of refined starches and oils replicate the binding properties of eggs. Specialized oil mixtures with factory-produced flavorings (and sometimes spectacular yellow-orange coloring) replace cheese. They are not the sort of foods you would find touted at a farmer's market as natural or traditional. For adults with food allergies, easy-to-eat and highly processed options are often necessary to balance basic sustenance with the responsibilities of family and work.

The Vaccine Connection

While vaccines were only rarely connected to food allergies by participants in my ethnographic research, they are another aspect of modernity that has been blamed for the rising rates of food allergies.[40] These concerns implicate parents, doctors, and caretakers who make decisions to administer or withhold vaccines for young children and potentially responsible parties for the development of food allergy. For example, Canadian food allergy mother Heather Fraser wrote a book arguing this point called *The Peanut Allergy Epidemic: What's Causing It and How to Stop It*. The book was well known within the food allergy community but inspired a good deal of skepticism because of Fraser's suspicion of biomedical protocols. Fraser argues that vaccinations are the overlooked cause of the rapid acceleration of peanut allergy incidence beginning around 1990. Her book catalogs biomedical etiological theories and argues that none could be seen as identifying the true root cause of the increase in rates of food allergies given the timing of that increase. What rankles her in particular is the hygiene hypothesis. The problem for Fraser is that "the hygiene hypothesis did not offer a purpose for allergy. . . . In positing that homeostasis was impossible without a burden of disease, the hygiene hypothesis gave little credit to the human body." Her alternative is more and better scientific research: "Perhaps technology and its concomitant toxicities deserve a closer look."[41]

For Fraser, the "toxicities" that explain the circa-1990 inflection point that she identifies in peanut allergy diagnoses include a number of vaccines and their component ingredients, fungal overgrowth in the body, unhealthy diets, castor oil supplements given to newborns, and the use of peanut oil in foods, medications, and cosmetics. But her main target is the *Haemophilus influenzae* type b (Hib) bacteria vaccine. According to the U.S. Centers for Disease Control and Prevention, Hib is administered to infants and young children beginning around two months of age to prevent a potentially fatal bacterial infection.[42] Healthy scientific debate about the possibility that the Hib vaccine is a key factor in triggering peanut allergy, Fraser argues, was "sidelined" by basic research on allergic diseases that was gaining traction in the 1990s, "a new and all-encompassing concept of allergy and immunity—the Th1/Th2 paradigm."[43] Fraser sees laboratory research focused on elucidating the specific physiological mechanisms of allergy etiology as a distraction from more structural questions about the changing nature of public health interventions and globalized food and cosmetic manufacturing supply chains.

Nowhere in Fraser's book is there a call for reversion to a utopian pastoralism, although she harbors deep mistrust of contemporary medical guidance. She argues instead that scientists need to do better science. For example, she cites the history of association between vaccine adjuvants and unexpected immune responses to substances, such as the well-documented history of adverse reactions to cottonseed oil in vaccines in the early twentieth century, as a warning that biomedical experts ought to heed. Had they paid attention to history, they might have been more open to accepting that more recently developed vaccines carry risks. For Fraser, past examples like this justify distrust of current vaccination recommendations. But a return to nature does not seem to offer an easy way out either. The flaw on the part of physicians and scientists is not simply that medical science has fostered an acceleration of technological sophistication. Rather, their shortcomings consist of ignoring particular pieces of evidence, especially evidence supporting the possibility that their own technologies are a potential cause of misfortune. The solution, Fraser suggests, is that scientists should become better at science. They should become better at suspending their disbelief to test out new ideas that contradict current models and best practices.

In the books by Robyn O'Brien and Heather Fraser, and in my interviews with Jenna, aspects of modern technology figure as likely triggers for food allergy in children and adults, but simply returning to the past is not the solution. Training attention on aspects of early life, including childhood vaccinations, early nutrition, and hometown environment, implicates contemporary parenting choices and the modern home as shaping the risk of children developing food allergy. This pattern of attention constitutes both a forensic search for understanding why this condition befell a particular family or individual and a continuation of the focus on the family and the home as a primary site through which food allergy can be understood, explained, and managed. O'Brien's, Fraser's, and Jenna's investigations seek to untangle the politics of biomedicine, food safety, and reproduction all at once. The next section will continue to elaborate this theme, showing how the biomedical prescriptions and theories about allergy etiology are not only actively negotiated by mothers of allergic children in particular, but also how they impact mothers' self-perceptions as good mothers.

MOTHER BLAME

The refraction of biomedical theories of food allergy etiology through individual illness narratives begged questions in the minds of many mothers of allergic children whether anyone could, or should, be held personally responsible for the disease. Similar to mothers of disabled children in other contexts studied by sociologists,[44] food allergy mothers are first in the crosshairs when something goes wrong with a child's health. In food allergy research, biomedical theories lend scientific credence to this cultural norm by naturalizing mothers' role in patterning their children's pathology. This research serves to link biological and social prescriptions for healthy and wholesome reproduction. In everyday food allergic living, mothers are typically the individuals in charge of cleaning the home of potential allergens, feeding infants, preparing meals for older children, and making decisions about medical care, all of which might pose risks for a reaction or the future development of allergies. Against the backdrop of biomedical expertise and community conversations about allergy etiology summarized in this chapter so far, many mothers ended up carrying around a great deal of guilt and self-blame for a child's food allergic condition. This guilt can be read as a consequence of being assigned a pivotal role in reproduction, whether they want to take it on or not.

Changes in medical recommendations, such as recommendations for the proper method and timing of childhood food introduction, have stoked the anxiety caused by managing food allergic children's unpredictable and potentially dangerous reactions. Eating is a fundamental need of young children (as indeed it is of everyone) as well as an activity that is heavily subjected to expert biomedical analysis and guidance. Failure to provide proper nutrition to infants and children risks moral and legal sanctions for faulty mothering. Increasingly, pediatric food introduction guidelines take into account whether a particular schedule will reduce the chance that a child will develop food allergies or asthma. Many parents of children who are already allergic and others with an interest in food allergy follow these developments closely, at times comparing new recommendations to their own feeding practices in the past. To make things even more fraught, the allergy-related aspects of feeding guidelines have been completely reversed in recent years. What may have been correct with an older child has become wrong for younger or future children. These changing recommendations provide ideal conditions for generating self-doubt and blame among mothers.

Feminist theorists have critiqued the ways that cultural scripts about gendered care work engender self-doubt and blame in the women who are expected to do it. The question of mother blame in food allergy worlds is an instance of a larger problem in the meaning of parenting in the United States. As Linda Blum puts it, "The mother-valor/mother-blame binary serves, in modern Western cultures, to hold mothers responsible for child outcomes and thus for the health of families, future citizens, and the nation."[45] Food allergy mothers distinctly feel the contradictory pull of this binary. On the one hand, they willingly engage in sacrifice of self-identity and career to care for their food allergic children. On the other, science and society alike would seem to hold them responsible for producing children who are at times seen by uninformed bystanders as weak or finicky.

The rationalization of housework and child-rearing by techno-scientific experts has heightened the demands on mothers in the United States since the early twentieth century. Ruth Schwartz Cowan recounts how rising expectations of cleanliness and technical proficiency created impossible expectations for mothers as more high-tech household appliances were introduced into American homes in the early and mid-twentieth century. Emergent popular hygienic ideals at the time "heightened the emotional context of the work," making an impeccably clean home a signifier of both technical accomplishment and a morally upright woman.[46] Taking one wrong step produced feelings of guilt. Luckily, if that happened, another new postwar technology, the tranquilizer pill, could conveniently restore a woman's easy demeanor in the face of unending, morally treacherous work.[47]

At stake was not just the family's continued well-being through the generations but also the nationalist demand that mothers and families provide the raw materials for crafting new and improved future citizens. This demand put reproductive politics on the national main stage, and it treated biological and social reproduction as inseparable. Biomedical experts starting in the Progressive Era were increasingly enforcing standards for the biological reproduction of "fitter families" and "better babies," the result of the rising influence of eugenics in family planning.[48] Against these histories, other recent ethnographic analyses that address mother guilt observe that it can be particularly acute for mothers of children with chronic illnesses or disabilities.[49] Guilt is compounded by high rates of medical and social services surveillance and threats of state violence for poor women and women of color, especially Black women. For example, Khiara Bridges's ethnography of a New York City public hospital referred to as Alpha shows how the poor women of color who use the hospital for prenatal care—including Black, Hispanic, and South

Asian women—are required to submit to extra, invasive testing and questioning about their private lives in order to access the standard of care available to privately insured gestators. The added surveillance is justified in the minds of many clinicians by theories of biological racial difference, including ideas about Black women's higher pain tolerance and Mexican women's natural fitness for birthing.[50] The stakes for failing to comply are high, as Dorothy Roberts shows: children can be treated as at risk of abuse at birth or soon after if mothers do not jump through hoops on schedule—and with what their wealthier and whiter caseworkers deem to be an appropriately accommodating attitude.[51] What is at stake in modern parenting for children with disabilities and chronic conditions is not only the moral hygiene of the mother but also a continued legacy of expectations concerning racial fitness for parenthood and the fitness of the nation. These linked contexts underwrite the anxiety experienced by food allergy mothers in the United States today.

The connection between breastfeeding and the development of allergic conditions is one major driver of anxiety for food allergy mothers. Beginning in the 1980s, several studies reported that food-derived proteins could also be transferred via breast milk, raising concerns that a child could develop allergies to milk, egg, or peanuts through consuming the breast milk of a woman who eats those foods.[52] Recommendations from the American Academy of Pediatrics followed, suggesting that mothers might change their diets by omitting common allergens like peanuts to prevent their children from developing food allergies.[53] However, further research contravened these findings.[54] In light of new evidence, a report by the American Academy of Pediatrics issued revised guidance in 2008 regarding maternal diet during pregnancy and lactation.[55] In this updated view, the evidence supporting the inclusion or omission of common allergens in maternal diets in order to prevent food allergies was deemed "insufficient on which to draw more general conclusions."[56] In two decades, medical science first established and then walked back the approach of controlling the diet of pregnant and breastfeeding women as an acceptable intervention for slowing the rise in rates of food allergy.

This concern with breastfeeding presents an opportunity to place the blame for a child's food allergy diagnosis on their mother. Many of the women I interviewed had breastfed while dietary restrictions were recommended, and some had followed the recommendations. This could be a stressful undertaking during a generally stressful postpartum period, when nutritional needs are particularly high and the time and ability to satisfy them especially scarce. One participant emphasized that breastfeeding is difficult enough to fit into this constellation of responsibilities, especially if the baby turns out to be an unenthusiastic feeder, if the parent is expected to return to work quickly, or if complications arise during or after childbirth. To then be told that the way she is doing something as basic as feeding her child is incorrect can be hard news to face.

A second mother who talked about this issue with me, whom I will call Joan, explained her frustrations with the feelings of guilt the breastfeeding theory triggered. Joan was an accomplished lawyer who worked in large law firms both before and after giving birth to her children. She liked to have control over her life as well as over the lives of her children. For her, buying into the idea that her careful choices about diet and breastfeeding ended up harming rather than helping by triggering food allergies would have added to her general feelings of guilt. Therefore, she chose not to consider these explanations in her own search for answers:

> Well you know what, to be perfectly honest, [the idea that allergens in breast milk can lead to allergies] is not part of my thinking, and I'll tell you why. Because, as a parent, we feel guilty for everything. Oh my gosh. I must have done this to her somehow. And the theories on that particular theory change so frequently and really do a 180.
>
> When I was pregnant and breastfeeding, I did not avoid any foods. And so there was this thinking for a long time that I might have quote–unquote caused her to become allergic by having her ingest those foods in utero and then through breast milk. And then the theory switched 180 and they were telling mothers, pregnant mothers and nursing mothers, you know what? Maybe if you eat these foods, you'll desensitize your kid and they won't have food allergies.

So the pendulum swung back and forth so drastically that I just decided to not listen to any of that, because that doesn't help my family personally. That might help future families in future generations, but I'm going to wait to see where they end up on that before my daughter talks about getting pregnant or, you know, having kids and breastfeeding. She can worry about where the current science lies then in, God willing, ten to fifteen years, because between now and then it's going to change so many times that it can't help her. And it's only going to make me feel guilty or not feel guilty. So I just choose not to even focus on it.

Joan's approach to parenting children with food allergies includes making an effort not to feel guilty for her past actions when biomedical recommendations change. Notably, scientific wisdom about the role of maternal diet and breastfeeding did "a 180" during the time her children were living at home. Such instability in what medical professionals regarded as actionable facts undermined Joan's confidence in the general idea that there is some link between breastfeeding and the development of allergies. The fact was that Joan had breastfed for as long as possible and made dietary choices while doing so that were not informed by the changing medical recommendations. Now that evidence backed a new finding, she had moved on with her life. It was no use to her to obsess over the role breastfeeding might have played in the development of her children's allergies. Instead, as she explained later on in our interview, she cast her lot wholeheartedly with another idea to explain her children's allergies: the hygiene hypothesis.

Ongoing debate about food introduction timing in the biomedical literature triggers similar guilty feelings as the changing research on breastfeeding and food allergy. For example, Robyn O'Brien describes the "mama guilt" she later felt about her choices to consume soy during her pregnancy and feed her children soy-based formula.[57] The research she conducted for her book had since convinced her that soy, particularly genetically modified soy, is a main culprit behind the rise of food allergies. Soy is present in obvious foods, like tofu and soy-based drinks, as well as in food thickeners and texturizers and, most troublingly for O'Brien, in so-called hypoallergenic infant formulas. O'Brien's guilt is connected both to the feeling that she did something wrong and to the fact that she allowed herself to be taken in by the promise that expert biomedical advice provided everything she needed to know about how best to raise healthy children. The alternative would have been to raise her children following her own "maternal instincts." As she writes, "The idea of 25 percent of all formula-fed babies being part of some giant science experiment made me shudder—particularly when you consider that it's a science experiment that neither they nor their parents ever knowingly signed up for."[58] Her unwitting participation in this experiment, she asserts, is the cause of her son's deadly allergies. It is her fault, and she feels guilty about it.

Although O'Brien's criticism of mainstream scientific thinking about food allergies is sometimes viewed with skepticism in the food allergy world, the resulting anxieties she experiences are common. O'Brien bristles at the way the breastfeeding hypothesis and the hygiene hypothesis can instill a sense of guilt in mothers of allergic children. She writes, "They're saying that we moms are the problem. If we'd only lighten up on the hand-washing, they suggest, the allergy epidemic would vanish right into that new layer of dust covering our formerly spotless floors."[59] This keenly felt "mama guilt" is a typical expression of the self-blame that is a staple of food allergy mothers' conversations online and in person. For her, as for Jenna and Joan, the whiplash between initially understanding that certain foods that are positioned as healthy for most eaters trigger serious illness in her children undermines her trust in expert advice. Blaming the modern food production system thus deflects the weight of blame from herself as much as it offers a plausible answer to the etiology question.

In response to the rising anxiety and self-blame among food allergy mothers, some are pushing back to applaud good-enough parenting. Take Heather Hewett's feature in the 2014 issue of *Allergic Living* magazine. Hewett, a women's studies scholar as well as the parent of an allergic child, writes about the "litany of self-recrimination" she experiences after a mix-up of glasses of soy and cow's milk that lands her daughter in the hospital with anaphylaxis.[60] Hewett's written account was the second version of the "mixing up the milks" story that I encountered. Hewett writes that she feared she was "a Bad

Mother" because she "[ate] too many peanut butter cookies during pregnancy . . . wait[ed] too long to introduce particular foods . . . [or didn't] expos[e my daughter] to enough germs and dirt." Being a "Good Mother" of a child with a disability in modern America means, in her reading, being a "fearless Warrior Mom" who never makes mistakes and always protects her child from all sources of harm. But food allergy mothers are ready for a break, she concludes, and deserve to be content with "good enough mothering," accepting mistakes and adapting to situations as they arise.[61]

The phenomenon of mother blame among food allergy families seems hard to avoid. Laboratory research on food introduction and cleaning techniques would seem to validate women's work in the home as the best tools for managing food allergy while creating clearer guidelines for how this work is to be done both in and out of the home. The rationalization of food allergy management in recent biomedical research on cleaning, maternal diet, and early food and pathogen exposure makes certain maternal choices seem scientifically correct, and others faulty and blameworthy. Modern food allergy mothers thus find themselves in a bind not so different from the homemakers of the 1910s and 1920s, who discovered that supposedly labor-saving technologies simply raised the bar for a clean and beautiful home. When technoscientific experts take an interest in home work, it validates the practices women have already undertaken for years or even generations. At the same time, by affirming what the "right" way to mother is, it makes these demands more inescapable than ever—and makes those who fail to perfectly embody the motherhood ideal more thoroughly blamable for the misfortunes of their families. It heightens the political stakes of mothering an allergic child by yoking care work to the politics of biomedical evidence and expertise.

BLAME, RESPONSIBILITY, AND MOTHERING

Allergy science has placed the home and the family under a microscope for the better part of a century, positioning it as a site where both risks and remedies for allergy are located. In the process, it has sharpened rather than attenuated the political tenor of reproductive activities like breastfeeding, infant food introduction, and home hygiene by linking care work to the politics of biomedical knowledge. Aspects of caretaking as mundane as the household products used to clean a table have been investigated in the laboratory, turning everyday practices into evidence-based interventions. The lived experience of heightened responsibility creates ample opportunities for feelings of guilt as well as the development of distrust in biomedical authority over child-rearing. In my interviews with food allergy moms, the women whose private lives were at stake in allergy science were well aware of what they were "supposed" to do, and critical of the mixed messaging delivered over time by the biomedical establishment. When narrating their decisions about caring for their children, they actively interpreted, selectively applied, and sometimes challenged the relevance and appropriateness of medical advice in their own lives.

One lesson for scientific experts to take from this is to take care when communicating scientifically informed best practices about caretaking. Authoritative statements that change over time sow mistrust. They can even prompt mothers to rely on personal experience, the experience of close contacts, and less reliable evidence to understand their situation instead. In response, mothers are skeptical of biomedical proclamations that do not map onto their own experiences. While practitioners might be tempted to understand this as a form of resistance or denial of their expertise analogous to vaccine hesitancy, this is better understood as "embody[ing] protection by means of suspicion."[62] In other words, critical reflection on biomedical expertise should be understood as an act of care in and of itself. Food allergy mothers truly want what is best for their children. Comparing their own experiences to biomedical recommendations demonstrates active engagement with biomedical knowledge while putting it in its place as but one important part of a broader entire set of practices and knowledges that make up caring for an allergic child.

Yet what is remarkable about food allergy advocacy is that despite misgivings and reinterpretations, the public face of food allergy advocacy—both individuals and organizations—remains closely aligned with biomedical experts and knowledge. Chapters 4 and 5 will show why this is consequential for food allergy activism. This is in contrast to antivaccination activists, for example, who actively seek fringe experts, publicly refuse to take medical advice, and challenge nonmedical institutions, like schools, to bend medical guidelines to allow for increasingly wide-scale refusal of preventive measures. Medical distrust largely remains a private matter, disclosed in support groups and one-on-one conversations. Public advocacy is instead focused on aspects of everyday management, like school disability accommodations, and medical interventions, like epinephrine auto-injectors, that most everyone agrees work reliably well.

In biomedical research on food allergy, domestic practices pass through the laboratory to become valid biomedical knowledge. For STS scholars, it is a truism that the laboratory is both a mundane space of material work and an obligatory point through which information must pass to become valid knowledge.[63] Pasteur's strategic manipulation of microbes in and out of the laboratory made the anthrax bacillus and effectiveness of vaccination into a real phenomenon.[64] Similarly, simulating domestic practices in the laboratory, using Bamba in clinical study protocols, and crunching the numbers on which breastfeeding women's children develop allergies and which do not all lend an aura of scientific truth to recommendations about how to care for home and children. Yet living up to the best practices as demonstrated by science might be impossible when faced with a fussy infant or when a potentially allergy-triggering food is all that is handy and appealing to eat postpartum. The transformation of everyday practice into biomedical fact thus presents new forms of ambivalence for food allergy mothers, as well as those with food allergy and other caretakers. On the one hand, studying everyday practices using clinical and laboratory protocols seems to validate the work that people do every day. On the other, it establishes officially correct ways of doing that work, which can add new forms of stress and even distrust. Socially reproductive work in the home becomes political in another way: It is now also subject to the internal politics of scientific communities of expertise.

The recent return to investigating the use of immunotherapy for food allergy continues the rationalization of caretaking in food allergy families by creating solutions that need to be scaffolded by intensive care work. For these treatments to deliver as promised, the family must continue to behave as expected, with multiple adult caretakers, one of whom earns a wage and health benefits and the other of whom is available for frequent doctors' visits, possible emergency school pickups, treatment of iatrogenic symptoms, and general surveillance of the child being treated. The family, and especially the responsible mother, are recentered as crucial social and biomedical institutions in this treatment paradigm.

This observation is not meant to discount the real promise of a life of reduced worry that long-acting treatments hold out for many food allergy families. However, it does raise important questions about the relationship of the American family to biomedicine and public health. Why, for example, are the solutions devised by biomedical experts targeted at self-management? Why are skin rashes and long waiting periods after daily treatments that take considerable time and support from caretakers seen as acceptable trade-offs for long-term reduction in food allergy? Why is the nuclear family seen as a readily available resource to deal with a widespread public health problem? The gender and care politics—and, as the next chapter will show, the racial politics—of the institution of the family appears poised to be drawn even closer into the politics of official biomedical knowledge with these new developments.

Scientific elaboration of the mother's pivotal role in food allergy management has important consequences for public food allergy advocacy work. As later chapters will show, the assumption that the family and the home are resources for food allergy management shapes the horizons of possibility in advocacy demands and strategies. For example, the role of allergy moms is used as a way to claim credibility in some campaigns, and the distribution of necessary health resources via nuclear family units, like health insurance coverage, is rarely questioned. Both gender politics and nationalist reproductive politics thus become part of the food allergy experience.

Before making those connections between home life and the public sphere, however, the next chapter builds on the questions of gendered blame and family responsibility laid out here. I will return to everyday practices in the home, this time with a focus on home hygiene and design, to develop the concept of the hygienic sublime.

Examining how the home is constructed as a pure and hygienic space requires reflection on the intersections of gendered care at home with race and class in society writ large. The very idea of home as a place of cleanliness and safety in the United States has developed with and through enactments of race and class distinctions concerning caretakers, hygiene habits, and consumer products. In turning to the home to find solutions to food allergy, then, we must question whom these proposed remedies are for, at whose expense they are promoted, and whose problems are overlooked in the process.

3

THE HYGIENIC SUBLIME

MAKING FOOD SAFE FOR PEOPLE WITH FOOD ALLERGIES

In life with food allergies, purity is paramount. The ordinary markers of a lived-in kitchen—crumbs on the counter, a thin sheen of oil on the stovetop, a dusting of flour on the shelves—present immediate dangers to someone managing an allergy to peanuts, wheat, or shellfish. To manage such ever-present threats, food allergy households turn to intensive management of home hygiene, including management of food sourcing, preparation surfaces, utensils, and other aspects of the domestic space. Meanwhile, the tidy, desirable home is modeled in media images of sparkling-clean, high-end kitchens and scenes of heteronormative domestic bliss. I call these figurations of perfect hygiene the hygienic sublime. The hygienic sublime prompts a confrontation with the limits of purity in the face of microscopic agents, like food oils and proteins. At the same time, the hygienic sublime contributes to the elevation of whiteness, heteronormativity, wealth, and nuclear families as the means through which bodily safety can be assured in the contaminated—and contaminating—spaces of modern life.

Food allergic people and caretakers face constant challenges to controlling the movement of oils, proteins, and chemicals, which are often present in such small quantities as to be invisible. The pursuit of purity in food allergic living is an attempt to domesticate the dangers of food substances through scrubbing, washing, wiping, separating, storing, packing, and transporting foods and the objects they contact in ways that create and maintain purity. Although the scale of concern is small, it is not small "on a human scale"[1] but on a microscopic one. It is thus not pastoral or beautiful in the sense of Edmund Burke's typification of the beautiful and the sublime, but instead dangerous at a different, nonhuman scale. In everyday practice, controlling tiny environmental contaminants perfectly and constantly through household hygiene is impossible. Hearing repeated stories about the impossibility of purity—about failures and mix-ups and the resulting episodes of illness—was the seed for this chapter. These failures further serve to remind individuals, often in traumatic ways, of the limited capacity of human control over things that are much smaller than human scale. The hygienic sublime yokes the reproductive politics of food allergic living with the material artifacts that so deeply shape the lives of people managing the condition.

As I briefly related in the previous chapter's discussion of allergy science and the home, hygiene has been the best medicine for managing allergies for over a century. This chapter will delve into this topic in more depth. It expands the examination of home management techniques to consider how gender and the family link to race and class. Because allergies have been notoriously difficult to reverse by medical interventions, controlling the environment has become the focal point for the management of many types of allergies in the United States since the nineteenth century. Some of these interventions have been focused on public space, like the anti-ragweed campaigns led by white, middle-class women in Chicago.[2] Wealthy nineteenth-century and early to mid-twentieth-century Americans would also travel to replace their ordinary environment with the forests of northern Michigan during hay season, or decamp to Arizona to treat intractable asthma.[3] Controlling the home environment also became, and remains, a key strategy for managing allergy, particularly respiratory allergy.[4] By the 1930s, the acquisition of specially marketed consumer goods was positioned as a solution to managing the disease that was attainable by the middle classes as well as the rich.[5] With access to remedies so consistently tied to purchasing power in the history of allergy, class positioning has been a central aspect of the reproductive politics of the condition. The home is also a site where technoscientific practice and innovation is intimately tied to the formation of subjects who are gendered, raced, and classed in intersecting ways. Historians have argued that household practices have been specifically aimed at cleansing and strengthening the social and physical body of the nation in a way that links both heteronormativity and eugenics.[6] Indeed, a frequently touted benefit of the hygienic home in the United States in the first half of the twentieth century was that it was private, free of potentially contaminated and contaminating people, and presided over by a woman whose entire life was devoted to caring for the family.[7] New household technologies allowed white women to do more household work without outside (and often undesirably racialized, foreign, or lower-class) help, securing the home as a private space where only the legally and genetically related family was allowed. In the process, it intensified mothers' moral duty to do housework and further naturalized the idea that a woman's place in the world was primarily as a caretaker. Contemporary food icons like Martha Stewart, as well as trends like foodie culture and the ubiquitous Starbucks pumpkin spice latte, continue to draw some of their cachet from the associations with white femininity that emerge from this longer history of home hygiene.[8]

This chapter argues that the hygienic sublime, as it is instantiated in food allergic living, positions the white, middle-class, heteronormative family as a resource for ensuring health in the contemporary United States. In the next section, I will further elaborate why aspirational home hygiene deserves to be considered a form of the sublime. Then I will analyze images from a popular food allergy magazine, *Allergic Living*, to begin describing the visual form of the hygienic sublime. *Allergic Living* was the premier food allergy print publication at the time of my ethnographic research, and its text and images represent widely held ideas about food allergies and what should be done about them. Then I delve into three interviews to explore how race, gender, family structure, and class intersect to shape how adults and parents manage food allergies in the home. The experiences of these

participants illustrate what the real-life pursuit of the hygienic sublime looks like, as well as the many complications and failures that
come along with its pursuit.

In closing this chapter, I consider how the hygienic sublime articulates with other, long-standing conversations in feminist technoscience studies about the ethics and implications of purity politics in
science, technology, and society. While the hygienic sublime is on the
surface a pragmatic response to the problem of "how to build yourself
a body in a safe space" in a contaminated world,[9] the historical record
shows that a politics premised on purity risks limiting the political
and ethical imagination of movements for recognition and inclusion. The politics of purity in the home are politically consequential
because they inform the stances taken in public advocacy campaigns
that will be discussed in depth in chapters 4 and 5. What happens
in the home is not magically separate from what happens in public
space, as feminist theorists and activists have long argued. It is also a
site for reproductive politics that can be flexibly applied and scaled up
in a variety of public settings. Thus, understanding the hygienic sublime in the food allergy home is necessarily part of the story of food
allergy advocacy on the floors of legislatures and elsewhere in public
discourse.

DOMESTICATING THE SUBLIME

The sublime as it has so far been conceived in philosophy and environmental humanities is a mode of experience that reifies gender norms
and national identity. But things identified as sublime have mostly
been large scale, outside the home, and coded as masculine: moun-
tain vistas, overcast prairie views, powerful waterfalls. Admitting impure countertops into the taxonomy of sublime landscapes represents
a decidedly feminist intervention into this scholarly tradition. The hygienic sublime has similar ideological effects in terms of reinforcing
gender norms and upholding a kind of racialized nationalism as a virtue. My use of the sublime breaks with some of the scalar conventions
of the sublime as it has been used to date, which focus on scales that
are much greater than and much smaller than human scale, to focus
instead on embodied experiences in domestic spaces.

Taking a cue from Edmund Burke's treatise on the sublime, originally published in 1757, scholars of environmental communication emphasize that the large scale and greater-than-human magnitude of landscapes, both pure and polluted, as key aspects of the sublime.[10] Within this literature, scholars have identified toxic sublimes meant to push viewers toward environmental activism, marketing-oriented recreational sublimes, and even domesticated sublimes, in which nature is tamed by viewing it through the technology of the camera lens.[11] Stormer enumerates a series of sublimes, including maternal sublimes and a hygienic sublime, characterized by a focus on highly gendered, nationalistic mental and racial hygiene.[12]

According to Stormer's analysis of Ansel Adams's photographic oeuvre, "sublime scenes" operate in mass media by "constituting a relationship between the spectator as a certain kind of human being and the sublime object as greater than human."[13] Stormer and other environmental communications scholars are especially interested in the "affective response" intended or experienced through viewing simultaneously dangerous and enticing, massive sublime landscapes.[14] Yet for Peeples, immensity is not the whole story.[15] Mystery, that which lurks off-screen, and a feeling of vertigo when confronted with differences in position and scale count for as much as human smallness in the face of the hugeness wilderness or nature. Peeples's description of the sublime invites a consideration of how the very small scale, like the very large, can trigger a confrontation with the limits of human mastery over nature.

Doing housework in pursuit of a hygienic indoor environment is often entirely overwhelming, yet in Miles's terms, for example, such a response to the presence of the sublime would not be admissible to a tradition of sublimity rooted in nineteenth-century literature and philosophy. For Miles (and Stormer),[16] what is sublime is always outside, exterior to the self, and public. Yet analogous to the response of the nineteenth-century American settler to perform masculine toughness in response to overwhelmingly vast landscapes, the call to perform housework is a never-ending task that demands action once affected by the hygienic sublime. Action must go on despite the feeling that the nonhuman scale overwhelms even the best of human intentions. The differences between the hygienic sublime and the existing sublime tradition lie in the direction of the difference in magnitude between humans and their threatening/enticing environs, and in the gendering of the particular activities performed in response to the stimulus of sublimity.

Sublime imagery and experiences of the sublime in U.S. contexts inspired normatively masculine feats of endurance and strength, recorded in the diaries and publications of historical colonizers, soldiers, and explorers.[17] Embodying masculinity on the frontier became linked with the enactment of Americanness, motivating generations of soldiers, politicians, and enterprising young men to expand the nation's territory. Masculinity was the proper response to sublime landscapes, and masculine feats of conquest and settlement exemplified an American vision of national progress. This form of progress was expansionist and concerned with the control of land in the nineteenth century; it shifted to emphasize the pursuit of technological advancements in the twentieth.

American technological sublimes in the twentieth century remained both racial and national, as David Nye describes.[18] The view of the Hetch Hetchy dam or a rocket launching into space from American soil connote progress and national unity for the masses. On the other side of the globe, and overlapping with the early years of Nye's analysis, the continuation of U.S. expansion through colonialism also created new terrains for investigating and enacting medical purity in locations like the American Philippines. In Warwick Anderson's investigation of the American colonial years from 1898 to 1946, for example, racial and bacteriological hygiene are linked and elevated to a subliminal coupling of threat for the colonizers and enticement for the colonized.[19] These technological achievements produced faith in the idea that life in the United States could only grow better, healthier, and stronger, and that it must do so through intensified deployment of the latest engineered inventions.

I situate the sublime in an everyday, domestic U.S. context in which race, gender, and class take on particular, intersecting formations. These configurations of power and identity are embedded in the imagery and experience of the hygienic sublime. The hygienic sublime is consequently political. It reproduces structures of power and visibility in U.S. society. Rather than emboldening wilderness adventurers, the hygienic sublime portrayed in food allergy publications targets homemakers—implicitly women—and entices them to make home improvements and invest in organizing systems, cooking tools, air filters, and allergy-friendly interior paint. It mediates a turn inward, an intensification of the regard paid toward private, domestic spaces and the families that inhabit them. The hygienic sublime is clearly classed as well; poor people need not attempt it, as the goods, time, and expertise require generously available time and capital. In the media version of the hygienic sublime, slim, white women smile and take care of children; they shine together beatifically in pure, filtered sunlight. In real life, women quit their jobs to cook, clean, and purify full-time, to ward off the dangers posed to their children by microscopic agents.

THE HYGIENIC HOME IDEAL

The hygienic sublime takes on its purest form in media images depicting the perfectly safe and pure food allergy home. Although media images often show an idealized experience of home and family, media analysis can nonetheless play an important role in understanding the sociotechnical imaginaries in circulation in a particular place and time.[20] Lisa Nakamura's examination of 1990s internet technology ads, for example, uncovers the colonial tropes used by technology companies that remain in circulation two decades later, although in modified forms, in practices and discourses about artificial intelligence "for good."[21] The hygienic home ideal portrayed in food allergy media frequently came up in partial ways in my conversations with food allergy moms, physicians, and advocates. Individuals even measure their success as caretakers against this ideal, as I will discuss. To understand how the hygienic sublime circulates as an unattainable yet desirable state, I therefore start with an examination of the ideal as presented in media and advertising imagery and text.

Central to the hygienic home ideal are a heteronormative conception of family, an assumption of access to middle-class or upper-middle-class financial resources, and the moral and aesthetic elevation of white women caretakers. Examining this ideal supports and extends my ethnographic findings. For example, throughout my ethnographic interviews and encounters, keeping children safe from food allergies was a duty almost exclusively assigned to members of nuclear, heteronormative families, particularly women. Extended family members like aunts, uncles, and grandparents were only periodically mentioned in interviews, and with only one exception, extended kin were said to be an impediment to the safety of allergic children and adults. The hygienic home imagery I discuss below echoes this lived reality in its depiction of mothers, children, and families. Furthermore, the idealized hygienic home in the materials I collected during my fieldwork was mostly populated by white people. (Later years of *Allergic Living* magazine shift the racial representation to be more inclusive of people of color—to the credit of the thoughtful, rigorous editorial staff.) Finally, the hygienic sublime interpellates a classed subject as well. The goods and environments portrayed as beneficial for people with allergies are more often than not spacious and made of high-end materials or involve costly specialty food products. The solution to allergy, in these images, lies not in a robust public health response but in the consumption practices of individual families with cash to spare.

The sources I will focus on here are 2014 through 2016 issues of *Allergic Living* magazine, the primary magazine of and for the English-speaking food allergy community. These are representative of news and advertisements I frequently encountered at conferences, in other publications, and in presentations about building a home safe for allergies. Headed by Canadian editor and food allergic adult Gwen Smith, *Allergic Living* magazine presents rigorously vetted health information from scientific experts alongside features about ordinary families dealing with food allergies. In addition, it includes updates on major food and environmental trends that might affect people with food and other allergies; provides recipes that omit major allergens; and features aspirational spreads about beautifully designed, allergy-friendly homes. Like all commercial print publications, it also contains a multitude of ads for products for allergy, asthma, and related health concerns. The magazine had a small permanent staff, and many of its columnists were scholars and independent food allergy bloggers whom I met, followed on social media, and interviewed during the course of my research. Depending on the page examined, the depiction of the hygienic home in *Allergic Living* provides a window into either what people with food allergies hoped to achieve in their own homes or what home products advertisers thought they should desire. It is a key site in which the hygienic sublime was documented and disseminated among people managing food allergies during the main period of my research, from late 2013 to early 2016.

Hygiene for Sale

The hygienic sublime in the home is advertised as a state of purity and peace accessible through the consumption of specialized and luxury consumer goods. This is a neoliberal vision of the home that makes individual families the bulwark against what might otherwise be considered a public health problem. As Arlie Russell Hochschild writes, care through consumption "strikes at a flash point between an advancing commodity frontier, on one hand, and the hypersymbolized but structurally weakened core of the modern American family, on the other."[22] Relying on consumption as a cornerstone of care also has consequences for which families can afford to follow expert advice to maintain health and which cannot. Care through consumption has the potential to deepen racial divides, for example, concerning access to necessary measures for health because families of color, particularly Black families, have lower average incomes and less wealth than white ones. The hygienic sublime represents strongly classed aspirations that articulate with ideals of racialized and gendered caretaking as well.

The fall 2014 issue of *Allergic Living* offers a compelling place to start unpacking these issues. This issue includes a seven-page feature article entitled "Kitchens that Cook" about designing an allergy-safe kitchen.[23] The recommended materials are as natural as possible— wood, stone, and glass—to reduce the possibility of volatile organic compounds (VOCs, found in higher proportions in plastics and certain paints) off-gassing into the home and irritating asthma or chemical sensitivity symptoms. The top-of-the-line design includes hardwood floors, low-VOC paint, wood cabinets, and stone and glass-composite countertops. Cabinets are spacious and plentiful enough to store the wide array of kitchen tools and basic grains, flavorings, and vegetables needed to easily cook all of a family's meals from scratch. The size and abundance of cabinets also make it easy to sort, see, assess, and choose the right products for different members of the family when their nutritional needs might vary. The finished kitchen is suburban luxury doubling as medical necessity—the highest expression of the hygienic sublime.

Such a contemporary union of disease mitigation efforts with a hygienic aesthetic has antecedents in the sanitarian movement of the Progressive Era. The ecological orientation of sanitarians, and before them much of nineteenth-century medicine, demanded that serious attention be paid to maintaining and improving the health of environments in which people lived.[24] Visual and olfactory cues—the absence or presence of visible waste and the smells of decomposition—were important indicators of healthfulness. Despite the shift of American medicine toward a microbiological understanding of infectious disease that sought to exclude, and later find and destroy, microbes, sanitation (and the aesthetic it promulgated) persisted as an important pillar of public and individual health.[25] Its persistence in theories of home management provides grounds for the limitless expectations of purity that characterize the hygienic sublime. In food allergic living, the heightened standard of order and purity proffered to food allergy families as a solution to their health problems dovetails with this fantasy of the home as a smoothly functioning and aesthetically pleasing machine.

Using images of the hygienic home to sell solutions to environmental allergies predates the uptick in concern about food allergy in the last two decades. Gregg Mitman documents a variety of technologies used by middle-class families to combat allergies in the nineteenth and early twentieth centuries. Mitman highlights how early air-conditioning manufacturers targeted allergy sufferers by promising a pleasant indoor climate in summer.[26] Ads promised that cool air could be had (for a price) within the hermetically sealed modern home, thereby keeping pollen away from those with susceptible constitutions. Carla Keirns connects marketing tactics surrounding allergy to the subliminal ideal of the midcentury American home as a zone of hygienic purity.[27] Professionals including allergists, home builders, architects, and reformers "joined together to create a new aesthetic of absolute cleanliness" as a proposed solution to the condition.[28] In the construction of a food allergy–safe home today, such precedents have served as useful models for managing unruly food proteins.

In other issues of *Allergic Living*, readers can find images that connect hygiene to a kind of otherworldly transcendence. One repeated ad for 3M Filtrete air filters for heating and cooling systems, for example, shows a white woman standing in a dim room looking upward into a glowing golden light. The light selectively illuminates her face, evoking the beatific imagery of saints and the Virgin Mary. The swirling dust in the air is beautiful, almost mystical—but also deadly dangerous for an allergy sufferer. The dust presumably could have been filtered out, had the woman purchased and installed the advertised filters. In other ads for 3M Filtrete products, a smiling preadolescent white girl with tidy, shiny brown hair and a white T-shirt is lying on white shag carpet. The blurred background varies in tone from white to a light gray patch in the shape and orientation of an open window. The ad features an endorsement seal from the Asthma and Allergy Foundation of America that reads "CERTIFIED asthma & allergy friendly™." These ads seem designed to instill a desire for health seeking and self-improvement via home improvement projects. The bodies and faces of white women and girls are offered as enticements, depicted as beautiful and pure—and potentially at risk in the home. These depictions of the hygienic sublime get across the larger-than-life stakes of the hygienic sublime while positioning specialized and expensive consumer goods as the markers of success.

Gender, Family, and Race in the Idealized Home

The expectation that appropriate health care can be achieved through aspirational consumption is mingled with images of idealized, white, heteronormative nuclear families in depictions of the allergy-friendly home. In advertising images, the ideal setting for using luxury and specialty foods and products is white and heteronormative, with either two parents of different genders and children or a mother–child dyad on display. White women and babies are depicted in soft focus or in light-colored, bright spaces decorated with high-end furniture. When families appear together, mother assumes either the role of family caretaker or of an infantilized child. Such representations of the heteronormative nuclear family reflect and reinforce the gendered, heteronormative experiences of my interlocutors, both men and women. They also tap into and help perpetuate a history of racialized and gendered caretaking expectations within families and homes that has figured prominently in the recent history of families in the United States.

The ads and features in *Allergic Living* often portray an idealized mother–child relationship as the seat of safety and purity in the allergic home. One fall 2016 feature about allergy-friendly flooring, for example, shows a white woman with long blonde hair sitting on a white leather couch wearing a white shirt, smiling down at a white toddler dressed in a pale denim onesie on a light gray concrete floor. The walls are white. In the background is a second, gray, minimalist couch and a 1960s-style sideboard stacked with blurred book spines.[29] The image depicts a home from which dirt and hard work are so reliably excluded that white furniture and clothes are a reasonable and comfortable choice. The household also seems to have disposable income to spend on an antique, decorative furniture item that could sell for $10,000 or more in my home of Brooklyn, New York, when the article was published. Other images emphasize the transcendental aspects of the mother–child relationship. A summer 2015 feature on designing "the better nursery," for example, depicts a light-skinned, black-haired woman of indeterminate race and ethnicity dressed in white and holding her baby up to her face in a white-washed, soft-focus child's bedroom. The room seems to be imbued with a mysterious glow, suggesting something divine about the mother–child connection depicted. These images, and many others, use literally white color schemes and careful staging and manipulation to recall medical-grade cleanliness. Further, they seem to suggest that the people depicted have attained a divine state of purity and safety.

The white, wealthy, heterosexual family also figures prominently, especially in advertisements. In the few ads that featured men, they appeared to be fathers. One was for the peanut-free and tree nut–free Wowbutter in the fall 2016 issue. The white mother is still in the foreground, although her back is to the camera. She is sitting at a small dining table in a sleek kitchen lined with hardwood cabinets and high-end countertops. The other participants in the scene interpellate her with the exclamation, "Mom! You have to try this." The white father stands across the table from mom with two young children, spoon-feeding her a taste of the "amazingly peanut free" food as though she were also a young child. Everyone appears uncontrollably happy. The mom is momentarily freed from her caretaking duties by a conscientious man, only to have him spoon-feed her like a child. In these images, the heterosexual nuclear family appears to be a safe and happy social element in the otherwise material enactment of the hygienic sublime.

Unspoken yet unavoidable in these depictions of the hygienic sublime are the entwined histories of structural and scientific racism in the United States. In the early twentieth century, the ideal hygienic home was constructed not only through the exclusion of certain materials but also through excluding or spatially limiting the incursion of racialized and classed bodies into the private space of the white nuclear family. As historians have documented,[30] the flames of moral panic concerning the disease-carrying nature of nonwhite immigrant and Black domestic workers helped drive advertising and sales of products designed for white, middle-class housewives. Public health officials and sanitarians meanwhile debated how to change epidemiological patterns in which diseases like tuberculosis and smallpox were endemic in crowded, urban immigrant communities. Behaviors and preferences associated with non-Anglo-American groups were often found to be at fault.[31] Whether these behaviors could ever be changed was additionally in question because many Anglo-American elites believed that a presumed inferior intelligence was hereditary and unavoidable for Southern and Eastern European immigrants. This racist history finds expression in the hygienic sublime in multiple ways: in the white, spacious, tiled bathroom; in the expectation that housewives will do their own cooking and cleaning in kitchens and bathrooms disinfected with Lysol; and in the pricy markets for the household products and services that help mother protect her family from wayward external influences.

Of course, some level of enactment of the hygienic home offers a necessary kind of purity for many people living with food and environmental allergies today. But the ideal solutions that are promoted in the pages of *Allergic Living* magazine (and elsewhere in allergy-related media) have their roots in a racist and patriarchal history that should temper enthusiasm for imagery of the modern hygienic home. My intent in drawing parallels between past and present is not to demonize the helpful solutions that families have developed; nor do I wish to discount the genuine goodwill that I know motivates people to share them through writing, stories, and images. Neither am I attempting to provide a comprehensive history of home hygiene or the heteronormative family, as this book primarily tells an ethnographic story. Rather, I wish to urge reflection about how imagery and discourse concerning the hygienic sublime are used, as well as whose experiences they depict and whose they ignore. In the next section, I will unpack scenes from three life history interviews to examine how overwhelmingly white, heteronormative, and expensive depictions of the hygienic sublime set up people managing food allergies in the home for feelings of failure, irresponsibility, and exclusion in their imperfect enactments of this ideal.

THE HYGIENIC HOME IN PRACTICE

The hygienic sublime entices caretakers and homemakers—especially mothers, or more rarely men who experience their role as caretakers to be distinctly feminized—to participate in histories of domesticity that assign responsibility for the health of a nuclear family to women, position people who are not classified as white as potentially contaminating and politically inconvenient, and infuse everyday family life with anxiety about class mobility. For food allergic people, eating foods that are considered safe because they do not contain ingredients that might trigger a person's specific physiology to become disordered—in other words, foods that are pure—is an extension of the basic reality that food is necessary to live. Failing to eat food that is free of one's allergens can lead to anaphylaxis, a serious, body-wide allergic reaction that can rapidly progress, with hives, trouble breathing, and low blood pressure quickly escalating to respiratory or cardiac failure and even death. In the United States, food safety and preparation have been constructed as comprising a broad set of demands placed overwhelmingly on women. This history shapes how food allergy households distribute responsibility for food purity in and within nuclear families.

Ruth Schwartz Cowan shows how the assignment of food preparation to women in nuclear households in the United States dates back to the colonial era.[32] In the eighteenth and early nineteenth centuries, food preparation included the growing, harvesting, cleaning, and preserving of raw materials like corn, wheat, and meat as well as cooking. But this work, even the work women did to complete the final steps of cooking that might today be recognized as domestic— hauling water, tending fires, and cooking in heavy iron pots—did not encode the same concerns about the delicacy of the female body that it would later on. According to Cowan, it was the development of more "convenient" household products and tools, starting with mass-produced milled flours, that supported the entrenchment of strongly gendered divisions of labor in the typical American home. By World War I, housework, including most food preparation, "was to be thought of no longer as a chore but, rather, as an expression of the housewife's personality and her affection for her family. . . . Feeding the family had once been just part of a day's work; now it was a way to communicate deep-seated emotions."[33] Hers was a necessary role within the heterosexual family, but a tightly circumscribed one. Conversely, when things went wrong, "she was entirely to blame, since remedies for those conditions were easily at hand and easy to apply."[34]

The food preparation techniques used to manage food allergies in the home continue this deeply gendered ordering of the work of social reproduction in and through the American home.[35] One need only glance at food allergy magazines to witness how this arrangement is idealized—so much so that it can be used as an enticement for the purchase of consumer goods. Food preparation has been subject to intense rationalization and regimentation as part of the effort to make domestic hygiene practices properly scientific throughout the twentieth century and at the start of the twenty-first century.[36] Alongside this process, the popularity of cultural icons like Martha Stewart has helped cement the association between order and white femininity more specifically.[37] What is more, domestic work like food preparation continues to drive the responsibilization of many women in the United States today, creating good caretakers through enticing engagements with, for example, foodie culture.[38] Cooking nutritious, pathogen-free, aesthetically pleasing food remains a central pillar of the domestic expectations for the homemakers and caretakers in food allergy families in the United States, and the stakes of success are especially high for these parents.

Mothering and Fathering

In practice, seeking to achieve the hygienic sublime in the home draws on and reinforces gendered caretaking roles. This section contrasts the experience of two mothers and a father in creating a safe and hygienic domestic space. Only one of these three individuals is a white woman. Including their varied experiences in this chapter helps to triangulate whiteness, femininity, and white femininity by its absence as well as its presence. It is ethnographic common sense to include multiple perspectives on a topic in order to show how even when specific experiences and views may differ, they are still culturally legible because they are positioned in relation to dominant or normative cultural forms.

For each person in this section, contamination and risk are negotiated largely individually, with extended family, colleagues, and friends all potentially posing threats to bodily health. Caretaking is thus experienced as highly individualized, with mother or father knowing best and shouldering the main burden of caring for allergic family members. However, their experiences diverge in how closely their lives as lived map onto their expectations of family life. For Alice, the mother, intensified mothering is unexpected but acceptable; for Michael, the father, becoming the primary parent of an allergic child upends his expectations of what adulthood would be like. Comparing their experiences side by side illuminates how subjective experiences of caretaking map onto expectations of how gender and care fit together in the context of family life.

One woman's story illustrates the stakes of purity for both health and social life for people with food allergies and how responsibility for maintaining purity is highly gendered. I met Alice over dinner at a conference for food allergy media professionals in 2014 in the southwestern United States. Alice's children were attending college and starting new jobs by the time we met. However, when her oldest son was diagnosed with food allergies in 1991, the condition did not have the same level of visibility and community support that it has today. He was often the first child with food allergies whom doctors, teachers, coaches, and other parents had encountered. Alice, a white woman married to a high-earning man, gave up waged work to be in charge of ensuring her son's safety at home, at school, and at play. The chance to focus on food allergy management in the home was presented to me by Alice as simply a logical choice. Yet her narration made clear that the hygienic sublime shaped the texture of her social worlds and became a benchmark of her own self-worth.

One of the biggest challenges Alice faced early on was the way that foods were labeled in the 1990s. Each of the eight most common allergy-triggering foods in the United States are simple ingredients found in a wide variety of foods: peanut, tree nut, milk, egg, fish, shellfish, wheat, and soy. Alice's son was allergic to peanuts, tree nuts, dairy, and eggs as a child. Because warning labels indicating the presence of these and other foods were rare in the 1990s, it was impossible to know with certainty whether a particular food was free of all of his allergens. To manage this uncertainty, she removed from her cabinets any packaged foods that might contain his allergens, and she committed herself to cooking all of his meals from scratch at home. Her pursuit of the hygienic sublime entailed keeping close control over her home and her son's body.

The issue of cross-contamination came up repeatedly in my conversations with Alice. In the 1990s, she and other allergy moms were on their own in figuring out how it happened and how to avoid it. She explained:

> There were a lot of things that today are sort of common knowl-
> edge in the food allergy world that we were just figuring out.
> Such as the idea, the concept of cross contamination. . . . We
> couldn't figure out why the kid kept reacting to things. I'd think,
> but that doesn't have milk in it! It didn't occur to me that he could
> react to what was on the knife, or what was on the equipment in
> the manufacturing plant. It didn't occur to me because there were
> no resources and there was no common knowledge.

Despite her vigilance, near misses and mishaps sometimes occurred, especially when other mothers tried to help her take care of her son. One day when her son was still a toddler, Alice left him with a friend whom she had trained to recognize and treat the symptoms of allergic reactions. After some time, her friend called, explaining that Alice's son was breaking out in hives on his face. Alice rushed to her friend's home and discovered that she had wiped his face with the same wash-cloth that she had used for her own son. In effect, "she had wiped allergens all over his face." The hives spread onto his legs, suggesting that the high chair he was seated in was also coated in allergenic food residue. Alice summed up these stories by lamenting, "Even if you find another mom who's willing to take him on and you send the food and you've gone through the emergency procedures, little details like that wouldn't occur to the average person." For Alice, purity became more than a material property of foods. It was an overarching concern that touched on many aspects of her social life as she sought to keep her son safe. Even well-meaning friends were not appropriately versed in the hygienic practices needed to keep her son safe.

A phone interview I conducted in 2014 with a food allergic adult, a man named Michael, offers another view of how the hygienic sublime is enacted in the home. As an exception to the general focus on women and mothers in this book, his experience brings into relief how gender expectations are built into the hygienic sublime, whether an individual likes it or not, as a result of gendered norms about who ought to do domestic versus wage-earning forms of work. Michael was one of only two men I interviewed who were the ones primarily responsible for managing food allergies in their homes, and his was the only family I encountered in which a man was the primary caretaker for a food allergic child. Michael had been diagnosed with allergies three years previously and spent his days looking after an infant daughter who was also developing food allergies.

In contrast to Alice, this did not feel like a choice to him. Being a full-time caregiver was not a responsibility he had even remotely anticipated taking on. He initially took on this role because his own food allergies and environmental sensitivities rendered him unable to work. Although being a stay-at-home dad had its rewards, he was still devastated by the inability to have what he considered to be a gender-appropriate social and professional life: to be regularly active outside the home and to bring in a significant, if not a majority, share of his household's income. Michael was much more willing to talk about the sense of mourning he felt in response to this change in his professional trajectory than most mothers I spoke to. The replacement of masculine expectations of success outside the home with a necessary focus on domesticity was a difficult part of his illness experience.

As we spoke by phone, he toured his kitchen and told me what he saw. Michael's version of the hygienic sublime was different from that of the mothers I spoke to thanks to the particular needs of his body. Yet even though his kitchen did not look sublimely pure, purity was still his reference point for comparing what he observed. His kitchen worked for him, but it fell short of what he knew others would expect. Boxes of onions, potatoes, and butternut squash from local farmers and his own garden sat on the floor shedding soil, banishing any hope of a "clean kitchen." There were "a few Crock-Pots here and there," and an extra freezer where he stored servings of bulk meals for days when he felt too ill to cook. Modern conveniences like prepared foods and high-tech materials were gone, replaced by stainless steel and boxes of basic, raw vegetables. It was, in his words, "no frills." His kitchen was not, as I envisioned from his description, particularly neat and tidy. It did not resemble the perfect visions of the hygienic sublime portrayed in the pages of *Allergic Living* magazine. Rather, it was pure in the right way to ensure his safety and health. His allergens were meticulously excluded, even though that meant that dirt was introduced. Nonetheless, his reference point for appropriate hygiene was the perfect vision commonly encountered in media portrayals of the safe and happy family home. By that metric, he knew he was failing.

Intersections of Race and Gender

A third parent's story adds another crucial perspective to understanding the hygienic sublime: how the gender politics of the hygienic sublime intersect with race. I use the verb "intersect" intentionally to index the Black feminist concept of intersectionality and thereby draw attention to the (sometimes inconsistently) interlocking systems of power and structural exclusion at stake in the hygienic sublime. Intersectionality was originally articulated by legal theorist Kimberlé Crenshaw in response to single-axis frameworks of analysis used in feminist, Black, and antidiscrimination theories in the 1980s. In these critical formations, one was a woman or not a woman, or Black or not Black; one could be discriminated against, in cultural theory and in legal practice, primarily as a result of race or gender, but typically not both at once. Intersectionality, by contrast, draws attention to how "Black women can experience discrimination in ways that are both similar to and different from those experienced by white women and Black men. . . . Yet often they experience double discrimination— the combined effects of practices which discriminate on the basis of race, and on the basis of sex."[39] When it comes to the hygienic sublime, the confluence of assumptions and exclusions regarding both race and gender in the tools that are available to caretakers heightens feelings of exclusion as well as the difficulty of everyday life managing food allergy.

Andrea was the mother of a food allergic child and leader of what she described as the only food allergy support group specifically addressing racial, ethnic, gender, and economic diversity and inclusion. She was the only Black person I interviewed during my research, and she was one of two Black people—both women—whom I corresponded with. In our interview, she chose to focus the discussion on issues of racial and ethnic diversity in food allergy support communities. She was the first (although not the last) person I spoke to who wanted to discuss this dimension of food allergy experience. Andrea started a support group in the southeastern United States to create a venue where both the direct health effects of food allergy and issues of ethnicity and racism related to food and health could be openly discussed. She had previously attended other support group meetings, but she found those meetings frustrating because she did not think that participants and leaders were willing to speak to how ethnicity and race shape the food allergy experience. The meetings struck her as "moms having tea," a phrase that evoked an image of white East Coast elites demurely assembled around porcelain cups. By contrast, she described herself as "more of an action person."

With food allergy, she saw a need for speaking more openly about the variety of racial and cultural attitudes that could shape the management of the condition. For Andrea, that included racial, ethnic, and religious biases as well as regional differences between people in the northern and southern United States toward food, child-rearing, and success. With food allergy, she explained, people of color and mixed-race people faced extra challenges in gaining recognition of the legitimacy of their condition and receiving appropriate accommodations in work settings. She reported that she had often heard the claim that "Black people don't get food allergies," despite limited statistical evidence.[40] In her network of Black friends, neighbors, and family, this attitude was complemented by a strong reluctance to seek medical diagnosis or advice for medical ailments across the board. This was due to what she described as an assumption, especially among older generations, that the "doctor was trying to take your money." Whereas the white parents I interviewed found strength and epistemic authority when they received a medical diagnosis, in Andrea's personal network, the medical profession was seen as parasitic and consequently avoided. This was one of many differences that could be salient to managing food allergies at work and in the home.

In public, she explained, people of color with food allergies did not only have to work against such stereotypes but also had to navigate "how to change cultural norms" around food and eating in social settings when they were already seen as a "newcomer [and] outsider." She could anticipate some of the issues that might arise for Black, Indian, or Jewish families in her southern city, for example. A wheat allergy would affect an Indian family's dietary changes differently than a Jewish family's, in her view. Different workplace or public accommodations might be appropriate for individuals from these backgrounds as well. But requests for legally required accommodations for a condition that was already considered biologically "illogical" by some were more readily interpreted as "rock[ing] the boat" coming from a racialized "outsider."[41] Her work—as a coach, consultant, and then support group leader—thus focused on helping families and individuals navigate their needs for accommodations by presenting their requests in a way that would neither unduly challenge the social norms nor exacerbate suspicions about the aggressiveness of racialized people.

My conversation with Andrea threw into relief how the common preoccupations with hygiene above all else in the food allergy world reflect, in part, a freedom from having to think about race, ethnicity, income, and other forms of oppression (with the notable exception of gender). Promoting a generic vision of pure food requires tabling a serious consideration of the different foods people eat and the different ways one might relate to food. There is also the very real way in which Black people like Andrea and other people of color I interviewed later in my research do not feel comfortable participating in white-majority conversations about how to raise food allergic children and how to maintain a hygienic home. In the absence of participation of people of color, the concerns built into media expressions of the hygienic sublime default to a white, middle-class perspective on how to live and eat well with food allergies. Pure, bland, sweet, starchy foods with no history, bought at a premium price, are often promoted as broadly appealing solutions. Strategies to adapt culturally specific and regional delicacies are only prioritized by a small number of people for whom these are everyday concerns.

Prioritizing white nuclear families as a site of safety and care, with all others viewed as threats, speaks to a history in the United States in which diverse family structures that include extended kin have historically been disciplined through the bureaucratic agency of white-controlled social institutions, including welfare and public housing.[42] It also speaks to a lack of imagination about the extension of kin networks beyond calculable blood ties.[43] Imaginative kin making has been both a necessity and a source of power for Black people in particular in the history of the United States, first as a way to manage the fracturing of families inherent in the chattel slavery system and more recently as a way to deal with the effects of state violence.[44] The family arrangements treated as normative for the hygienic sublime thus reflect and reproduce the gendered roles within the household while simultaneously reproducing an ideology of whiteness at the heart of the normative American family.

PURITY, POLITICS, AND SOCIAL REPRODUCTION

The hygienic sublime fuses necessary requirements for purity and safety with gender-, race-, and class-inflected aspirations of appropriate social relationships. Maintaining a certain degree of purity is a concern for people living with food allergies for good reason: An unexpected encounter with allergens can trigger an allergic reaction, and in some instances, allergic reactions can cause serious bodily harm. Yet an uncritical pursuit of material purity comes with risks. The purifying impulse can easily jump from the materials people use or avoid, or the work these materials do or eschew, to the people themselves. Furthermore, it is a leap to move from observing that a certain kind of purity is needed to keep food allergic people healthy to the current reality as I observed it in my research, where women are almost exclusively the primary caretakers of allergic children, where wealth is a prerequisite for adequately safeguarding the home, and where white nuclear families are portrayed as the ideal support system for managing allergy. Biological needs must be filtered through strong cultural sieves in order to land on this sorting of domestic expectations and responsibilities.

The deployment of technoscience-informed hygienic techniques in the home is particularly salient in current feminist scholarship about the political effects of the idealization of purity of kin and kind. Donna Haraway laid out these concerns over twenty years ago.[45] She critiques the reinscription of eugenic impulses among both scientists and laypeople in maintaining the purity of categories like species and blood relations in 1990s biotechnology. Such moves, she argued, reflect a Western ontological obsession with purifying nature from

culture,[46] a binary that has cascading oppressive effects for those species, landscapes, and individuals deemed to fall closer to nature than
to culture.

Among those who have taken up Haraway's critique of purity politics, Alexis Shotwell's pointed address in *Against Purity* calls out purity as an unjustified simplification of "our ethical and political situation in the world."[47] In contexts as varied as the ways that trans people
interface with the U.S. state, or the idealization of sexually dimorphic
frogs as a sign of healthy waterways, Shotwell diagnoses the North
American fascination with purity of type as oppressive to people, organisms, and landscapes that are not seen as pure enough. Shotwell's
broadly intersectional statement against the Western fascination
with purity usefully connects with Reardon and TallBear's critique of
scientific uses of Native American DNA.[48] Scientists' preoccupation
with the assumed purity of kin and kind makes Native DNA especially
valuable while erasing from view centuries of violence toward, theft
from, and forced resettlement and enslavement of Indigenous people throughout the Americas. While food allergic adults and food allergy parents are not aiming to enforce genetic purity through their
pursuit of the hygienic sublime in their homes, the priority placed on
close blood relations, the semiotic and historical roots of what "clean"
and "pure" look like, and the enticing offers to own consumer goods
in food allergy media all indicate how purity in the home is noninno-
cently embedded in eugenic, classist, and xenophobic histories.

Moreover, following Shotwell's observation that a focus on purity
oversimplifies a broader array of possible ethical and political solutions, focusing on purity in private homes distracts from a number
of broader systemic issues that make the modern food supply risky
for people with food allergies. For example, it distracts from addressing the lack of preventive regulatory enforcement concerning food
safety, especially allergen contamination, provided by U.S. regulatory
agencies. It largely distracts many activists from understanding the
historical and contemporary political interests that have shaped lax
regulatory oversight of food safety and limits the pressure to change
these systems. It occupies attention that could be spent understanding the problems produced by the long and complex multinational

supply chains that deliver food to the tables of U.S. households. In-stead, the hygienic sublime offers a solution to food allergy manage-ment that demands the responsibilization[49] of individuals and nu-clear families to each tackle the problem of impure food on their own. It parasitically relies on normative ideas about gender, race, class, and the ideal family. It posits a politics of white, wealthy heteronormativ-ity as a safe space for allergic bodies.

In food allergy advocacy, this narrowing of vision extends beyond the home into activists' legislative, regulatory, and legal interventions. The next chapter will examine how the reproductive politics in the home and the centering of the family sketched out in these first three chapters shape activist demands and strategies. Familial networks connect patient activists to people in positions of power, funneled through the networks of famously white and wealthy towns and clubs. These mostly white, upper-middle-class, family-mediated networks provide the basis for making claims on the state. In turn, these claims often explicitly invoke family, motherhood, and private care as pil-lars of the solution to food allergy even when it is conceptualized as a public health problem. It is reproductive politics all the way down. As Hi'ilei Julia Kawehipuaakahaopulani Hobart and Tamara Kneese put it, the "neoliberal model of care as one of moralized self-management produces the body as a site in which idealized citizenship coalesces as an unachievable goal that, simultaneously, glosses over the political, economic, and ideological structures that do the work of marginaliza-tion."[50] What happens in the home is ultimately contiguous with what happens in the food allergy advocacy on the public stage. Whether this is good or bad depends on how closely one's family and home ad-heres to the historical ideal of U.S. domestic life.

4

ACTIVIST POLITICS

DISABILITY LAW, LEGISLATIVE ADVOCACY, AND PUBLIC MOTHERHOOD

On November 13, 2013, President Barack Obama signed the School Access to Emergency Epinephrine Act into law. The law encouraged states to enact legislation making epinephrine auto-injectors more readily available in public schools for use on any person on the premises who experiences an allergic reaction. Children were front and center in this moment of political theater. The federal law was, in Obama's statement, "something that will save children's lives."[1] While signing the bill, Obama revealed that his daughter, Malia, had been diagnosed with peanut allergy, suggesting that it would help children and families like his own. While the bill addressed a public health issue, food allergy, that affects people of all ages and in a variety of family situations, the bill targeted children in schools, a longtime site of negotiation and struggle for food allergy parents. Moreover, it invoked children and families as the prime beneficiaries of this change in public policy. It was thus emblematic of the reproductive politics of food allergy advocacy. This chapter will show how these politics show up in many aspects of food allergy advocacy. It will also put this moment in the context of the recent history of food allergy advocacy by parents on behalf of individual children at local schools, as well as in public and in state and national legislative bodies.

The law, while enacted at a federal level, placed the financial responsibility for food allergy management on the shoulders of states and local school districts. States would be responsible for requiring or incentivizing school districts to procure epinephrine auto-injectors; to train teachers, nurses, and staff to use it; and to keep the devices on site at all times. Those states that did not have a "stock epinephrine" law, as these bills were called colloquially, were incentivized to develop them; states that had such laws under consideration were advised to quickly enact them. Food allergy advocates already working locally in each state pushed for passage of these local bills through the network-building activities of national patient advocacy organizations and their pharmaceutical corporation allies. The law motivated states with the carrot of access to federal medical research funds, including the Children's Asthma Treatment Grants Program, as a prize for passing state-level stock epinephrine legislation.[2] Advocates and states rapidly responded to the challenge. The final state to pass a stock epinephrine bill, New Hampshire, approved Senate Bill 25-FM, "Relative to the administration of epinephrine," less than three years later, on April 5, 2016.[3] It was signed into law by Governor Maggie Hassan on May 3, 2016.

This chapter uses this landmark moment of the signing of the School Access to Emergency Epinephrine Act as an entry point into examining the reproductive politics of food allergy legislative advocacy. The politics of food allergy embedded in legislative solutions are influenced by the kinds of heteronormative, whiteness-infused, mother-blaming domestic experiences that make up everyday life for many advocates and food allergy moms. As the last chapter showed, these experiences are shaped in turn by U.S. cultural expectations of the appropriate allocation of caregiving work within society and within the family. What is more, the site of schools is significant: schools are sites of reproductive politics par excellence, primary sites in which children are made into citizens and trained as workers.

The stock epinephrine solution to food allergy safety that advocates pursue through legislation is multiply privatized. This solution relies on market logics to incentivize legal requirements for caretaking in schools; mothers are elevated as the appropriate spokespeople for problems affecting children thanks to their caretaking role in the home; and the solution proposed, stock epinephrine, creates new markets for sales of epinephrine auto-injectors for which municipalities are typically on the hook to pay. The networks assembled during these campaigns are consequential beyond stock epinephrine advocacy as well. As chapter 5 will show, how these networks accomplish their goals may shape the kind of political debates with which advocacy organizations will subsequently engage. When food allergy advocacy strategies are considered alongside disability justice movements, questions arise regarding whether this form of health advocacy has the potential to make truly radical political claims about the place of disabled people in society.

To make this argument, I connect negotiations around disability and care for food allergic children in schools before the stock epinephrine push led to these legislative campaigns. I start by recounting the ways that food allergy parents have used disability legislation at the local school level since the 1990s to seek school accommodations for food allergic children. This part of the story synthesizes many individual accounts to highlight some of the most common strategies, worries, and wins shared with me across dozens of interviews and conversations. Then I narrate key moments from two state-level stock epinephrine campaigns, primarily on the basis of two interviews with key activists. Because these accounts are based on personal recollections, they tell us about these two individuals' versions of the facts as well as the lived experience of conflict and of intentionally gendered self-presentation. Their strategic positioning of the issue extends the reproductive politics of parent negotiations with local schools onto a much larger stage.

In focusing on what happens in families, schools, and legislative bodies, I take a different approach from other analyses of patient activism in STS. Much previous work has focused on understanding how patients and patient organizations interface with scientific experts and communities to shape research on their conditions.[4] However, this chapter focuses instead on how health activists shape the legal and legislative standards that in turn influence everyday life with food allergies. I draw on many primary sources to tell this story, which spans nearly thirty years, leading up to the passage of state stock epinephrine bills in the mid-2010s. These include interviews with parents and advocates, news reports, social media posts, legal advice webinars, and participant observation in food allergy patient- and family-focused conferences. Nonetheless, this chapter remains ethnographic at its core. It takes seriously the recollections of food allergy mothers, my core participants, as reliable and central to the story of food allergy advocacy. Taken together, these varied sources tell a complex story about how disability law, corporate interests, state and local labor politics, parenting norms, and food allergy are negotiated by some of the people most directly affected.

FOOD ALLERGY AND/AS DISABILITY

Before turning to my empirical material, I want to address the relationship between food allergy advocacy and the broader terrain of disability activism. Parents' use of disability law to seek accommodations for food allergic children, which I will discuss at length in the next section, has consistently prompted the following questions from other scholars: Do food allergy advocates and mothers see food allergy as a disability? Is food allergy even a disability? I have received such questions most often from scholars in STS and anthropology whose work does not engage with disability studies.[5] Allison Carey, Pamela Block, and Richard Scotch offer a typology of "organizations led by parents" that can help characterize the relationship between food allergy advocacy and broader disability activism and disability justice movements. Food allergy advocacy most closely fits their frame of "medicalized support of the social model," or "a limited medical model to support what is primarily a social model" of disability. As the authors put it, such movements "are concerned with issues of social participation, opportunities, and rights, but also use the medical system to claim rights and access to funding and services to support participation."[6] In food allergy advocacy, reliance on biomedical tools and preexisting bureaucratic structures for support is further conjoined with gendered norms of care, creating a powerful, yet also highly normative, advocacy tool kit.

During the main period of my research, from 2013 to 2016, the status of food allergy as a disability was contested in the networks where I conducted research. Some people embraced the status of disability for themselves or their children because it was a broad category that encompassed related conditions like asthma, stomach conditions, and the unexpected nature of food allergy symptoms. Others preferred a designation they saw as less stigmatizing, like "condition," "illness," or the simple specificity of "food allergy." In interviews with caretakers of food allergic children, I was sometimes told that I had chosen the wrong word and that it made the participant uncomfortable, so I began to regularly ask participants what term they preferred to use to talk about a food allergy diagnosis. Some participants even changed their minds on terminology within or between conversations with me. One blogger, Maya Trimner, discussed the question head on in a 2013 blog post titled, "Are Adults with Food Allergies or People with Gluten Intolerance Disabled?"[7] Yet no matter where parents fell in terms of their preferred terminology, every parent I spoke to embraced the limited protections of disability law in the specific context of schools.

Even though much of this chapter is about how people with food allergies use disability legislation to seek accommodations, I will not settle the question of whether food allergy is a disability. I leave it instead for food allergic people and advocates to continue to (self-)define as a community and movement. I defer this question in a spirit similar to Laura Mauldin's recognition that few parents of deaf and hard-of-hearing children who use cochlear implants embrace the technology as a comprehensive solution to their child's deafness.[8] Instead, they experience what Mauldin calls ambivalent medicalization, a phenomenon where "individuals are both empowered by and surrendering to the process of medicalization."[9] This medical technology can be both a tool for living how one wants and expects (or for making one's child live how one wants and expects them to live), as well as a constraint on individual bodily agency and a reminder that one's child is not normal. Similarly, I would suggest that at the time of my research, many of my participants related to food allergy as an ambivalent disability. The legal tools of disability and stock epinephrine law, like the biomedical tool of the cochlear implant in Mauldin's research, were used strategically but were often separated from the politics of disabled identity and cross-disability solidarity movements.

Autism self-advocates and feminist disability studies scholars argue that this approach of holding the politics of cross-disability solidarities apart from the pursuit of technical solutions is common in parent-led health advocacy undertaken on behalf of disabled children but is ultimately harmful to disabled adults and disability justice. For example, autism self-advocates and researchers alike have attacked the parent-led organization Autism Speaks as promoting medical "cures" for autism through fearmongering tactics. Calls to cure or prevent autism by parent-led organizations are heard as eliminationist and eugenic by autistic adults, reinforcing the sense of social abandonment.[10] Adam Rosenblatt, drawing from literature about postgenocide reconciliation efforts to refer to the feeling of being ignored and abandoned by the broader society, terms the harm of such efforts ethical loneliness.[11] Therapeutic cures like applied behavior analysis, promoted to parents as necessary for both their children's future and their own social standing, are experienced as abusive, enforcing not only neurotypical behavior but also other forms of normativity, like gender normativity.[12] By contrast, autistic people themselves frequently promote a neurodiversity framework that recognizes and values, but does not pathologize, sensory, cognitive, and bodily differences. Outside of advocacy organizations, mothers themselves often adopt this more inclusive stance when choosing therapies or support for their children.[13] They do not necessarily narrowly adhere to biomedical strategies that aim to "fix" their children instead. Still, public efforts by mothers to center their children, or children like theirs, to drum up sympathy and donations for organizations that self-advocates see as distinctly harmful has done much to shape a broader public discourse around autism that distinctly infantilizes autistic people, further justifying their exclusion from ordinary, public life.[14]

Parent-led advocacy, whether for food allergy or autism, is not an uncomplicated good for disabled people. Nor is it necessarily aligned with the aims of self-advocate-led disability activism and justice. As Carey, Block, and Scotch note, disability justice self-advocacy has often been guided by the motto, "Nothing About Us Without Us," which "demands self-determination [and] which is potentially under-cut by the power of parents to determine disability policy." Their social movement–informed analysis frames this tension as one of "divergent or competing interests."[15] However, some disability self-advocates frame it less as a question of interests and resources, and more as a question of (re)producing other futures: as an issue of "the future that we must guide ourselves toward," or even a question of "dreaming."[16] In contrast to parent-led movements focused on treatment and cure, Leah Lakshmi Piepzna-Samarasinha describes disability justice as an intersectional, queer feminist movement that is wary of the state in-stitutions that parent-led organizations often appeal to: "Our focus is less on civil rights legislation as the only solution to ableism and more on a vision of liberation that understands that the state was built on racist, colonialist ableism and will not save us, because it was created to kill us. A movement where, in the words of Sins Invalid, 'we move together, with no body left behind.'"[17] "This [disability jus-tice] is radical," Piepzna-Samarasinha writes. "It is a radical rewriting of what care means, of what disability means, taking anarchist ideas of mutual aid and crip-femming them out."[18] Disability justice would undercut, overthrow, burn down, and revolutionize state institutions that purport to help disabled people, in contrast to parent-led move-ments that are often satisfied to work within them.

Led by advocates who are separated from, or possibly unaware of, such radical disability justice movements, biomedical and insti-tutional expertise is a more salient feature of food allergy advocacy in my research. Food allergy mother-advocacy more resembles the "expert patient" model of activism pursued by the Treatment Action Group (TAG) offshoot of ACT UP, or the "expert parent" model of vac-cine skeptics, than the more oppositional models of disability or AIDS activism.[19] There were no "sledgehammer-wielding activists" physi-cally dismantling the infrastructures that failed to consider or include people with food allergies, as there were, at least apocryphally, in the Berkeley disability rights scene of the late 1960s.[20] Nor were food al-lergy activists hosting spectacular, intentionally unsettling events like die-ins in health care facilities or legislative buildings, like ACT UP's more radical elements routinely organized into the 1990s. Like antivaccine moms, another contemporary, health-related "mother's movement,"[21] food allergy activists during my period of research were granted entrance to elite circles as a reward for decorous behavior and cooperation with elite political and biomedical experts. There, like vaccine-refusing mothers, they "construct[ed] themselves as experts on their own children" and were allowed to speak on behalf of all children and families, even though they were predominantly white and middle or upper middle class.[22]

Food allergy mothers thus brought their expertise as mothers, a form of gendered and often classed embodied experience, onto the floors of state legislatures and made claims on the state as mothers of food allergic children. As mothers—perhaps, to play on Epstein's coinage, as expert mothers—their authority went uncontested. However, outside of this narrow lane, they largely deferred to medical, political, and corporate experts to make claims about why new measures were medically necessary and how they could be made politically palatable.

In the absence of radical disability politics and cross-community solidarity, food allergy mother activists work with available resources. This often means relying on class privilege and gender roles in their appeals, even though this reproduces the very relations that make food allergy management difficult for so many. For example, situating the family as the site of care and mothers as selfless caretakers reinforces the status of a food allergy diagnosis as a private problem best managed within families in which caretaking labor is divided along the lines of gender. Obama administration–era approaches to health care did little to challenge these dynamics. Instead, they incentivized participation in competitive markets over direct funding for public health measures—not only in the landmark Affordable Care Act but also in legislation like the School Access to Emergency Epinephrine Act.[23] That is to say, they reinforced the act of mothering disabled children and mother-led activism as "a troubling form of contradictory neoliberal feminine subjectivity."[24] Consequently, access to the public health benefits established by this law required unpaid labor by activists and reliance on the deep pockets and extensive networks of pharmaceutical companies and lobbyists. Gendered relations of care—specifically the figure of the mother as a fierce protector of children who presses her case, ideally politely and quietly—typecast women and mothers into specific roles in stock epinephrine campaigns as they pursued the shaky protections offered by the neoliberal U.S. state. Rather than challenge their roles, those whom I spoke with generally inhabited them, often uneasily, in the service of the greater good.

In many ways, working within the existing channels and with a narrow focus on food allergy reproduces the classed, raced, and gendered organization of access to appropriate health care and disability accommodations. By working within the halls of power, activists assume a position where they are often limited to using heteronormativity and the nuclear family as rhetorical resources. In the end, accepting the role of expert mother (which has, to be sure, granted food allergy activists short-term gains) reinforces the expectation that the nuclear family is the appropriate site for ensuring safety and care for food allergic children. It helps to reproduce the gendered arrangements through which care is organized in the United States. This chapter and chapter 5 show how mother-advocates' engagements with policy makers, pharmaceutical companies, school districts, and food allergy organizations do a kind of reproductive politics that privileges biomedicine as a path to normalcy and entrenches gender and the white, heteronormative family as optimal adjuvants to care.

FOOD ALLERGY IN SCHOOLS

Stock epinephrine bills are a tool in the legal and legislative maneuvers that parents have used to ensure the safety of children with food allergies in schools. To understand why they were an obvious point of intervention for advocates, this section summarizes the loosely coordinated care work taken on mainly by mothers since the 1990s to gain recognition for food allergies as a health condition worthy of disability accommodation in U.S. schools. Well before President Obama signed the School Access to Emergency Epinephrine Act in 2013, parents relied on disability legislation to seek safeguards for food allergic children in public schools. Beginning in the mid-1990s, the pioneering mothers who connected with one another through local food allergy support groups and electronically networked, cross-country food allergy advocacy groups began learning and teaching each other how to use existing disability legislation to seek accommodations for their children. Without any clear state or federal guidance, requesting and winning accommodations proceeded family by family and school by school. These women became expert mothers. Their expertise was shaped through the experience of raising food allergic children, through teaching themselves the relevant aspects of biomedical research, and through familiarizing themselves with the legislation, state and district policies, and procedures relevant to keeping their own children safe at school. In the process, the role of women as mothers, caretakers, and protectors of children remained a necessary complement to the technical specifications of the legal regime of disability.

There are three laws that provide the legal basis for seeking disability accommodations in public schools in the United States: Section 504 of the Rehabilitation Act of 1973, the Americans with Disabilities Act (ADA) of 1990, and the 1975 Individuals with Disability Education Act.[25] The first two pieces of legislation figured most prominently in interviews with and trainings by food allergy mothers and activists that I participated in during my ethnographic research, so they will be the focus of this section. The ADA sets the legal standard for providing disability accommodations in public and nonreligious private schools. While public schools must do everything necessary to provide accommodations, private schools do not have to take on an "undue burden" to provide accommodations. Additionally, the ADA only provides grounds for legal action against most entities (educational and otherwise) when appropriate measures are not taken. That is, it provides grounds for redress after a violation of access expectation occurs, but it does not prevent such violations from occurring. Those affected by inaccessible schools can only threaten future punishment of the school by taking them to court on the basis of the ADA, and winning. Section 504 is more practically useful than the ADA, but it only covers public schools and private schools that receive federal funding. Section 504 requires schools to do more to identify, appropriately place, and accommodate students with disabilities. Further, it outlines the procedures for designing and enforcing a 504 plan, which is a legally binding document that lays out the accommodations to be provided to a child with disabilities. This document is drawn up on the basis of medical records and school assessments, with the close involvement of parents who must take time off work to take their children to doctors and develop, provide, negotiate, and verify the relevant documentation. A second kind of document, an individualized health care plan, can also be used to describe a child's desired accommodations, but it is not legally binding.[26]

Figuring out how disability law applies to a particular child can be, and has historically been, difficult for both parents and schools to navigate and enforce. In all cases, the burden falls on parents to demonstrate that their food allergic child meets the federal definition of a person with a disability. As defined by the Americans with Disabilities Act of 1990, an individual with a disability is someone who has "a physical or mental impairment that substantially limits one or more major life activities of such individual."[27] Whether food allergy meets this threshold can depend greatly on context. If children only become ill when they come into contact with a specific food that is allergenic for them, are they always experiencing a "physical . . . impairment that substantially limits one or more life activities"? If a typical day in the classroom is not officially expected to involve food and eating, but another parent sends in cupcakes or candy for a birthday and food allergic children cannot participate in that part of the school day, are their life activities "substantially limit[ed]"?

While these questions are now generally decided in the affirmative in the case of food allergy, it took years of advocacy by parents of allergic children for schools to become accustomed to recognizing these highly contextual scenarios as meeting the legal threshold of disability. In addition, the type of school—public or private, and if private, religious or nonreligious—matters for determining what documentation needs to be provided or will be produced, as well as what procedural and judicial recourse parents would have, should accommodations prove unsatisfactory or fail to be followed. Even then, laws aren't necessarily the whole story. While private schools do not need to follow Section 504, for instance, some mothers told me that they can still be a good option for food allergic children because private schools may also have more staff per student and may empha-size a more personal touch for each child's education.

The solutions commonly offered by school districts to satisfy legal requirements are not always seen as optimal compromises of safety and social inclusion by parents. Peanut-free tables in lunchrooms are one common strategy that schools use to accommodate children with peanut allergies, the most common type of food allergy. The peanut-free table has reached an almost iconic status as a marker of the sudden rise in food allergies and its emergence as a public prob-lem.[28] Peanut-free tables are designated areas in school lunchrooms where children are not allowed to sit if they have lunch items contain-ing peanuts. They are typically guarded against contamination by the surveillance of lunchroom attendants and specially cleaned between mealtimes or days of the week. Yet this solution often draws ire from parents. Sitting at these tables keeps children safely away from pea-nuts and allows them to attend school, but it can also prevent them from sitting with their friends. The price of physical safety is a new form of social exclusion that, in the eyes of many parents, is more ob-vious to peers than the condition of peanut allergy itself.

In recent years, food allergy researchers and organizations have stepped in to provide standardized guidance to parents and school officials regarding the implementation of disability law for food al-lergic children. The two largest food allergy advocacy organizations, FARE and Kids with Food Allergies (KFA, which at the time of writing was a division of the Asthma and Allergy Foundation of America, or AAFA), now provide guides on their websites, archived recordings of webinars, and in-person conference sessions on this issue. These doc-uments have been produced through decades of collected community knowledge circulated informally via support groups, social media, and online forums, including online support forums hosted by KFA. These two organizations—as well as other, smaller ones like the Asthma and Allergy Network (AAN) and Food Allergy and Anaphylaxis Connection Team—emerged as grassroots, parent-led organizations in the late 1990s and 2000s. In the early 2010s, when they codified lived expe-rience and person-to-person advice into physician-reviewed docu-mentation, many mothers and other family members of people with food allergies were still on their staff. KFA and FARE documentation can thus be thought of as an artifact that reflects the views of expert mothers themselves.

In 2013, the U.S. Centers for Disease Control and Prevention picked up on this momentum and published a nonbinding set of guidelines outlining the best practices for U.S. schools to follow to manage and accommodate food allergies among children.[29] Several key pioneers from the food allergy community—including physicians, advocacy organization staff, and expert mothers—were named to the panel and coauthored the final document. It made a strong statement that regulatory and scientific experts recognized these specific mother-advocates as capable of participating in the formation of official knowledge concerning food allergies. Significantly, all of the mother-advocates acknowledged in the report were white, and their names were all accompanied by current or prior affiliation with legally recognized food allergy advocacy nonprofit organizations. Gendered caretaking expertise once again became part of the official scientific and regulatory knowledge about food allergies through inclusion in the formal guidelines writing process. However, it wasn't just any mother's expertise that was admitted, only that of white mothers with official institutional recognition.

In addition to navigating complex and inconsistent disability protections, food allergy parents frequently confront outrage from other parents who bristle at being asked to help protect food allergic children. Parents of nonallergic children often complain when they are told they cannot send their children to school with a peanut butter sandwich or can only send in wheat-free cupcakes for a classroom party. Other parents and visitors to the school often forget to comply with such rules, don't know how to do so, or, rarely, intentionally undermine them by sending or bringing forbidden foods into schools and classrooms. Internet comments on a regular Huffington Post parenting series about food allergies exemplify the resistance to food allergy accommodations in schools from other parents. For example, one 2015 article, "No Sandwich Is More Important than a Child's Life" by Heather Spohr, received over 2,700 comments in under four months. Many of the comments used sarcasm and ad hominem attacks to accuse parents of food allergic kids of being overprotective and finicky. One commenter's remarks in particular bristled at the idea that some parents could "dictate" the choices of others:

> You could have chosen to home schoool your daughter or done a million other things but you choose to go to a school that did not have a strict policy forbidding peanut butter . . . that was your choice. Now you are affecting everyone elses choice and belive the life of your daughter is more important than their choices. . . . Your "holier than thou" mantality as just as wrong as "I can do what I want" mentality. There is a middle ground but instead of find that middle ground you want to dictate to others what is right and wrong.[30]

Such commentary, online and off, makes food allergy parents nervous that other parents will disregard accommodations that involve restrictions on foods in schools and classrooms. Protections nominally ensured by disability legislation remain both difficult to secure and too easy to undermine.

Stock epinephrine auto-injectors held in classrooms and school offices would seem to offer an alternative to accommodations that rely on other parents to take care with the food they send to their children's schools. In theory, stock epinephrine would reduce the responsibility of other parents for food allergic children. Instead of relying on food allergic parents' advocacy and community efforts to prevent the exposure of food allergic children to their allergens, stock epinephrine policies enlist teachers, coaches, school nurses, and other school staff to deal with the potentially serious consequences of exposure and allergic reactions when they occur. In this way, stock epinephrine schemes are indicative of a biomedical approach that treats individual bodies in a reactive fashion when they become ill rather than remaking social and physical environments to provide proactive safety for all, as disability justice activists might call for. The individual child is centered as the point of intervention and the object of protection. This would seem to maintain the child's problems as a private matter and reflect a distinctly neoliberal approach to ensuring health.

Ironically, the efficacy of stock epinephrine plans still depends on the reconfiguration of the social environment. Rather than enlisting the entire community of parents at a school as responsible for the well-being of food allergic children, stock epinephrine intensifies the responsibility of feminized educators and care workers in schools. Epinephrine auto-injectors require adults in schools to be trained in how to use them appropriately. Because they require more training and new responsibilities for many workers, their rollout became a new front line in labor struggles between teachers unions and state governments in states like California. Stock epinephrine creates new legal liabilities for feminized workers like teachers and school nurses as well, while interpellating their presumed interest in children's well-being as a reason why they should comply without complaint. While adults and children in the community are, in theory, off the hook, school staff become enfolded into the community of responsible actors along with food allergy parents.

In practice, the obligation to care is redistributed beyond the individual whose health is at stake with the introduction of stock epinephrine in schools. Within schools, the burden falls on workers who are already under siege by budget austerity measures, rhetorical attacks on their expertise and labor rights by state and federal politicians, and ever-expanding job responsibilities. Accommodations limiting the introduction of allergenic foods are combined with stock epinephrine devices and plans. School nurses and teachers are thus not only responsible for learning how to use these devices but are also still called on to do the bureaucratic labor of managing and communicating requests that community parents do not send in allergenic foods. They must also continue to do the emotional labor of educating frustrated parents of nonallergic children about the steps they must take to help safeguard the health of allergic children.[31] Nonetheless, as I will discuss below, mothers sometimes view educators and other school workers as adversaries when they ask for support for this added labor. This has been especially acute when education staff unions demand funding for training and increased staffing. The experience of mothers who do care work without compensation—or who even give up wages to do it—seems to inform expectations for doing similar work in schools, even though school-based care workers are typically under contract to receive pay for this labor.

Schools have thus emerged as a primary target of stock epinephrine laws for a number of reasons. For one, mother-advocates were already working with schools and learning what existing disability legislation could and could not provide through hands-on engagement. Advocacy organizations fostered the organized collection, sharing, and communication of this knowledge. By the late 2000s, many mothers knew what couldn't be achieved in schools under existing legal frameworks and were interested in designing legislation that could do more and be legally enforceable. Beyond what they learned through collective experience navigating disability laws in schools, savvy parents recognized that framing stock epinephrine bills as a way to protect children would be a politically expedient way to achieve legislative success. Many reasoned that politicians could hardly refuse to support a bill that potentially saves children from death. Starting with school epinephrine bills was politically strategic and was built on existing relationships and expertise.

Most advocates and activists during the period of my research anticipated that school epinephrine laws would be the first in a planned progression of campaigns. They would begin with those interventions they thought to be on the most indisputable moral footing; stock epinephrine in schools to protect children was one such intervention. They expected to then turn to settings subject to more complicated moral and political forces, like stock epinephrine in lightly regulated industries, like summer camps, churches, and in industries with politically and economically powerful representation, like restaurants and the hospitality industry. As of the time of this writing in 2020, however, schools have remained the most successful site for pressing programs that protect the health of food allergic individuals in the United States. The success in schools, and the slow progress in other domains, perhaps reflects not only the power but also the limits of reproductive politics. In a context where children's well-being offers moral and rhetorical justification for a wide variety of political interventions, it is relatively easy to motivate others to act on their behalf. However, in institutions serving a wider array of stakeholders or customers, perhaps such appeals carry less weight.

NEGOTIATING LIABILITY AND CARE

Family, children, and the mother–child bond were front and center in arguments about why state-level stock epinephrine legislation was necessary to protect people with food allergy from 2013 to 2016. These campaigns, as they were narrated to me by food allergy advocates, were led by food allergy advocacy organizations like FARE, individual mother-advocates, and pharmaceutical company lobbyists from companies like Mylan that make epinephrine auto-injectors. Mothers were positioned as key witnesses to the dangers of food allergies, and their politely delivered testimonies with and on behalf of their children were a key tool for advocacy campaigns in statehouses across the country. While children's lives as lived among nuclear families provided the ostensible motivation for these bills, the bills were notable for how they reconfigured expectations of responsibility. By enlisting nurses and teachers as potential frontline protectors of children, they had the potential to expand responsibility beyond mothers and nuclear families. Yet in the process of making their case, mothers were positioned again and again as the best caretakers for food allergic children. Confrontations between mothers, pharmaceutical company lobbyists, and feminized workers did not ultimately prevent the bills from being passed, but they revealed fractures among different actors with an interest in taking care of allergic children.

As the vanguard of food allergy activism in schools shifted from navigating disability law to advocating for stock epinephrine bills at the state and federal levels in the early 2010s, the focus of food allergy advocacy shifted from inclusion and normalization of food allergic children through disability provisions to the creation of spaces of legal exception for the management of acute health crises. Some stock epinephrine bills were written to create exceptions in prescribing rules that allow epinephrine auto-injectors to be prescribed to an organization or a place of business rather than to an individual. Some relaxed legal liability for the person or people who might use an epinephrine auto-injector on an individual to whom it is not prescribed. This was sometimes done by adding specificity to existing Good Samaritan laws. Some stock epinephrine bills did both at the same time, depending on state law, case law, and regulations. In some states, these laws require epinephrine auto-injectors to be "stocked," or prescribed, to entities like public schools. They also typically make it permissible for stock auto-injectors to be used by a wider variety of adults—including teachers, coaches, or even bystanders—to treat someone having an allergic reaction on the premises. Relaxing liability was explained to me in interviews with mother-advocates as a way to incentivize organizations to stock and prepare staff to use epinephrine auto-injectors on their premises by removing fear of lawsuits in the event that something goes wrong.

The creation of such exceptions responds to two structural pressures that deeply shape the U.S. health care system today: tort law and the financial windfalls of disaster.[32] Providing exceptions to liability is a logical response within the U.S. context, where tort law has been extensively used in cases of medical malpractice and to pursue compensation for suspected vaccine-derived injury by autism mother-advocates.[33] It works as a way to pin blame on someone when something goes wrong within the country's medical system; conversely, removing the threat of fines or other sanctions could, in theory, make taking risks in hopes of helping someone more palatable. The use of tort law in U.S. health care has become a significant problem in certain medical specialties. For example, the field of obstetrics and gynecology faces a shortage of practitioners in part because of the high fees for financial insurance against damages.[34] In stock epinephrine negotiations, nurses and educators in some states clamored early on for release from liability, often via union-organized statements and lobbying. Thus, the combination of this national context and pressure from educators and school nurses meant that stock epinephrine bills displaced and reduced liability for prescribers and certain users. Removing the fear of tort action and liability would presumably allow rational actors in the health care system to choose to prescribe and use these devices as needed.

Along with the issue of tort law in U.S. health care, a disaster orientation is used to enlist public attention and legislative support for stock epinephrine campaigns.[35] It is the specter of personal disaster, and the claim that any of the approximately fifteen million people with food allergies in the United States could have a serious allergic reaction at any time, that makes stock epinephrine seem like a measure that works in the public interest. These appeals are reminiscent of autism mother-advocates who claim that they are working to prevent the disaster of "losing" more children to the condition and to "recover" those who have already been lost. These discourses are seen as damaging and violent by people with autism because they center the fear that neurotypical and able-bodied people harbor about neurodivergent and disabled people, rather than working toward remaking society to be inclusive of everyone.[36]

Yet despite the potential harm for disabled people and disability justice efforts, the disaster orientation is potentially quite profitable for those in power. The massive potential scale of the need for stock epinephrine devices promises significant profits from increased sales and improved corporate image for pharmaceutical companies who support stock epinephrine campaigns. In some cases, EpiPen maker Mylan even donated epinephrine auto-injectors to schools after bills were passed to ease the transition to stocking epinephrine—which could make it harder for schools to stop stocking epinephrine in the future, when they have to pay for the devices themselves, without losing face with their communities. The creation of exceptions thus created a new market for this important "drug for life,"[37] enlisting pharmaceutical companies as allies to activists and sponsoring lawmakers. Epinephrine is, paradoxically, "for life" both in Dumit's sense of being a lifelong companion to individuals with food allergies that must be repurchased on a predictable schedule, and in the sense that the drug is only used in emergency circumstances where a person's life is potentially in the balance. Successful use of the disaster orientation in food allergy advocacy would seem to provide strong incentives for pharmaceutical companies that make the devices to align with stock epinephrine campaigns.

Activists and advocacy organizations often use a disaster orientation that focuses on the desire of mothers to protect children. This is exemplified by what one of my participants called death talk, which I discussed in chapter 1. Mothers are often positioned as ultimately responsible for ensuring that food allergic children do not become victims of disaster—an expectation reinforced through media, science, and the food allergy community itself. In this frame, as in other disaster discourses of late capitalism,[38] incipient catastrophe lurks ubiquitously, to be controlled through planning and preparedness at both institutional and individual levels. This contrasts with the social model of disability that has been part of managing food allergies for schoolchildren under disability law. In the social model, the mechanisms of social inclusion and exclusion, such as the peanut-free lunch table, are significant concerns; they are seen as remediable through a shift in cultural attitudes toward difference.[39] The disaster orientation offers a more urgent appeal yet might ultimately undermine inclusion and justice by emphasizing vulnerability and incapacity instead of capability and kinship. However, standing between children and disaster at many crucial points are careful mothers and caretakers in femininized workplace roles, like teachers and school nurses, who are most often the people elevating concerns about food allergy in the public sphere.

Advocacy organizations pushing the cause of stock epinephrine in schools primarily relied on a combination of fear and entreaties to protect vulnerable children to get their message across. Through its Kids with Food Allergies (KFA) division, the Asthma and Allergy Foundation of America (AAFA) was one of the leading food allergy organizations that supported these campaigns. (They also supported other measures designed to improve the health of people with allergies and asthma, including tightening air quality standards, improving asthma health outcomes, and improving food safety standards for people with food allergies.) In 2013, AAFA released a statement regarding stock epinephrine bills that featured strong language about the lifesaving potential of epinephrine: "Anaphylaxis is a serious medical condition, which can be life-threatening if rapidly developing symptoms are not treated promptly. . . . With prompt injection, epinephrine is nearly always effective in the treatment of anaphylaxis. Delay increases the risk of poor outcomes and even fatalities. . . . The facts are simple: when available, epinephrine autoinjectors save lives." The press release continued, emphasizing the necessity for schools to protect the children in their care: "Children spend a sizeable amount of their time in school, whether for daily instruction or recreational activities. Therefore, schools must be prepared to address the safety of their students."

The document then appeals to fear by recounting a story about a Virginia first-grader who died from anaphylaxis during school recess in 2012. Within the food allergy community, this case was seen as a watershed moment for stock epinephrine legislation. It triggered a parent-led movement to pass school stock epinephrine legislation in Virginia. This led to success in the state, and it also created a playbook and a pool of parent experts for groups in other states to draw on when trying to pass their own bills. In the KFA press release, this incident was used to underscore the necessity of stock epinephrine legislation to protect children: "[The first grader] was rushed to the school nurse and 911 was called. By the time the ambulance arrived, she had gone into cardiac arrest. She died a short time later at a nearby hospital. Her tragic passing instilled a sense of urgency in Virginia to protect school children and Virginia passed a law requiring schools to maintain a supply of epinephrine auto-injectors."[40] This sort of death talk was meant to demonstrate the importance of epinephrine's lifesaving properties. In these documents and stories, stocking epinephrine in schools offers a new kind of hope for people with food allergies—a hope closely shadowed by illness and death. The specific focus on children is sensible; because the legislation focuses on spaces where children spend their days, these stories highlight children. Yet at the same time, the focus on children in schools is also a focus on reproductive politics.

FARE's messaging took a less personal and more population-focused approach to portraying stock epinephrine as a crucial public health measure. While they asserted that food allergic children would remain in danger as long as stock epinephrine bills were not passed, they also emphasized that such measures could benefit those who might not yet know they have a food allergy.[41] However, the primary impetus for adopting stock epinephrine remained the threat of death, which was in this case depersonalized and treated as a matter of statistics. In 2015, FARE's web page about epinephrine in schools explained that stocking "undesignated," or stock, epinephrine auto-injectors is a way to "help save the lives of those who experience an anaphylactic reaction and don't have a prescribed epinephrine auto-injector." The page also cites the statistic that "approximately 20–25 percent of epinephrine administrations in the school setting involv[e] students or staffers whose allergy was unknown at the time of the event."[42] The reader is meant to understand that stock epinephrine is potentially a significant public health intervention, especially considering that most children in the United States attend public school for half of more of their waking hours.

Individuals from patient advocacy groups aligned with major nonprofits also spoke out in favor of stock epinephrine bills on online platforms, including blogs and personal Twitter feeds. Leading up to a legislative vote for stock epinephrine bill SB 1299 in California in May 2014, for example, food allergy advocates from around the country posted a steady stream of messages on Twitter urging followers to vote in favor of the bill. User @CaAdvocatesFA was especially prolific in the days leading up to the vote. The user publicly directed messages at politicians and regional news outlets, and posted both original appeals to action and retweets of other users' messages. On May 20, @CaAdvocatesFA posted a series of messages about the importance of stock epinephrine, one of which included the entreaty, "A child's life is worth the cost of stock epi."[43] Another original message stated, "We can either save the next child with stock epi or wish we had."[44] Accompanying this message was an image that was subsequently widely shared. The image was bounded by a simple black rectangle, and the words were written in a sans serif font, imitating the style of recent internet memes. In the bottom right corner of the image is a cartoonish line drawing of a person standing with an open mouth and a red heart set against the light blue of its shirt. The message from this user (and many others) was clear: Requiring epinephrine in schools is a lifesaving move. To think otherwise is to condemn innocent children to death.

These sorts of press releases and texts from allergy advocacy organizations and individual activists position stock epinephrine availability as necessary to save the lives of children. Within the food allergy community, such messages are forwarded from parent-led support group e-mail mailing lists, debated in food allergy discussion groups on Facebook, and circulated between official nonprofits and their followers on social media platforms like Twitter and Pinterest. As messages are amplified through these channels, writers, creators, and organizations enlist allies and set the stage for legislative action at the state and federal levels. Perhaps most importantly, because of the reach and community credibility of some of the organizations, these messages play a role in standardizing the messaging and language that are ultimately used in direct, state-level legislative advocacy for stock epinephrine bills. The specter of the disaster of child death haunts their messaging, tapping into U.S. cultural anxieties about the fragility of providing appropriate care to children when they leave the safe space of the home and the nuclear family. In seeking to expand responsibility through legislation, the nuclear family home remains the default site of safety and care in the midst of rampant inattention to safety that can only be tamed through the law.

Advocacy organizations' and public campaigners' emphasis on children as the primary beneficiaries of stock epinephrine programs asserts reproduction as a key justification for food allergy awareness and activism. Focusing on children centers the hopes and fears that parents, communities, and society at large place in nurturing the next generation. It also implicitly focuses attention on caretakers. The stories discussed above portray schools and childcare workers as neglectful—in contrast, one is left to assume, to the responsible parents who willingly send children to communal care and learning settings each day. Legislating stock epinephrine is positioned as a kind of stopgap remedy for the oversights of nonkin caretakers.

Yet at the same time there is radical potential in this proposal. Easy access to epinephrine, coupled with general awareness campaigns about the dangers of food allergy, could very well help distribute the responsibility of caring for food allergic children, as well as food allergic adults. Indeed, the hope of many food allergy advocates pushing for stock epinephrine legislation was simply to be able to have more trust that teachers, school nurses, coaches, and others could appropriately care for food allergic children and respond to emergencies. However, as the next two stories about state-level stock epinephrine campaigns will show, both narrated to me by mother-advocates, this goal of expanding responsibility is at odds with rhetoric and strategies that center mothers as naturally the best caretakers of allergic children, with others—even feminized care workers like school nurses—perceived as potential adversaries.

Industry Alliances

Norms of femininity infused the advocacy strategy narrated to me by one mother-advocate, whom I call Denise, who worked to pass a stock epinephrine bill in a small state in 2012. Both gendered norms of comportment and claims to authority that were based on being a mother were instrumental to this advocate's work that supported passage of the bill in key ways. In addition, access to networks of political and economic elites via family and community networks offered important entry points to the halls of power. Here I tell this advocate's story to understand the intertwined role that family and gender played in one successful state campaign. I contextualize these dynamics in a brief consideration of past feminist health movements to take a critical view of the central role played by normative white femininity in supposedly postfeminist or postracist contexts. This episode in food allergy legislative advocacy underscores how mother-advocates perform the role of feminine, morally upright guardians of the next generation who appropriately occupy their time fighting for the good of their children.

Food allergy advocacy is far from the first instance in which women have been instrumental in raising awareness about access to medical care. The history of women's health in the twentieth century is filled with instances where women have pressed medical professionals and policy makers to acknowledge the expertise of women themselves in tackling problems of public and individual health. As a result, women's embodied experiences, especially the experiences of white, middle-class women, have often become a primary platform for their scientific and political activism.[45] Alongside such movement, in feminist theory, experience has also been theorized as a kind of evidence that stands apart from, but can be put into conversation with, the evidence of other knowledge-making systems, like biomedical science.[46] However, experience as the evidential basis for activism presents a conundrum for movements that attempt to represent a wide swath of society. Whose experience of a gendered body or of a particular condition counts as authoritative in this situation?

One helpful precursor to consider is the rise of radical feminist health activism in the United States in the 1960s and 1970s. Michelle

Murphy's work in particular highlights how the intersections of gender with race and class shaped whose voices counted as authoritative and universal in these movements.[47] Sharing experiences in the context of consciousness-raising groups at this time offered a way to connect as women as well as sufferers of gendered bodily ills. By raising consciousness in multiple, loosely connected groups over time, these groups laid claim to a supposedly objective understanding of women's health. Although it was not scientific in an institutional sense, Murphy argues that the knowledge women created was objective because it was grounded in the embodied experience of illness and society and was discussed and recorded systematically.

However, knowledge production in this movement was not immune to fractures along the lines of race and class within women's movements and organizations. Women who were white and middle to upper middle class were most often the ones with the time and financial resources to build durable platforms and widely distribute materials about their findings and politics—by, for example, creating protocol-driven practices tied to specific, often proprietary devices.[48] The concerns of white women with ample resources and wide-reaching platforms, such as the positioning of abortion care as the end-all, be-all of reproductive rights and justice, have often been treated as the concerns of women of all classes and races.[49] Such patterns of access to resources and political recognition persist in activist movements led by women today, including in food allergy activism.

The story of Denise's legislative advocacy work illustrates how a combination of gender and class positioning is enacted in practice and how it can shape the course of a patient advocacy campaign. Denise is widely credited as a national leader in the push for stock epinephrine legislation. In her sparsely populated state, a stock epinephrine bill was introduced and passed in just a year and a half—a remarkable feat given that the state's legislators only convene in session every other year. Denise had been active in the food allergy community since her teenage son was about two years old. He and Denise's younger daughter both developed allergies in infancy, including nut, flaxseed, and sesame allergies. She became a recognized voice in the food allergy community in part thanks to her blog, which she started in 2011. Through this platform, she offered advice to other parents of food allergic kids, ranging from tips on dealing with school policies to recipes for how to bake delicious, nut-free desserts. By the time stock epinephrine legislation became a cause célèbre in the food allergy community, she had been negotiating with her school district concerning their food policies for over a decade. She got involved directly in stock epinephrine advocacy after the Virginia bill was under way and used some of the tactics that others had used before. More than anyone, she became an important hub for knowledge and connections related to food allergy legislative advocacy.

Denise got involved in stock epinephrine legislation in April 2012 via her then-preteen son's interest in the issue. He attended a national organization's Kid's Congress advocacy day in Washington, D.C., where he and Denise met a prominent U.S. senator. When Denise asked the senator how she could help advocate for school stock epinephrine legislation, he recommended that she look into advocating for state-level bills. After the trip, she did some research on state legislators in her home state who might be interested in sponsoring such a bill. To pitch the idea, she got in touch with a legislator who was known for his work promoting education policy and who sat on a number of committees relevant to such a bill (including judiciary, education, and health and human services committees). The senator was supportive, but there was still plenty of work for Denise to do to support the effort—much more than she originally anticipated. She quickly set about enlisting allies, including fellow parents and a lobbyist friend in her state who donated his time to advise Denise, and reviewing early drafts of the bill.

The supportive and enthusiastic tone changed that summer when an unexpected player entered the scene: Mylan, the maker of the EpiPen brand of epinephrine auto-injector. In Denise's recounting, Mylan seemed surprised to find that mothers and legislators in her state were already working on stock epinephrine legislation. Mylan entered the state with plans to put forth a preformulated bill that did not take into account the specifics of existing state law and politics.[50] Without changes, it likely would have been doomed to failure. Initially, they viewed parent advocates, according to Denise, as "bonbon-eating moms. . . . . They literally wouldn't look me in the eye. They were pissed! They had a bill, and we were messing it up." In Denise's view, "they were not kind . . . they were pretty hostile," despite their being welcomed as a powerful ally in the process by the parents and grass-roots activists already on the ground.

Mylan had much to gain from joining the stock epinephrine scrum—not only the possibility of thousands or millions of EpiPens sold to schools and other entities, but also a boost to its image as a company with a sense of social responsibility toward its EpiPen customers. By 2012, however, some in the food allergy community were already beginning to view Mylan ambivalently thanks to its aggressive pricing strategy for the EpiPen—a growing suspicion that turned out to be warranted. Mylan's preformulated bill, which they initially tried to advocate for without making adjustments for local conditions, caused problems until the company's representatives began to cooperate with state-level actors. Crafting a state-level bill required a careful understanding of sometimes idiosyncratic state policies and legislative vocabulary. This was expertise that Mylan's people initially lacked, but that advocates in each state could access through their local and familial connections.

This was one point where Denise's knowledge of the local situation—beyond her personal experience as a mother of an allergic child—became invaluable to the process. On the basis of her research of existing state regulations, Denise had narrowed the advocacy strategy in the state to require stock epinephrine in K–12 schools. The Mylan bill initially specified that "any campus" would have to carry stock epinephrine, but in this state, school buses were considered part of the campus. Denise and other grassroots advocates anticipated that requiring stock epinephrine on buses would prevent the bill from passing, thanks to the additional supplies and training it would require. Mylan's bill would have additionally required a wider variety of educational institutions—including preschools and universities—to carry stock epinephrine. However, state-based advocates determined that including those entities would open the bill up to being killed in committee, before it could come to open debate on the floor of the state legislature. Finally, state nursing statutes also shaped how certain provisions could be worded, which the outside bill did not originally take into account. Throughout the process of negotiating these points, Denise's contributions to identifying key groups of stakeholders and reaching out to include them in the writing process helped build consensus and collective understanding of the proposed legislation. Consensus turned out to be crucial when the bill was completely rewritten the Sunday before its committee hearing. Because agreements had already been reached concerning the bill's scope, the task was now doable, if demanding.

After the bill was rewritten, it landed in committee in February 2013, where mother-advocates and reproductive politics took center stage. Although they had already done a great deal of research, negotiation, writing, and editing behind the scenes, rubbing shoulders with professional lobbyists, it would be their public performances as responsible, selfless mothers that stuck in the collective imagination. To win over legislators, the coalition combined testimonials from parents that stressed feminine charm and effusive expressions of parental concern with testimony from food allergic children. All of the parents had been coached ahead of time to stay within time limits, to address lawmakers in the audience using appropriate honorifics, and above all to be both "professional" and "sweet" at all times.[51] Denise explained that in order to counter resistance from the teacher's union to using epinephrine auto-injectors on the grounds that they were difficult to use, she had her own nine-year-old daughter demonstrate the device. While a physician testified on the medical dimensions of epinephrine auto-injectors, a nurse spoke about her experience with parenting a food allergic child. Other parents from the major city in the state spoke about their emotional reactions to reports of children dying from allergic reactions, bringing death talk onto the floor of the legislature as a political tool. At this moment, reproductive politics came to the fore with the prominence of children as the chief beneficiaries of the legislation, and mothers and women professionals assuming responsibility for speaking on behalf of the next generation.

The priority placed on "professional" and "sweet" comportment for mother-advocates suggests racial as well as gender politics at play in the debate of the bill on the floor of the state legislature. Niceness and whiteness are linked in the Western—and especially U.S.—political and cultural imaginary. As anthropologist Setha Low argues, invoking niceness is a way to police who is allowed to occupy a space.[52] For example, in her work on suburban communities, niceness is invoked when homeowners and real estate agents do not want to specifically mention race, for fear of legal or social sanctions, but want to keep Black and other people of color out. Cheryl Mattingly offers a glimpse into what this means in the context of Black mothers advocating for health care for their children.[53] When a mother does not appropriately perform whiteness and niceness when seeking medical care, requests for aid for their children can be dismissed out of hand, potentially deepening racial disparities in health care. Niceness evokes associations in the U.S. cultural imaginary with whiteness and femininity. When those norms are not upheld, resources including real estate and health care can be withheld. In food allergy advocacy work, this lesson seems to resonate, whether or not it was consciously intended. It suggests that in this context, full consideration and adequate political representation is more easily granted to those who are white, or who have the correct demeanor, skills, and biography to pass in white society.

Combining nice femininity with the local knowledge and negotiation skills of mother-advocates was successful. The bill passed in committee. It then sailed through both chambers of the state legislature to be signed into law on June 3, 2013. In Denise's words, the testimony convinced Mylan that "food allergy parents are a force to be reckoned with—and a good force." Mothers would always be part of the process in future state and federal campaigns. It would be up to Mylan, as Denise put it, to "earn their keep" as these bills were introduced state by state, rather than steamroll and exclude mothers from the process.

Denise's experience illustrates how the public face of food allergy advocacy is often represented by mothers advocating politely on behalf of their children, not women agitating militantly on behalf of themselves and their embodied experience, or disability justice advocates aiming to revolutionize normative structures of care. Mothers position their work as altruistically devoted to their children and appropriately feminine. As described in this and previous chapters, many food allergy mothers do this by putting their careers on hold, either temporarily or permanently, to make caring for allergic children their full-time jobs. Getting involved in the legislative process offers them a way to combine this selfless devotion with their professional skills from before they became mothers, but the public performance may still stress motherhood above all. Being a mother-advocate is a socially and morally appropriate exercise of professionalism. However, it comes at the expense of broader solidarity projects with other health and disability activist communities and capitulates to working within the boundaries of naturalized gendered roles in the home and in public life, as the next section will illustrate.

Mothers versus Nurses

Another mother-advocate's recollections of a different stock epinephrine campaign illustrates that not all socially reproductive care work for food allergic children is valued similarly. The passage of this second bill, which took place in 2013 and 2014, was one of the most high-profile and contentious negotiations over stock epinephrine bills in the United States. As the campaign unfolded, mothers faced off against the state's politically powerful teachers union, who raised questions about expanded job duties and training. This episode showed how the demands of mothers with the right kind of connections and an apparently altruistic investment in children's health can overshadow the labor rights concerns of feminized workers, like teachers and school nurses, who are tasked with caring for allergic children at school. It revealed fissures between the value placed on work done by caretakers whose role is unpaid and naturalized, and work done by caretakers whose role is compensated with a wage. Mothers garnered support for stock epinephrine with the public through media campaigns. At the same time, paid care workers, like teachers and school nurses, were at times portrayed unfavorably when they argued that the roll-out of stock epinephrine exceeded their contracted job duties and required further pay or negotiation. The sides ultimately reached a compromise, although not without a public fight. This episode shows that the reproductive politics of food allergy advocacy prioritizes the care work of unpaid mothers over the waged care work of paid laborers. It suggests a hierarchy of care, in which "natural" caretakers are more sympathetic figures than those who do some of the same work for pay.

Here I focus on the fight for stock epinephrine in one of the most populous U.S. states in 2013 and 2014, as narrated to me by a mother-advocate I call Cindy. In Cindy's narrative, she turns family ties, professional skills and relationships, and her status as a mother into politically valuable tools for food allergy advocacy. Cindy's family's financial stability also allowed her to leave the workforce to raise her food allergic son and gave her the time to pursue these sorts of campaigns in the first place. Her familial and professional networks gave her personal access to lobbying experts, legislators, and prominent media figures. These connections were key in pushing back against strong opposition from the state's large and politically powerful teachers union. The union vigorously objected to requiring members to provide new forms of care to schoolchildren without additional training or compensation, pitting waged, publicly supported caretakers against unwaged ones who work in the private space of the home.

From the start, Cindy's involvement in legislative advocacy was shaped by family ties. The seed was planted in the summer of 2013. Cindy was working with a fellow food allergy parent whose son had died of an allergic reaction to organize a food allergy fund-raising walk in conjunction with a food allergy nonprofit. The parent's personal tragedy motivated him to work on the national bill encouraging states to pass stock epinephrine legislation, the School Access to Emergency Epinephrine Act of 2013. Now he was itching to update the legal framework in the state where he and Cindy both lived. The state had had a voluntary stock epinephrine law in place for a decade, but few schools had invested in the training and supplies necessary to make stock epinephrine availability widespread. His belief, and later Cindy's, was that only a mandatory state law—one that compelled schools to carry stock epinephrine, rather than allowed them to on a voluntary basis—would be effective in meaningfully broadening access to epinephrine in schools.

Cindy's interest was piqued by their encounter, and subsequent events facilitated moving ahead with the idea. That fall, a state senator visited Cindy's son's elementary school class to talk about the legislative process. The senator encouraged the students to bring "really, really good ideas" for new legislation to his office. Cindy's son proposed the idea of a stock epinephrine bill. By November 2013, she had worked her personal network to score a series of meetings at the senator's office to promote the concept. They were already loosely connected by family business ties. She had worked for the senator's father at his family business when she was a teenager. The senator decided to take up their cause, ultimately sponsoring a state bill with another legislator from the opposing party who had been considering introducing a similar bill. The bill was introduced to the state senate late in February 2014.

With bipartisan support and enthusiasm from her senator contact, Cindy anticipated that the process would go smoothly until the bill was passed. In the meantime, she took on the role of handling media requests, public relations, and social media in a grassroots capacity to engage the public in the process. Her partner for this mission, another mother-advocate based in her state, liaised with the legislative sponsors' offices and FARE. FARE assisted by encouraging their mailing list subscribers to show the state's legislators their support for the bill through writing letters and posting messages on social media. Together, the two advocates and the advocacy organization positioned the process to unfold in public view.

Soon, however, Cindy's team began hearing rumors of resistance from the state's teachers union. Their complaints with the bill focused on teachers' lack of training for administering a powerful emergency medication, concerns that there were too few school nurses to train teachers and staff, and worry that teachers could be held liable in the event of a child's injury or death. Frustration with the union's resistance joined frustration with the lack of interest in the bill within the state—even, in Cindy's view, within the state's food allergy community. To draw more attention, Cindy contacted a reporter friend at a local news station with a request to report on the union's resistance to a bill positioned as beneficial for children, and the reporter broke the story in their high-density part of the state.

This moment exposed a fracture between teachers and mothers. Specifically, it marked a split between the kind of care work teachers were willing and able to assume in addition to their existing duties as defined in employment contracts and the kind of care work mother-advocates like Cindy expected them to take on out of a moral obligation to care for children. Cindy expected them to do more simply because it was the right thing to do, no matter what they were paid for. She did not see this moment as a struggle over working conditions for teachers but as an opportunity to point out what she saw as a failure of the teachers union to be fully committed to protecting children's health. The coverage, as she saw it, exposed an apparent contradiction in the union's position. It showed that teachers perhaps didn't care as much about children as they might claim, because they were apparently unwilling to support this new measure designed to protect children's health. According to Cindy, this new round of media coverage made all the difference: "The story broke. It was out in the open that the [union] was opposed. [That was when] the grassroots movement really took off." After the story's appearance, grassroots support for the campaign—in the form of letters, phone calls, and social media entreaties to state legislators—became more consistent and widespread among state residents.

Cindy's own efforts at this time were often focused on negotiating a truce between reproductive politics and labor politics. Now that media coverage had forced the union to the negotiating table, food allergy advocates and legislators sought to assuage teachers' fears about liability. Rather than go on the defensive in their now public disagreements with the teachers union, the bill's sponsors and their advocacy allies also designed what Cindy called "a classic example of a compromise." The bill as originally conceived would have added responsibilities for teachers and school nurses that went above and beyond their contracts, adding duties without taking away others or adding compensation. It could also place other sorts of unreasonable demands on teachers and school nurses. Some schools did not have an assigned nurse to oversee training, stocking, and administering epinephrine auto-injectors. In others, a single school nurse could be in charge of overseeing an entire district of thousands of students in multiple different locations. Nurses would, in all likelihood, be stretched too thin trying to train teachers to use stock epinephrine. Yet rather than side with them to make demands to state legislators and the public for more nurses and resources, advocates treated their interests as being antagonistic—as something to overcome or, in the last instance, negotiate around.

To achieve what the advocates wanted without undermining the capacity of school nurses to provide appropriate care, they eliminated the mandatory provision, even though it had been the original impetus for the campaign. Instead, only schools with a district or school nurse would be expected to carry stock epinephrine. The nurse would be expected to carry out training with teachers and staff, and to maintain the epinephrine auto-injectors in the school. In schools without a nurse, another staff member could implement stock epinephrine by volunteering to take on the responsibility of training and maintenance. With these changes written into the bill, the state's governor signed it into law in September 2014.

In Cindy's eyes, this bill was only the first step toward providing stock epinephrine in public spaces in her state. When we spoke about stock epinephrine in 2015, a new bill was in the works to improve food allergy mortality reporting and expand stock epinephrine bills beyond schools to a wider array of public spaces and businesses. Cindy was not directly involved in this new effort, but she was watching from the sidelines. Spearheading the push for the new entity bill, as these more generalized bills were called, was Mylan, maker of the EpiPen. Mylan's involvement in stock epinephrine legislation to date had been uneven and at times adversarial with the food allergy community. Entity bills were just beginning to be introduced and would extend stock epinephrine provisions to churches, restaurants, and other public places that were frequented by adults as often as children.

Cindy saw both opportunity and troubled waters ahead in expanding stock epinephrine legislation. More generalized entity bills would shift the debate away from the reproductive politics of caring for children to the less sympathetic politics of adult consumption and leisure. On the one hand, the entity bill called for better reporting of incidents in which children died from allergic reactions, which could better inform legislators and the public about the political and public health expediency of stock epinephrine. On the other, she believed restaurant industry organizations would pose significant resistance to the move to expand stock epinephrine requirements to places of business and public facilities beyond schools. Because an entity bill would be much less exclusively focused on protecting children, she reasoned that the moral arguments for passing it would be less compelling than the school bill. With school epinephrine, she explained, it was understood that children would be the prime beneficiaries. As she put it, it was much more difficult for politicians to say "just let the kid die" and vote against a bill focused on school safety than it might be to put in place new protections for adults that inconvenienced the hospitality industry. Adults are generally expected to be individually responsible for their health and life, whereas children are recognized as needing extra care and concern.

Cindy's misgivings about entity bill expansions to stock epinephrine in her state provide another clue to unraveling the reproductive politics of food allergy advocacy. Her misgivings indicate how children's lives are treated as more worthy of sacrifice and care than the lives of adults, echoing the consistent emphasis on children in a wide variety of advocacy campaigns. Moreover, her reflections suggest how different industries garner different levels of support in U.S. politics and culture. For-profit, private employers in the leisure and hospitality industries are formidable opponents who are expected to easily resist moral appeals to demonstrate care for their customers. Feminized care workers paid through public funds, like teachers and school nurses, however, are seen as having little right to refuse new caretaking responsibilities. They are even maligned as a group in the media to force them to compromise around employment contracts and concerns about workplace fairness and safety if needed. Broader entity laws protecting restaurant patrons and enforcing new requirements on chefs and food service workers are not likely to carry the same moral weight, so these campaigns are the second line of action in food allergy advocacy. A hierarchy of industries—for-profit industries are more politically powerful than publicly funded ones—and a hierarchy of care workers—naturalized, unpaid mothers who put their children above all before waged workers who maintain an interest in their own well-being—shapes food allergy advocacy approaches and priorities.

In advocating for safety for children and publicly demonstrating an openness to compromise in these two campaigns, mother-advocates positioned themselves as flexible and appropriately selfless "feminine warriors" in their roles in the home and in public life.[54] Mothers who did not have to work outside of the home, or who had a great deal of flexibility in how they did so, fully embraced their feminine roles within the nuclear family to become advocates for children like their own. Yet in advocates' approach to negotiating with the teachers union and school nurses, feminine norms of self-sacrifice for the sake of children were weaponized against public school workers who were doing care work for a wage during the school day. Ultimately, motherhood proved more effective in bending legislator and public opinion toward supporting their cause than the opposition. Denise's and Cindy's narratives suggest that food allergy advocacy is aligned with disability justice. Disability justice recognizes care workers as deserving of concern and protection equal to unpaid caregivers, brings together advocates across the lines of disabilities and conditions, and aligns with gender justice movements.[55] Food allergy advocacy, by contrast, is a mother's movement that prioritizes nice femininity and that is antagonistic to the interests of feminized workers. It is a mother's movement for some, but not necessarily for all.

WHO BENEFITS FROM THIS MOTHER'S MOVEMENT?

Dense reproductive politics are at stake in the evolving legal protections for food allergic children and adults. From disability accommodations to stock epinephrine bills, there is a real effort to more broadly distribute responsibility for the health and well-being of allergic children in particular beyond mothers and the nuclear family. Yet when push comes to shove, mothers' interests take priority over those who do care work beyond the family. These hints, suggestions, and direct claims about the special status of children and mothers echo the media messaging, experiences, and discourses concerning food allergy management by parents in the home: Mothers are uniquely responsible for taking care of food allergic children. While this accomplishes the immediate job of securing accommodations for individual children or passing state-level school stock epinephrine bills, it ultimately positions mothers as the people uniquely and solely responsible for their children. Without ties to broader disability justice movements, for example, food allergy mothers are often on their own with epinephrine access advocacy, no matter how tired of lobbying they might become. Such narrow, parent-drive, biomedical intervention–focused disability politics have had violent consequences in other contexts, like autism advocacy.[56] Happily, that does not seem to be the case in food allergy advocacy. However, at the very least, going it alone would seem to undermine the hope that new legislation and enforcement of existing disability law could truly broaden the network of people who assume care for food allergic children.

Disability scholars and advocates have raised these concerns about mother-led movements before. Expert mothers, like food allergy moms, often advocate for certain things focused on the specific needs of their own children and prioritize biomedical interventions over social revolution. Food allergy advocacy efforts bear a closer resemblance to the "radiation brain moms" who questioned government food policy in Japan after the Fukushima nuclear disaster in 2011 or the antivaccination activists described by Anna Kirkland who sought out their own experts to argue in court against vaccine researchers than they do to broad-based disability justice activism.[57] Rather than justice for all, food allergy mothers focus on access for their children and for families like their own, justifying demands for children like theirs using their specific expertise as mothers. Families like those of many of the mother-advocates I encountered in my research, however, make up a shrinking slice of all families in the contemporary United States, as salaried, well-paid jobs that provide affordable health care for chronically ill dependents and the ability for one parent to opt out of paid work become a greater and greater luxury.

Within neoliberal, market-based logics that position health as a private and individual matter and slowly chips away at workers' rights, measures like stock epinephrine bills and parental insistence on proper implementation of disability statutes create new kinds of individual responsibility for feminized professionals like teachers and school nurses. Prior chapters have argued that the private, domestic space of the home is reproduced, in practice and rhetoric, as the one safe space for people with food allergy. In stock epinephrine legislation, the family home is still the safest place for allergic children by default; all other places, and especially schools, are demonstrated time and again to be sites of unacceptable risk. At the same time, feminized workers like teachers and school workers are enlisted as potential medical caretakers, whether they like it or not. The economic aspects of privatization are also at stake. Private corporations with an interest in the expansion of markets are satisfied by the mechanisms of food allergy advocacy because they expand the potential market for medical products like epinephrine auto-injectors.

Health care access and costs were among the next issues to come to the fore in food allergy advocacy, starting in 2015 and with increased urgency in 2016. The rapidly rising price of Mylan's EpiPen, at the same time that state-level stock epinephrine bills were successfully passing around the United States, was one of the key instigators of a national debate about the cost of health care. Mylan became an emblem of what was often referred to as a crisis in the rise in cost of health care, alongside Elizabeth Holmes, the founder of disgraced medical diagnostics company Theranos, and Martin Shkreli, a serial health care entrepreneur charged with fraud by his investors. This health care affordability crisis almost perfectly segued with the passage of the final state-level stock epinephrine bill in 2016 and directly implicated one of the heroes in that story, Mylan. In that drama, as documented in the news media at the time, many new tensions between public and private responsibility for food allergy children came to the fore. Advocacy organizations in particular found themselves in a double bind, stuck between maintaining alliances with powerful pharmaceutical companies and the growing criticism of those companies and those who benefited from their support. The food allergy activism world had to quickly adapt to this changing landscape. Yet as

I will discuss in the next chapter, close relationships with the pharmaceutical industry seemed to shape the response of activists and advocacy organizations to the affordability controversy.

As with stock epinephrine advocacy, the priority in the next chapter of food allergy advocacy was to work within existing systems and relationships. In the process, niceness, compromise, and deference to biomedical expertise remained key tactics. The priorities of the comfortably middle-class family once again remained unexamined and unquestioned, with families and the short-term safety of children taking precedence over larger structural concerns with health care access and cost. With templates, tactics, and networks established through the push for stock epinephrine legislation, the food allergy advocacy world would continue to do its work in a way that positioned the family unit as the pivotal object of concern for health care and policy in the United States.

5

THE EPIPEN PRICING SCANDAL AND THE FUTURE OF FOOD ALLERGY ADVOCACY

On September 21, 2016, the CEO of Mylan Pharmaceuticals, Heather Bresch, appeared before the U.S. House of Representatives. In nearly four hours of testimony, Bresch was asked to account for the rapid rise in the price of the EpiPen in previous years. In his opening remarks, Jason Chaffetz, a Utah Republican representative and chair of the House Oversight Committee who presided over the hearing, contextualized the need for the hearings by saying, "Here you've got a drug, it's been on the market for about a hundred years. Costs roughly a dollar. . . . But the price of this has gone from roughly $99 for one to more than $600 for two in a very short amount of time." Chaffetz went on to emphasize that the EpiPen, at that moment, "generate[d] about ten percent of their revenue" while overburdening people who needed to keep multiple devices on hand. Chaffetz then implied personal motivations for the price increase on the part of top executives: "What doesn't add up to a lot of people is that the company had five executives in five years that earned nearly $300 million in compensation, and this is, by all accounts, by best I can tell, one of their biggest revenue drivers and one of their biggest revenue items." "Family," "families," or a "mother" were cited ten times in the three-hour, forty-five-minute-long hearings as parties directly injured by the price increases spoke, indicating the centrality of reproduction in the politics of food allergy.[1]

The EpiPen pricing situation had gained widespread national attention in the months leading up to Bresch's testimony. Public interest was triggered by the release of a thoroughly reported pair of articles by Bloomberg Business News in late 2015 and 2016, which were subsequently picked up by a wide variety of U.S. news outlets, including the *New York Times, The Atlantic,* and NPR.[2] Bloomberg's reporting came on the heels of their coverage of price increases by other drug companies, most notably Martin Shkreli's decision to hike the price of the antiparasitic medication Daraprim (pyrimethamine).[3] While Representative Chaffetz's opening remarks at the Mylan hearing suggested that Bresch was a bad apple, an executive only in it for the money, Mylan's EpiPen pricing strategy was actually just the latest example of what was coming to be perceived as a systemic national crisis in pharmaceutical drug costs in the United States.

The politics at stake in this moment of political theater were not only financial but also reproductive. Concern for the impact of high prices on families and children was evident throughout the congressional hearing as well as in other media appearances and announcements by Bresch and Mylan. The needs of families and mothers were invoked five times by Bresch, and several more by lawmakers, to suggest that she had compassion for users of her company's product, even while she claimed to be unable to do anything further to help them. Price increases across the board, as she explained, enabled safety improvements to the device and the ability to provide discounts to some families judged to be deserving of price breaks. Outside commentators like *New York Times* health columnist Tara Parker-Pope cast raising the cost of an EpiPen as a public crisis by highlighting the effects of high prices on the bottom lines of families with food allergic children in mainstream news outlets.[4] Such concerns were amplified and brought to the attention of lawmakers and the media through the efforts of some of the same mother-advocates and advocacy organizations who participated in the legislative advocacy campaigns described in chapter 4.

The second half of 2016 was also notable in the world of food allergy advocacy because one of the major goals of the previous four years had just been accomplished. As of May 2016, all fifty U.S. states had passed stock epinephrine legislation that either mandated or allowed for expanded use of epinephrine auto-injectors like the EpiPen in public schools. With this goal accomplished, many of the high-profile initiatives and anticipated milestones that remained concerned the development of new drugs for treatments to diminish the severity of food allergies and prevent reactions altogether. Public anxiety about the price of the EpiPen emerged at this pivotal moment, even though some food allergy bloggers and organizations had been calling attention to the rising price of epinephrine auto-injectors since at least 2012. Although there is an element of chance in the timing, it is useful to look at the public statements made by Mylan and its representatives, food allergy advocacy organizations, journalists, food allergy bloggers, and others about the EpiPen's price at this moment. Doing so reveals how logics of care, family, and markets were closely intertwined as some advocacy energies shifted from legislative advocacy to supporting pharmaceutical research.

My contention in this chapter is that the reproductive politics of food allergy so far discussed at length was not simply eclipsed by new priorities after the signing of the final state stock epinephrine bill. Rather, reproductive politics continued to shape public discourse about food allergy, and continued to be shaped by advocacy strategy and messaging. In this instance, reproductive politics were entwined with the privatizing impetus of U.S. pharmaceutical innovation and marketing, which affects both markets for treatments and the resources available to ordinary people to manage their health. With public awareness about the recently inflated cost of the EpiPen rising, food allergy advocates and advocacy organizations had to grapple with questions about the relationship between privatized care and corporate profits, sometimes in public. As the controversy reverberated from the media into food allergy advocacy organizations, longtime alliances were tested, and the emphasis of advocacy work shifted from legislative advocacy toward facilitating clinical research on food allergy treatments. However, increasing support for research still raises questions about who is served by health advocacy, much as the account of mother-advocates' legislative efforts did in chapter 4. Such efforts, in this case, support the profit-seeking and market-making goals of for-profit pharmaceutical companies without challenging the social and economic orders that privatize responsibility for the health of people with food allergy.

This chapter departs from the ethnographic methods of prior chapters to analyze public statements made by Mylan, Bresch, and food allergy advocacy organizations, as well as the investigative press coverage of the uproar around EpiPen pricing, to tell a microhistorical story about the stakes of growing the market for this drug, which had been central to food allergy advocacy for several years. Analytically, I carry through the concepts and themes of previous chapters to show how they appear in public advocacy and public relations campaigns. Doing so reveals how markets for drugs are reproductive in several senses. Building markets sustains and reproduces complex, often close, relationships between for-profit drug companies and nonprofit patient advocacy organizations. These close relations are justified by appeals to children and the family, who are positioned as both the injured parties of the pharmaceutical industry and the potential prime beneficiaries of cooperation between advocates and for-profit companies.

My intent is not to criticize the hard work of individuals and organizations in this space. Rather, this final analytic chapter demonstrates how difficult it is to think health activism as outside capitalist reproductive politics by showing how thoroughly the politics of social reproduction infuse both advocacy involvement with U.S. pharmaceutical markets and pharmaceutical research and development. This episode and subsequent shifts in advocacy efforts raise thorny questions about how to do health activism otherwise, in ways that challenge the social necessity of nuclear families, the privatization of care, and heteronormative roles within households. These are questions relevant for food allergy advocates and food allergic people as well as every individual and community struggling for high-quality, appropriate, and financially accessible health care in the United States today.

ADVOCACY AND THE PHARMACEUTICAL INDUSTRY

The relationship between patient advocacy organizations and pharmaceutical companies establishes some of the conditions of possibility for health advocacy, including the reproductive politics embedded in advocacy strategy and messaging that chapter 4 and much of this chapter focus on. Before recounting and unpacking the specific events that surrounded the EpiPen pricing controversy previewed at the start of this chapter, I here lay out some of the previous literature and general context surrounding these industry–advocacy relations as a starting point for subsequent discussion. Two converging trends are key in shaping how pharmaceutical companies and health advocacy organizations occupy shared social worlds. The first is collaboration between pharmaceutical companies and professionalized patient groups, and the second is the institutionalization of corporate social responsibility programs. In the context of food allergy, corporate social responsibility and collaboration with patient advocacy organizations are closely entwined. Closer analysis shows that appeals to children and family can easily be subsumed to corporate interests in raising prices and expanding markets while still allowing organizations and companies to claim they are operating in the best interests of patients.

Professionalized Patient Advocacy

Engagement with patient groups has become an integral part of pharmaceutical company practices because of the collected knowledge, experience, and desire for treatment that such groups have learned how to channel. As Vololona Rabeharisoa, Tiago Moreira, and Madeleine Akrich explain, the "experiential knowledge" these groups hold can be used as a tool for industry actors to find inspiration for new products and markets as well as a way to cheaply troubleshoot the designs of products under development through faster trial enrollment and consultation with patient representatives.[5] In the food allergy world, patient advocacy groups that are officially recognized by the U.S. government as nonprofit organizations are one of many modes through which experience is shared and collected. Formats like online forums and in-person support groups, which are used by many health communities with or without nonprofit representation, typically lack official legal recognition or tax status yet also provide infrastructure for building shared community among people managing food allergies.[6] It is the larger nonprofit groups with professional staff that are most useful to the health care industry. They tend to be better organized and already play a gatekeeping function regarding who can be said to appropriately speak for people with a medical condition.[7] It is also more efficient to learn about patient experience via a large advocacy organization because they claim to speak on behalf of large groups of patients, like everyone with food allergy in the United States, rather than, for example, representing the issues at play in a specific locality as an in-person, unincorporated support group might do. When working with volunteer advocates, organizations actively select which community voices to elevate through allocating funding through grants and collaborations and airtime via their formal communications channels. Opinions that would be distasteful to industry actors can thus easily be screened out, if that is a priority.

The kind of professionalized patient advocacy that occupies much of the rhetorical space of food allergy activism has significantly different political stakes than Paul Rabinow's widely cited idea of biosociality. Rabinow defines biosociality as "a circulation network of identity terms and restriction loci, around which and through a truly new type of autoproduction will emerge." In Rabinow's work, such circulation coalesces around "the new genetics" that encourages patient identification with their genetic risk and disease profiles.[8] Food allergy does not fit Rabinow's precise definition because it is not easily detectable through a blood-based diagnostic test, be it genetic, genomic, or otherwise. Nearly everyone with food allergies first finds out about them through an actual reaction to the food rather than through the measurement of a biological marker. Nonetheless, if biosociality is understood as a more general mode of sociality, where shared biological dysfunction, risk, or illness brings people together, it can be considered a relevant point of comparison for this discussion of food allergy advocacy. However, in addition to a kind of autoproduction in which individuals choose to associate and find shared meaning, professionalized patient advocacy in the 2010s also turned shared suffering into big business for nonprofit organizations, event planners, tax specialists managing the money of the wealthy who support nonprofits through donations, and the pharmaceutical industry.

FARE, the largest food allergy nonprofit in the United States, is a relatively small and new patient advocacy organization. It lacks the high-profile visibility of the American Cancer Society, which had an annual budget of $724,208,000 in 2018.[9] Yet FARE's 2016 revenue of $12.3 million, disclosed in its publicly available 2016 annual report, was still nothing to sneeze at.[10] Its five top staffers drew a combined $1,733,878 in reported compensation. Its total assets that year were $63.5 million, a figure boosted by the value of its holdings in a pharmaceutical startup company that had gone public in 2015, a matter I turn to later in this chapter.[11] These numbers indicate that some of the most prominent spokespeople for food allergic people are not simply self-appointed representatives of an impromptu assemblage of patients and their loved ones trying to survive with a dangerous disease. They are highly paid professionals. With such large budgets to manage, it is unlikely that just anyone would be chosen as a leader of a nonprofit organization and a spokesperson for a patient community. Leaders must have the financial acumen to engender trust in large donors who are donating thousands of dollars or more to an organization and the skills to manage budgets in the tens of millions of dollars. Another clear indication of the professionalization of FARE and other food allergy organizations has been the hiring of successful executives, lobbyists, and entrepreneurial scientists with private-sector experience, like former CEO James Baker, to lead the organization and many of the specialized functions within it.

The sociality of food allergy organization events, which I witnessed several times during ethnographic research trips, are another indication of the warm relations with industry. Industry sponsors are generally warmly welcomed at advocacy-focused events. They often pay sponsorship fees to support event operations, and in return, their logo features prominently in brochures, and they sponsor physical booths in designated exhibition halls. Companies can feel secure knowing that the organization will spend their money following similar decision-making frameworks as their own directors and executives while gaining access to the collected patient experience that the organization represents. With this dynamic as background—product marketing and extraction of patient knowledge in one direction, financial dependence in the other—certain topics can easily get cordoned off from critique. The rising price of the EpiPen is a prime example of how a problem felt by many families affected by food allergy remained mostly under the radar in major food allergy advocacy campaigns—at least, that is, until journalists and others highlighted the price hikes and subsequently became curious about advocacy complicity with pharmaceutical companies. Then demands to make public statements about markets and costs were no longer avoidable for industry-friendly organizations.

Corporate Social Responsibility

The second important piece for understanding Mylan's involvement with food allergy advocacy organizations is the rise of corporate social responsibility, or CSR. In studies of extractive industries and pharmaceutical manufacturing, CSR programs present a friendly face of the company to the public, consumers, and shareholders as a way to short-circuit activist critiques of the effects of the company's products and processes.[12] In the particular case of Mylan's involvement with food allergy advocacy, the rising price of the EpiPen would seem to be an obvious target of critique. Indeed, individuals articulated these concerns from person to person in hushed voices—including to me between breakout sessions at conferences—and wrote about them on their individually authored blogs. However, they were slow to be addressed in public by food allergy advocacy organizations until they were more widely publicized by the Bloomberg reporting and a congressional hearing.

CSR in the pharmaceutical industry is reminiscent of gift economies, such as the postwar "detail men" and their contemporary descendants, pharmaceutical sales representatives.[13] In Jeremy A. Greene's account, in the 1950s, these salespeople—exclusively men—

strategically leveraged gender, vocabulary, cultural references, attire, bodily comportment, and other aspects of self-presentation to present an authoritative but nonthreatening persona to the physicians they coaxed into prescribing their company's drugs. Through strategic class positioning with respect to the physician's self-image and offers of carefully delivered advice about how to use drugs, detail men set into motion a complex economy that inspired product loyalty and promised to keep physicians on the cutting edge of medical science. As Michael Oldani describes in his account of contemporary drug sales, gifts are now a standard part of the encounter between drug reps and doctors. Gifts can range from samples to free lunches and dinners accompanying continuing medical education sessions to honoraria and paid travel for speaking at medical conferences. These gifts help to grow and sustain the moral economy of pharmaceutical knowledge and sales that was established as a normal part of medical practice in the postwar period.[14] With contemporary CSR and crackdowns on direct physician gifting by professional societies and laws like the Affordable Care Act in the 2010s, pharmaceutical companies now often gift donations to patient advocacy groups to support their public activities rather than, or in addition to, providing gifts directly to prescribers. In exchange, they receive mainline access to aggregated patient experience, invitations for company representatives to mingle at doctor- or patient-centric events, and willing participants in clinical trials.

Mylan's publicly available 2015 Corporate Social Responsibility brochure offers a window into their CSR efforts. Because Mylan is a highly diversified company and one of the largest generic drug manufacturers in the world, the brochure discussed CSR programs designed for a wide variety of geographic regions, communities, and conditions. In the "Combating Anaphylaxis" section, Mylan highlights their involvement in food allergy advocacy by stating, "We have spearheaded and supported multiple efforts to help raise anaphylaxis awareness, preparedness and access to treatment."[15] The programs in this section include legislative advocacy for stock epinephrine in schools and in other community spaces, a partnership with Disney to "increase awareness of anaphylaxis" in their parks, and a list of "community allies," including medical and education unions, food allergy advocacy nonprofits, medical societies, and the American Red Cross. They also devote a page to their EpiPen4Schools program, which "provides four free EpiPen or EpiPen Jr (epinephrine injection) Auto-Injectors to qualifying U.S. schools along with additional training and educational resources for schools."[16] The top half of the page is taken up by a soft-focus picture of the Mylan-branded cabinet where the free devices can be stored by school staff until they are needed in an emergency.

Their involvement in stock epinephrine as a CSR initiative thus has two sides: assisting in lobbying efforts to make the EpiPen more ubiquitously available and providing a small number of auto-injectors for free to entities who might be affected by stock epinephrine legislation. The former strategy could expand the consumer base for the device in the future by putting schools in a position where they might face local pressure to buy more of the devices when the free samples get used or expire, while the latter is a way to short-circuit critiques of the high price of the device. Advocating for stock epinephrine legislation in the United States demonstrates that they are on the side of food allergy advocates, who were still focused on legislative advocacy in 2015. By donating epinephrine auto-injectors to some entities, like schools, the company shows that they care about their consumers— that they are a socially responsible entity. Yet by the same gesture, they create potential future revenues by getting a foot in the door with the new entities who will be required or allowed to purchase from them, should stock epinephrine campaigns succeed (which indeed they later did). One mother-advocate articulated the risk of such an arrangement to schools and other community entities when she told me in an interview that Mylan was "under no obligation . . . eventually, that [program] stops."

Using CSR, Mylan can write its own future by creating new markets. By supporting the creation of these markets through gifts of free EpiPen devices, they can also position market making as a form of care for people with food allergy. During the stock epinephrine legislation push, mother-advocates and advocacy organizations who lobbied alongside the company's representatives became stuck. Instituting stock epinephrine legislation and getting epinephrine auto-injectors into schools and other community locations could go a long way toward relieving the mother guilt and other well-founded anxieties felt by those managing food allergies. However, resources leveraged by pharmaceutical actors to write a desirable future via these collaborations put stock epinephrine advocates in what Kim Fortun calls a double bind: enmeshed in "fields of force and contradiction . . . the double binds that position enunciatory communities within new world orders."[17] The new world order at stake in this case is one in which pharmaceutical industry actors continue to profit while the ability of patients to access crucial medications diminishes, despite small-scale patches administered through narrowly targeted programs. The baseline situation in which patients are asked to pay high out-of-pocket prices for health care is not especially novel for the U.S. health care context. But the configuration of actors in play represents a new way of maintaining the status quo. Accessing funds to raise awareness and pass crucial safety legislation for people with food allergies requires advocates to align with pharmaceutical companies like Mylan. Yet this alliance also puts an implicit stamp of approval on the company's activities, even when they work against broader access to epinephrine in other contexts.

Nonprofit Capture

The story of the relationship between pharmaceutical companies like Mylan and food allergy advocacy organizations is one of industry capture of voices and organizations that claim to represent patients' best interests. Professionalization and CSR are two important mechanisms through which this is accomplished. The idea of private industry actors "capturing" another organization has been developed in political science and sociology to explain the perceived undue influence of private corporations over governmental regulation, a phenomenon referred to as regulatory capture.[18] The aim of regulatory capture, according to Abraham and Ballinger, is for profit-seeking companies to shape the priorities and rulemaking procedures of the targeted agency to lighten regulation while "enabling industry scientists to define commercial concerns as matters of techno-scientific progress."[19] In the pharmaceutical industry, changes like reductions in the number of safety tests that need to be conducted for a new drug application reduces the time to get a new product to market, which accordingly potentially accelerates the realization of profits.

By analogy, I want to suggest that food allergy advocacy nonprofits were sufficiently captured by industry before the breaking news about the price of the EpiPen that it was hard for organizations to disavow Mylan's pricing strategy or to imagine advocacy strategies that did not serve to lighten the load for pharmaceutical companies. I call this nonprofit capture. While the captured nonprofit organizations discussed in this chapter are not governmental agencies, the strategy of a for-profit industry gaining influence over the policies of an outside, non-profit-seeking organization to benefit private corporations makes the comparison apt. In this case, as in regulatory capture, the alignment of the interests of industry with patient organizations positions nonindustry actors to act in ways that ultimately benefit the industry, intentionally or not. This is the case both during and after the height of the EpiPen pricing controversy in the summer and fall of 2016.

Professionalization and CSR sustain complicities between organizations that claim to speak for patients and industry interests. While previous work has examined how advocates take adversarial relationships toward industry and government to force them to respond to the needs of patients and disabled people, in the food allergy case, I argue that patient advocacy works in a way that is complementary to, and even supportive of, industry interests in growing markets and sales. For this reason, while the rising price of the EpiPen became a public controversy, it did not trigger a consequential reckoning with the partnerships between industry and food allergy advocacy organizations. Instead, the focus of cooperation just changed. The next sections follow Mylan and FARE in particular because they are two of the largest actors in the food allergy world, and they carefully document their changes in strategy and policy through robust public communications channels like websites, press releases, and other statements to the media. These sources are both publicly accessible and widely distributed, shaping how other organizations make decisions, and are thus important for understanding how the climate around food allergy advocacy shifted overall.

EPIPEN PRICING AND THE POLITICS OF AFFORDABILITY

The news of the rising price of the EpiPen first hit the mainstream U.S. media in 2015 amid growing restiveness over the high price of pharmaceutical drugs in the United States and expanded into a major public controversy in the second half of 2016. Here I recount the unfolding of the public response in detail on the basis of reporting, press releases, television interviews, and other public documentation of the episode. On its face, the controversy pitted Mylan, who claimed that rising prices allowed them to create a better product and support food allergy advocacy, against critics in the media, lawmakers, and food allergy advocates who claimed that the company's policies were causing financial harm to ordinary people. Reproductive politics arose in public discourse and the logic behind proposed solutions. Actors on all sides appealed to the well-being of families and children as justifications for their positions. Bloggers and parents quoted in journalists' reporting, for example, reported concern about the effect that rising prices for the EpiPen would have on the finances of their family or families like their own who cared for one or more food allergic children. Mylan in turn sought to defuse the tension by developing programs that they claimed would help people, including the EpiPen4Schools program and copay discount cards. The public back-and-forth between the company and its critics suggests how malleable appeals to the needs of family and children can be as political tools. This episode shows how reproductive politics offers unstable ground for advocacy on behalf of the financial well-being of ordinary people because it can also be invoked by corporate actors whose activities threaten the ability to provide care for sick and disabled people.

The story starts well before 2016, although that will be the focus in the coming pages. One plausible starting point is 2007, when Mylan acquired the full rights to develop and market the EpiPen from Merck when they took over the company's generic drugs business. From 2007 to 2016, the out-of-pocket price had risen from about $50 for a single pen to as much as $600 or more for a two-pack, which by 2016 was the standard way the devices were sold. As the price rose, some insurers declined to cover all of the increases, leaving some buyers covering larger proportions of the cost. Some plans only covered one two-pack per year, so any extras bought for school or a family member's house—typical scenarios my research participants had told me about in interviews during my ethnographic research—had to be paid for entirely out of pocket. The shift toward higher deductible health insurance plans in the United States also meant that some individuals and families had to pay several thousand dollars of health care costs out of pocket before any coverage would kick in. Because epinephrine easily breaks down when EpiPens are exposed to heat and other environmental conditions, experts recommend replacing them each year. For the many people who are unlucky enough to purchase a pen that expired sooner, left it too long in a hot or cold car, or had a deductible to meet, they would most likely be paid for completely out of pocket.

The first detailed reporting on rising EpiPen prices outside of food allergy circles, by Bloomberg Business News, came out in September 2015.[20] The release of additional reporting by the *New York Times*, Bloomberg, *The Atlantic*, NPR, and numerous other news outlets in August and September 2016 made the EpiPen a focal point for national discussions about health care costs. Families and children featured prominently in media coverage from the start of the late summer and fall 2016 wave of reporting. For example, in an entry on the *New York Times'* Well blog entitled "How Parents Harnessed the Power of Social Media to Challenge EpiPen Prices," health columnist Tara Parker-Pope interviews several mothers of food allergic children about rising prices. She calls it "a lesson in the power of social media to help create a groundswell." Parker-Pope also notes how different this moment looked from others in food allergy activism: "What's so unusual about the pricing furor is that it has been orchestrated almost solely by parents and family members of people who use EpiPens. Patient advocacy groups, which typically are vocal on all issues related to food allergies, have been largely silent."[21] In other coverage by Parker-Pope and other journalists, parents were featured as interview subjects to testify to the power of epinephrine, concern about the company's actions, and the impact of rising costs on their families and children.[22]

The EpiPen price increase hit a nerve because it was another confirmatory data point for a felt reality for many individuals and families: The cost of pharmaceutical products was seemingly out of control on the unregulated U.S. market for medical care. It broke through in a heated political moment in the U.S. health care landscape and followed numerous other pricing and fraud scandals in the U.S. medical marketplace. The Mylan congressional hearing mentioned in the opening of this chapter happened less than two months before the 2016 U.S. presidential election—an election in which the continuation of the Affordable Care Act, passed under President Barack Obama, drew a great deal of pundit commentary. It was the summer of pharmaceutical industry wunderkind Martin Shkreli's securities fraud trial, based in New York City and broadcast worldwide. It was also the beginning of the end for medical testing company executive Elizabeth Holmes, who, the public was learning, had swindled wealthy investors out of millions to create a medical testing platform that didn't work as advertised and had caused clear harm by delaying appropriate treatment to dozens or hundreds of individuals. Against this backdrop, the story of a generic medication that had been on the market for decades suddenly jumping in price seemed primed to become an object of national attention.

Mylan Offers a Partial Solution

To defuse the growing tension, Mylan appealed to the well-being of families and children in announcing a new program, $0 copay cards, and reminding the public about an existing CSR initiative, the EpiPen4Schools program. The company announced the new $0 copay cards via a press release on August 25, 2016—just three days after the August 22 release of the first of a string of *New York Times* pieces about Mylan and the price of the EpiPen.[23] The company announced this program "in recognition of those patients who are facing the burden of higher out-of-pocket costs."

The cards could be used to help purchase an EpiPen or EpiPen Jr. two-pack at a pharmacy. When presented at checkout, a discount card reduced the price the user would have to pay out of pocket for people with insurance by up to $300. Mylan would also "doubl[e] eligibility for our patient assistance program to 400% of the federal poverty level," meaning that "a family of four making up to $97,200 would pay nothing out of pocket for their EpiPen® Auto-Injector." Mylan would also allow some patients to buy the devices directly from the company. Finally, they reminded readers that the company would "continue to offer the EpiPen4Schools® program," which had "provided more than 700,000 free epinephrine auto-injectors and educational resources to more than 65,000 schools nationwide." During my ethnographic research, the cards—typically small booklets folded to approximately the size of a credit card with a glossy card-stock cover—were handed out at food allergy events and available through company websites and by phone to users who directly requested them. As a participant-observer at food allergy advocacy conferences in 2015, for example, I received copay cards for both the EpiPen and Auvi-Q epinephrine auto-injectors from exhibitors at events I attended as well as in bags of samples and announcements provided to all participants.

Copay cards are a uniquely neoliberal invention of the U.S. health care system. They place the responsibility for monitoring and controlling the price of pharmaceutical drugs on families and individuals rather than treating drug pricing as a systemic problem that is subject to national or state policies or regulation. In the U.S. health care system, a copay is a payment a person makes for a prescription drug at the point of sale. Copays are a portion of the full price of the drug. They are often a small amount like $0, $5, $20, or $35 for common medications, and hundreds to thousands per prescription for more specialized medications. Copays do not scale to the price of the medication; they are set by insurance plans for all drugs that fall into different insurer-defined categories. The insurance company then pays the difference between what the user pays and what the insurance company has negotiated as the total price for the medication with the manufacturer. As drug prices rise, and as health insurance increasingly shifts the costs of drugs and other health care items to consumers through rising copays, premiums, and deductibles, lowered costs at the pharmacy checkout is a welcome but very small, relief.

Copay discount cards are emblematic of neoliberal solutions for high health care costs in the United States that favor those who are already relatively secure. By linking benefits to insurance plans, these copay cards are not universal by design. Rather, they extend the benefits afforded to people who receive health care benefits through the employment of a household breadwinner. Because some of their benefits are tied to health insurance, the help they provide is designed to help people who already have the most security possible in the precarious U.S. health care landscape. Even for those families and individuals who are insured in alignment with card benefits, there are strings attached, such as caps on how much of total out-of-pocket costs will be covered (still limited to $300 per two-pack in June 2020). Still, the cards were welcomed by people with food allergy who were seeking any kind of financial relief when purchasing EpiPens, and they were positioned by the company as meaningful interventions on a systemic problem. Yet access to the EpiPen, even when it was supposedly made easier in the face of controversy about its financial inaccessibility, was not designed to be universal.

Mylan's 2016 copay card program spoke to the reproductive politics of food allergy advocacy in implicit and explicit ways. The ways the cards interacted with insurance plans presumed a household breadwinner, a role that has historically been aligned with men's social role as providers in the United States. They also centered families in their marketing. This was not the first time the company had offered copay cards, but now it was the company's way of taking "immediate action" to "[expand] already existing programs."[24] The program was announced within days of the company's coming under sustained media scrutiny for how much families were being asked to pay out of pocket for the devices by pharmacies. In citing a "family of four" as their benchmark, they signaled to their audience that they were especially concerned with the impact their policies were having on the archetypal family of two adults and two children. In announcing this program, the company also positioned it as part of a broader portfolio of acts of care for people with food allergies, like the EpiPen4Schools program. In that program as well, the interests of children took center stage. In both ongoing CSR campaigns and crisis response strategy, addressing the needs of families and children was supposedly a primary logic behind Mylan's actions.

While accounts of the rise in the EpiPen's price by major news organizations like Bloomberg Business News and the *New York Times* brought the issue to the consciousness of the general public, some food allergy bloggers had been writing about EpiPen costs and copay discount cards for several years. Bloggers typically refrained from blaming the company for high prices, instead praising small measures like copay cards as beneficial for families managing children's food allergies as they were announced. For example, Caroline Moassessi, who writes the blog Grateful Foodie, wrote about the out-of-pocket costs of EpiPen as early as 2013. In a February 2013 post entitled "Affordable EpiPens! Really," Moassessi explained that Mylan was offering $100 copay reduction cards for EpiPen two-packs. She expressed enthusiasm and gratitude for this offer on behalf of her family: "Wow. This is a big deal for families like mine. We are self insured, have a high deductible and to add insult to injury, our prescription plan does not cover auto-injectibles (and that is another conversation for another day). The icing on the cake is that the '$0 Co-Pay Offer' will help reduce my annual $700–$800 epinephrine tab."[25] In July 2013, two more posts on the Grateful Foodie blog tracked the continuation of Mylan's program and the introduction of $0 copay reduction cards from a new EpiPen competitor, Auvi-Q, designed by the founders of startup medical device company Kaléo and marketed in the United States at the time by Sanofi.[26] Later posts on Grateful Foodie, like those in January 2015 and June 2015, demonstrate the long-term interest from food allergy advocates in programs and tools that reduced the out-of-pocket cost of epinephrine auto-injectors.[27]

The interest in "families like mine" in Moassessi's post shows how the reproductive politics of Mylan's messaging is shared by parent-advocates. Such shared attitudes make this framing a potentially successful tool for uniting parent-advocates and for-profit companies. The two sets of actors can—or even ought to—get along because at the end of the day, they are both trying to keep children safe. At the same time, it can obscure the difference in motivation, with companies seeking expanded profits and markets and parents hoping for durable relief from high prices. Invoking families and children as a strategy to press for affordable health care is thus a tricky game. The language can be flexibly adapted both for parents who make demands for relief and for industry actors who make tweaks with many strings attached without pursuing systemic change in health care delivery. In short, reproductive politics is perhaps a more dangerous tool than parent-advocates fully realize.

Congress Seeks a Scapegoat

As the public controversy unfolded, the media sought to hold Mylan CEO Heather Bresch personally accountable for the rise in the price of the EpiPen. In cable and nightly news interviews in late August 2016, Bresch was grilled on why users were paying much higher prices for EpiPens that they had in previous years. Interviewers at times engaged her in conversation about the broader issue of rising drug prices in the contemporary United States. In one particularly rocky interview with CNBC on August 25, for example, Bresch articulated similar points as those the company would later announce in the August 29 press release that placed the blame outside Mylan.[28] While the interviewer suggested that the company alone was responsible for raising prices on the EpiPen, Bresch repeated the message that blame did not lie only with her company but with other actors in the supply chain that helped to deliver finished pills and medical devices into the hands of users and patients. In the United States, this chain includes subcontracted manufacturers, the company whose brand marks the product (Mylan's role, in this case), billing middlemen called pharmacy benefit managers who coordinate billing between patients and health insurance plans, and insurers and prescribing providers. The complexity of the system meant that no single person should be blamed.

Toward the end of the interview, Bresch repeated another frequent pharmaceutical industry argument: that high prices in the United States enabled innovation for new and improved products worldwide. As she put it in the interview, "The reality is we do subsidize the rest of the world innovation. We do subsidize. And as a country, we've made a conscious decision to do so. And I think the world's a better place for it. But that doesn't excuse an outdated, inefficient system and we can't hide behind that."[29] Bresch's statement made it clear that it should be considered a point of nationalist pride for people in the United States to pay significantly more than people in other countries for their medications. U.S. EpiPen users had a duty to subsidize global EpiPen users, and perhaps users of Mylan's other drugs, around the world. When real individuals and families within the United States bore the brunt of high prices, the metaphorical American national family could then provide improved products to the rest of the world, boosting the nation's standing as a leading innovator.[30] Such a suggestion seems contrary to other aspects of the company's messaging that U.S. families and their children were a strategic priority, like the EpiPen4Schools program and their involvement with school stock epinephrine legislation. Bresch nonetheless calls on food allergic people in the United States to subsidize the company's operations abroad. However, despite her company and customers bearing the uniquely American responsibility to innovate, Bresch also emphasized, "as a mother" in addition to a CEO, that "the last thing that we would ever want is no one to have their EpiPen due to price." Reproductive relations were again invoked as part of the calculus of company strategy, this time with Bresch herself as a symbol of how the two domains were interlinked.

In a final attempt to address public anger over the price of the EpiPen, the company turned to creating a new generic market for epinephrine auto-injectors. Four days after the CNBC interview, and seven days after *New York Times* articles about the price of the EpiPen started to come out, on August 29, 2016, Mylan announced that they would release a generic version of the name-brand EpiPen for a list price of $300 per two-pack. This would be a roughly 50 percent reduction in the $600 or more price per two-pack commonly cited at the time for the name-brand version when it was not covered by insurance. The company again sought to shift blame for the branded EpiPen's high price away from itself and onto the supply chain and health insurers with the statement attributed to CEO Heather Bresch in the press release:

> We understand the deep frustration and concerns associated
> with the cost of EpiPen® to the patient, and have always shared

the public's desire to ensure that this important product be accessible to anyone who needs it. Our decision to launch a generic
alternative to EpiPen® is an extraordinary commercial response,
which required the cooperation of our partner. However, because
of the complexity and opaqueness of today's branded pharmaceutical supply chain and the increased shifting of costs to
patients as a result of high deductible health plans, we determined that bypassing the brand system in this case and offering
an additional alternative was the best option. Generic drugs have
a long, proven track record of delivering significant savings to
both patients and the overall healthcare system. The launch of a
generic EpiPen®, which follows the steps we took last week on the
brand to immediately reduce patients' out-of-pocket costs, will
offer a long-term solution to further reduce costs and ease the
burden and complexity of the process on the patient.[31]

Once the EpiPen pricing story broke, it remained in the headlines
as September arrived, culminating in Bresch's testimony to the U.S.
House of Representatives on September 21. By this point, the price
of the EpiPen, a crucial and meaningful device for food allergic people, had become a mainstream political issue. Bresch testified before
the U.S. House of Representatives on September 21, 2016, at the invitation of several representatives. She ended her opening remarks by
saying, "I wish we had better anticipated the magnitude and acceleration of the rising financial issues for a growing minority of patients
who may have ended up paying the full wholesale acquisition cost, or
more. We never intended this, we listened, and focused on this issue,
and came up with an immediate and sustainable solution."[32] In the
more than three subsequent hours of remaining testimony, U.S. representatives called on Bresch to explain this supposedly excessively
complex pharmaceutical distribution and billing system, the company's inability to anticipate it, the benefits she might have personally
gained from the rising price, and the company's involvement in stock
epinephrine campaigns.

In the course of the hearings, Bresch used talking points about
"access and awareness" that were already familiar from food allergy
advocacy campaigns that centered children as the prime beneficiaries

of increased EpiPen sales. As she put it, the company "started help-ing" with legislative advocacy because "only a handful of states [had] started to recognize that epinephrine auto-injectors could be in a school's name and not a child's name."[33] The company then started the EpiPen4Schools program and distributed "seven hundred thou-sand free pens to over 66,000 schools with no strings attached." She explained that they had also donated to school and school nurses' associations—the very unions who had resisted them in state-level campaigns, as explained in chapter 4—for training on recognizing anaphylaxis and using epinephrine auto-injectors.

The questioners even dug into Mylan's marketing budget for the EpiPen, which offered suggestive figures for the scale of its spending on stock epinephrine campaigns, EpiPen4Schools, and other CSR ac-tivities aligned with food allergy advocacy organizations' programs. For example, in her testimony, Bresch noted that the company had spent $1 billion on developing EpiPen since 2008. In the first hour of testimony, Representative Elijah Cummings noted that the company had submitted documents showing $97 million spent on marketing in 2015. Bresch then explained that four million two-packs had been sold, and approximately $105 of the $274 the company received for each two-pack went toward research, development, patient assis-tance, and marketing in 2015, which would come out to $420 million. These costs, according to her testimony, included patient assistance programs (which could include programs like copay discount cards) and awareness campaigns. Her testimony thus suggested a budget on the order of tens of millions of dollars for "awareness and access" work related to the EpiPen in 2015, although Bresch said she was not sure exactly how the $105 per two-pack was broken down into different types of spending.[34] On the basis of the company's self-reported CSR work and their ubiquitous presence at food allergy events, it is evident that at least some of this budget was used to position the company as being on the side of families, schools, and children.

Overall, the 2016 media drama concerning the price of the EpiPen spoke in important ways to the reproductive politics of food allergic life and food allergy advocacy discussed at length throughout this book. Families, children, and schools were again positioned as the key beneficiaries of the EpiPen and of Mylan's corporate social responsibility work that the company highlighted when criticized for the device's rapidly rising price. At the same time, the company sought to deflect responsibility for rising prices by citing a complicated system for manufacturing, distributing, and receiving payments for pharmaceuticals and medical devices in the contemporary United States. The company thus positioned itself as not responsible for certain financial pressures placed on families and at the same time responsible for programs and policies that benefited select families with certain kinds of health insurance or with children enrolled in schools.

In light of the scrutiny on the price of the EpiPen, and with the wrapping up of stock epinephrine campaigns, food allergy advocacy was at a pivotal point by the end of 2016. Many food allergy advocacy organizations, and many individual advocates, had been comfortable with the relationship between companies like Mylan and nonprofit and parent-led food allergy advocacy. However, the company's assurances that it had the best interests of EpiPen users at heart were not enough to completely halt criticism. During the pricing controversy and after the school stock epinephrine wins, there were significant shifts in the public alliances between advocacy organizations and pharmaceutical companies. Public attention on the high price of the EpiPen dovetailed with increasing support for new drug development from food allergy advocacy organizations. Instead of supporting the creation of new markets for existing drugs, a foreseeable effect of the expansion of stock epinephrine in schools, these efforts help to establish new markets for new drugs in addition to supporting research.

The latest collaborations between industry and advocacy speak to another dimension of the notion of social reproduction: the maintenance of capitalist social relations. In this case, what is maintained are the established relationships between nonprofit advocacy organizations and their corporate sponsors, in which advocacy organizations take on work that can expand markets for for-profit companies. While the shift from stock epinephrine campaigns to medical research draws on different forms of expertise and deemphasizes families, schools, and children in some ways, these changes do not fundamentally change the fact that pharmaceutical companies stand to gain considerably from working with food allergy advocacy organizations. In the meantime, the financial needs of families and individuals for cheap, high-quality medical care remain mostly out of the spotlight of large-scale food allergy advocacy campaigns.

SHIFTING PRIORITIES

As the EpiPen pricing controversy unfolded, food allergy advocacy organizations repositioned their public priorities and relationships to pharmaceutical companies. The cluster of events that bought the EpiPen price increases to public attention marked the moment when the "political dimensions of illness [became] discernible to the wider public."[35] The previous section argued that these politics were reproductive in nature because families were used as a rhetorical device in appeals for both remediation and forgiveness: Both the company and its critics claimed that they were doing what was best for families and children. This section examines how food allergy advocacy organizations' public statements and initiatives to support clinical research in response to and after the controversy continued to treat food allergy treatment as a private problem that individuals were responsible for managing by choosing among a variety of appropriate solutions within a marketplace. Such commitments do little to challenge the role of families and mothers as the ultimately responsible actors for the safety and well-being of the next generation. New directions in advocacy strategy simply maintained established relations, both within advocacy work and within the homes of food allergic people, just in a different guise.

With food allergy now a mainstream political matter, and with public attention focused for a moment on food allergy experts and organizations, some kind of response had to be made to demonstrate to food allergy advocacy's new audiences that advocacy organizations considered the high cost of health care a serious matter. Advocacy priorities had been focused, until just a few months before, on the passage of stock epinephrine bills state by state, which had been passed with the help of pharmaceutical company lobbyists and donations.

When passed, these bills had the effect of not only increasing safety for food allergic people but also creating new markets for epinephrine auto-injector sales to schools. A rapid pivot to public discussion of the price of pharmaceuticals drew food allergy advocates into preexisting conversations about patient access to affordable health care, such as long-term discussions about the cost of treatment for HIV/AIDS and emerging questions about the cost of insulin for people with diabetes. It could have been a moment in which cross-movement disability justice solidarities against high prices were forged. But this did not happen. Speaking out on behalf of affordability could have meant alienating industry allies and cutting off funding sources for the organizations that had provided the people to perform much of the on-the-ground advocacy work so far. It tightened the double bind that advocacy organizations found themselves in.

Corporate Support in a Moment of Controversy

Food allergy advocacy organizations found themselves in a double bind when news of the rising price of the EpiPen hit the mainstream media because they had directly benefited from cooperation with pharmaceutical companies for years. In my ethnographic research trips, I often witnessed that it was standard practice for pharmaceutical companies, along with specialty food companies, other food allergy–related businesses, and even other nonprofits, to sponsor food allergy family and advocacy-focused events. Brochures I collected at the 2014 FARE conference near Chicago, Illinois, for example, listed pharmaceutical companies Mylan and Sanofi among the conference's "Premier Exhibitors."[36] Elsewhere in the brochure, the FARE Walk for Food Allergy program included a note that it was "Presented by Mylan," and indicated that Sanofi was also an "Elite"-level sponsor.[37] The 2013 Food Allergy Bloggers Conference website listed thirty-five sponsors on its website, including Mylan and Sanofi.[38] When I attended the conference in 2015 in Denver, Colorado, the conference goodie bag included a copay discount card for Mylan's EpiPen. Pharmaceutical company names, logos, discount cards, and marketing messages were a constant feature of food allergy gatherings. However, when Mylan faced public scrutiny, advocacy organizations tried to carefully distance themselves from specific companies and discuss the impact of pricing policies on families without critiquing individual companies.

The financial entanglements between food allergy nonprofits and the pharmaceutical industry are hard to overstate. In at least one case, a nonprofit organization played a supporting role in building an early-stage, for-profit pharmaceutical company focused on developing therapies for food allergy. In a press release dated November 21, 2013, Allergen Research Corporation (ARC, renamed Aimmune Therapeutics in May 2015) announced the completion of a $17 million Series A, early-stage fund-raising round, which was "led by Longitude Capital . . . and included support from Food Allergy Research & Education (FARE), the nation's leading nonprofit focused on food allergies."[39] While the nature of this support was not publicly elaborated on, it was a strong statement about the intimacy of financial relations between the nonprofit and a new corporate entity.

Press releases from ARC/Aimmune and financial statements from FARE from subsequent years suggest that a close relationship was maintained for some time after this early milestone. In 2014, FARE's then-CEO, John L. Lehr, was quoted in a 2014 ARC press release as stating that the nonprofit was "pleased to be supporting progress toward commercially available treatments."[40] ARC and Aimmune press releases in 2015 and 2016 included links to FARE's website as a resource for learning more about food allergy. The company's chief medical officer appointed in 2016, Daniel Adelman, MD, had previously served on FARE's research advisory board.[41] The relationship was financial as well as personal and rhetorical. In 2015, the year the company changed its name and had its initial public offering of stock, valued at $168 million, FARE reported a one-year increase in investment assets from holdings in Aimmune, from $150,505 to approximately $47,485,577 in its 2015 audited financial statement.[42] With yearly noninvestment revenue of approximately $12.8 million that same year,[43] such an investment could potentially create long-term stability for the organization—if, that is, the stock price of the company was maintained at a reasonably high level. As a consequence of its early support of Aimmune and investment holdings in the company, at least part of FARE's future stability as an organization would be tied to the company's success.

In light of this kind of close relationship between advocacy organizations and the pharmaceutical industry, it was notable when some organizations publicly spoke out against the high price of the epinephrine auto-injectors. Even though the triggering event for such statements was the EpiPen pricing coverage, organizations tried to speak out without singling out any particular company. FARE, for example, made the following announcement on August 24, 2016:

> FARE strongly believes that all these entities need to justify the increased cost of epinephrine to consumers and identify solutions that will help to ease the financial burden currently faced by patients who need epinephrine. FARE's role is to represent the voice of the patient in this process, and where possible help facilitate the dialogue and process by which solutions can be identified and implemented. We cannot accept the status quo.[44]

The release goes on to describe six measures FARE had taken over the past year to "try and ensure all individuals with food allergies have access to epinephrine." These steps included meeting with pharmaceutical companies marketing epinephrine, encouraging foreign manufacturers to sell competitor products in the United States, "offer[ing] support" for a relaunch of a competing device, Kaléo's Auvi-Q, "offer[ing] support" to pharmaceutical companies' FDA marketing applications, conducting studies on "access and affordability of epinephrine," and sponsoring a scientific report on food allergy in the United States to be released by the National Academies of Science, Engineering, and Medicine.

While the organization positioned these actions as representing the interests of people with food allergy in the face of reproachable corporation actions, four seem to involve a continued working relationship with pharmaceutical companies. Two of the actions offer support to an unspecified number of companies, including Kaléo. FARE's commitments in this moment focused on creating a more competitive and crowded marketplace of options for treatment and dietary needs for people with food allergies. However, such interventions would do nothing to directly address the structural complexities of sales pathways cited by Mylan or the deeper structural issues that make medical care so much more easily accessible to the wealthy in the United States, like expensive insurance copays and deductibles. In FARE's future of a more competitive market, the responsibility for affordable and appropriate care would still fall on the individuals and caretakers in charge of everyday food allergy management. The responsibility to choose wisely as a discerning consumer among the options available for purchase would be even further intensified as more options became available.

As pressure on Mylan and scrutiny on food allergy advocacy organizations mounted thanks to relentless press coverage, FARE soon vowed to stop accepting financial support from companies marketing epinephrine auto-injectors. However, these promises were limited in scope and still displayed faith in the efficacy of market-based solutions. On September 7, 2016, FARE announced that it would stop accepting money from Mylan until more steps had been taken to reel in the price of the EpiPen. FARE's press release was signed by the organization's then–chief executive officer and chief medical officer, Dr. James R. Baker Jr. It stated:

> The current situation relative to epinephrine auto-injectors has given us pause. FARE is committed to leading the charge for improving access and affordability to lifesaving drugs like epinephrine, while promoting competition and innovation in the market. To do this, we must build new relationships with partners and policymakers who share our desire to truly put patients first. FARE views a single child's injury or death because they cannot afford an auto-injector as a preventable tragedy. We have therefore decided that until meaningful competition exists in the epinephrine auto-injector space we will no longer accept donations from companies marketing these devices.[45]

While implicitly taking a step back from Mylan, which was the only company marketing a branded epinephrine auto-injector in the United States at the time, the last sentence of this statement underscores FARE's commitment to market-based solutions to food allergy.

The language also leaves much to interpretation. It does not specify the metric for "meaningful competition" or the "we" who has decided on this benchmark. Further, the scope of the statement is notable for how narrowly it defines the sources of financial support that are now off-limits. FARE won't accept money from "the epinephrine auto-injector space," a qualifier that excludes companies who market other kinds of devices and medications for the treatment of food allergy, like allergy immunotherapy or diagnostics. This disavowal of the pharmaceutical industry is thus narrow in scope; it still allows the organization a great deal of leeway in accepting donations from other companies in the pharmaceutical industry.

Direct financial relationships between Mylan and at least one nonprofit, the Asthma and Allergy Network (AAN), reportedly continued into September 2016 despite the EpiPen's pricing controversy. While Mylan was faced with public pressure over the price of the EpiPen, it was also pursuing a new campaign that would force insurers to pay for the full cost of the device. In an interview with the *New York Times*, the CEO of AAN acknowledged receiving "compensat[ion] to ensure access to epinephrine" while leading a campaign to add the EpiPen to a federal list of preventive medical services that insurers would be required to cover in full. This would protect users from copays and deductibles while requiring insurance companies to pay for the device in full, no matter the price. Such extra spending by insurance companies could later be passed on to all of an insurer's customers in the form of higher copays, deductibles, and monthly premium payments. By contrast, one of the leading scientific allergy organizations, the American College of Allergy, Asthma, and Immunology, offered a statement through their medical director that there was "no way that we could do that." FARE, while still holding equity in Aimmune, said of working on this project with Mylan, "We just don't feel, given the structuring, that it fully aligned with our role as a patient advocate" through its CEO. While it is difficult to determine exactly which organizations received support from the outside, and exactly how much, Mylan did share in the same September 16 *New York Times* article that it had donated $1.8 million in 2016 to nine organizations "in support of anaphylaxis awareness and education initiatives," including $227,500 for preventive medical services advocacy.[46]

Close relationships with the pharmaceutical industry persisted in the wake of the EpiPen pricing scandal. FARE's website in June 2020 did not list Mylan as a supporter, but it did list Kaléo. It also lists Aimmune Therapeutics, Genentech (maker of a number of costly injectable drugs for autoimmune conditions and asthma, commonly experienced by people with food allergy), DBV Technologies (an allergy immunotherapy company and competitor to Aimmune), and Janssen Pharmaceutical Companies (a division of Johnson & Johnson), in addition to a number of specialty food companies.[47] The Food Allergy and Anaphylaxis Connection Team, or FAACT, lists scientific organizations, food industry groups, and pharmaceutical companies as supporters, including DBV Technologies, Aimmune Therapeutics, Genentech, Kaléo, Mylan, medical technology startup Nima, Sanofi Genzyme, Regeneron, and Takeda. Uniquely, FAACT specifies which programs the funding from each company supports. Mylan supports numerous education, advocacy, and networking programs, including "FAACT's education and peer programs, which includes Camp TAG (The Allergy Gang), Food Industry & Research Summit, Leadership Summit, Civil Rights Advocacy Program, and Behavioral Health Resource Program."[48] The AAN disclosed support from AstraZeneca, Amgen, DBV Technologies, Mylan, Novartis, GlaxoSmithKline, Sanofi Genzyme, and Regeneron for their "Allergy & Asthma Day Capitol Hill 2020," an annual lobbying event that was held virtually in 2020 as a result of the Covid-19 pandemic.[49]

These relationships underscore an important dimension of the reproductive politics of food allergic living, namely the privatization of care. On its face, decisions to accept industry support may appear simply to concern the relationship between nonprofit organizations and the for-profit pharmaceutical industry. They also reflect the faith that markets for pharmaceuticals will appropriately regulate access to treatment and that no move toward broader public funding for health care and disabled people is necessary. Yet bigger markets also create more options—and more complexity—for individuals and caretakers to navigate in the future. Choosing appropriate tools to care for themselves and their loved ones then requires more behind-the-scenes self-education. At the end of the day, growing markets as a solution to the high cost of treatments for food allergic people maintains the status quo of access to medical care.

Despite the media blitz singling out Mylan as a bad actor in the pharmaceutical industry, the company maintained close ties with some food allergy advocacy organizations throughout 2016 and beyond. Those that eschewed ongoing support, like FARE, nonetheless expressed confidence in the market system in which it participated, and the organization recommitted to supporting the development of larger and more complex markets. In the end, little changed. Mother-advocate, advocacy organization, and pharmaceutical company appeals to drug access and the well-being of children supported the continuation of a high-priced, market-based system for delivering essential health care to food allergic people. This episode thus maintained the market organization of U.S. health care and the symbiotic relationships between pharmaceutical companies and patient advocacy nonprofits rather than rupturing them. Advocacy organizations navigating this terrain were in a double bind: They could operate on behalf of food allergic people in part as a result of the support of industry actors, but the decisions of those industry actors create difficult economic situations for food allergic people and their kin.

The Rise of the Clinical Network

The double bind faced by nonprofits persists in another popular model for food allergy advocacy organizations that was not obviously affected by the EpiPen pricing controversy: offering support for the development of new pharmaceutical products. This often takes the form of research funding for clinical investigators or granting access to networks of patients, providers, or researchers to research sponsors, including pharmaceutical companies. This model has been increasingly emphasized by food allergy advocacy organizations since the passage of stock epinephrine laws in all fifty U.S. states. Such work would appear to benefit patients in an uncomplicated way; indeed, patient involvement in pharmaceutical research has indeed been treated as an uncomplicated good by other STS scholars.[50]

However, accelerating research on drugs that will be introduced into the U.S. treatment market extends the logic of private consumption as a primary solution to public health problems, much like the privatization of care in the home that I discussed in chapters 2 and 3. Aiding clinical research by facilitating participant recruitment, for example, shortens the time it takes to create new markets for their sale and use, which reduces the cost for companies of developing new drugs. This section examines the aims and proposed benefits of one such program that is exceptionally well documented in public-facing materials, FARE's Clinical Network.

FARE's Clinical Network was founded in June 2015, well before the May 2016 completion of state-level stock epinephrine campaigns and slightly over a year before the EpiPen pricing scandal hit. As stock epinephrine became less of a focus in food allergy advocacy, the network became a larger part of the organization's messaging. It is designed as a two-sided registry of centers carrying out food allergy treatment research and people with food allergies to facilitate enrollment into clinical trials and to vet trial centers on behalf of people with food allergy. The centers side includes a number of teaching hospitals where high-profile researchers conduct medical research on food allergy. The other side is a registry of people with food allergy who are pre-screened and willing to participate in clinical trials.

As FARE described it on their website in June 2020, the Clinical Network had five primary objectives that emphasized novelty, knowledge, and efficiency:

raise the quality of care for food allergic patients nationwide

reduce discrepancies in care across providers

make comprehensive care accessible and available for all food
   allergic patients

investigate the biology of food allergy

develop new therapies and new diagnostics for food allergy[51]

The network underwent an expansion, announced in June 2020, that further differentiated participating centers according to whether their focus lay in novel research or in everyday patient care.[52] After the expansion, it included forty-four sites in twenty-two states and

Washington, D.C. The centers had already collectively participated in forty-four major clinical trials by June 2020. Soon after the expansion was announced, the program website further explained the ambition of the network in this way: "By increasing the locations available for multi-site clinical trials, the expanded FARE Clinical Network will facilitate the development of new therapies, diagnostics and prevention strategies and will make experimental treatments more accessible to a broader number of those living with potentially life-threatening food allergies."[53]

The public face of the network emphasizes sharing as a crucial activity for clinical research, and an activity that both researchers and food allergic people should engage in to advance the development of treatment options. Member medical institutions have access to a patient registry, created in 2017, and a data commons portal to facilitate participant recruitment and gain access to study data. In turn, institutional researchers are expected to contribute to these data banks: Members "will contribute to the development of the data commons . . . through privacy-protected data sharing." The landing page invites people with food allergies to "share your food allergy story with researchers." People browsing the page are enticed to join the registry with notices like "your life holds important clues for food allergy researchers," "breakthroughs are possible from your living room," and "the registry enables ground-breaking food allergy research collaborations." The patient registry page explicitly links participation to the provision of data to industry, explaining that the platform "encourages collaboration between leading food allergy research institutions, clinicians, pharmaceutical companies, and others seeking to deepen their understanding of the everyday burden caused by food allergy, improve patient care and education, and lead the way for the discovery of better treatments and a cure."[54] By signing up for the registry as a potential study participant or using it as a clinical investigator, users can expect to advance—indeed, speed up—the food allergy treatment research conducted in both academic and industry contexts.

However, there is a deeper story—and higher-value stakes—behind this patient registry/clinical network matrix than just an altruistic tool to aid medical researchers to get new treatments to users faster. In the pharmaceutical industry, one of the biggest hurdles in research and development is participant recruitment to studies.[55] This process involves finding individuals who meet stringent standards of health, have used minimal medications to treat the condition under study in recent weeks or months, and have symptoms that are neither too severe nor too mild. This process is so exacting that there is now a global clinical trials recruitment industry, which often opens up poor people, especially in the global south, to exploitation to develop drugs they often could never afford to use once fully developed.[56] After passing biological and life history screenings, participants must be able and willing to participate in the rigorous schedules, routines, and technical tasks necessary to be given or self-administer an experimental drug. Experimental drugs are often not offered in their final, commercial form, and can thus be more difficult to take. Finally, participants must be able to keep up with numerous physician check-ins and be prepared to potentially spend time and money dealing with any adverse effects of treatment.[57]

Streamlining participant screening by centralizing and sharing participant health status and willingness to enroll promises to reduce the time it takes to complete a study and reduce the direct costs to companies running the studies. This is the value proposition of FARE's research data and registry platform. By making screening more efficient, it promises to ultimately shorten the time it takes to receive marketing clearance for new products from regulatory agencies like the FDA. Recruitment is especially key for many food allergy treatments currently under development in part as a result of the complexity of administration. New treatments under investigation and just reaching the market include food additives with precise administration protocols and skin patches that frequently trigger adverse effects, making administration more nuanced than simply taking a pill or injecting a liquid. Most protocols also screen out potential participants with conditions related to allergy, like asthma, that could make possible adverse effects more dangerous. Patient registries could thus play an outsized role in reducing the time to market for new food allergy therapies. Yet at the same time, companies do not seem to be required to make specific promises about the prices of new products in proportion to the resources saved by using the system. They are allowed to save time and money with the help of nonprofits like FARE while offering nothing certain to food allergic people in return.

The specificities of many food allergy treatment protocols currently and recently under development underscore that the benefits of patient registries accrue to companies. At the same time, the treatments themselves produce new forms of care work for users and their caretakers. Many therapeutic agents for food allergy treatment are derived from food and thus present comparatively fewer technical challenges to produce than many other types of new drugs, such as those based on food allergy immunotherapy (described in chapter 2). Efficient participant enrollment is therefore a relatively larger slice of the cost of conducting food allergy studies. However, studies for food-derived products like Aimmune Therapeutics' Palforzia and DBV Technologies' Viaskin Peanut report numerous adverse effects, some of which required medical attention. In 2019, *Science* magazine reported, for example, that across two studies of AR101, the investigational version of Aimmune's Palforzia, seventy-four participants out of seven hundred needed to use epinephrine, and 20 percent dropped out of the studies as a result of adverse effects.[58] In the PEPITES phase 3 study, 59.7 percent of participants in the treatment arm who received the Viaskin Peanut skin patch experienced adverse events, most commonly skin swelling and irritation at the patch site; 34.7 percent of the nontreatment control group experienced such events as well.[59] To enroll in studies with such high rates of adverse events, participants need to have work or school schedules that are both predictable, to account for regularly scheduled treatments and doctor's visits, and also flexible, in case of discomfort or an emergency like a rash or anaphylactic reaction. Participants, or their caretakers in the case of children, must be prepared to care for reactive bodies. The high rates of anaphylaxis and skin irritation suggest that frequent discomfort and advice about managing symptoms made up the day-to-day experience of many participating in these trials.

Rapid recruitment, no matter the tools used to achieve it, can also create its own kind of news, contributing to the development of a market before a product is even ready for sale. Researchers I

interviewed during my ethnographic research called the phenomenon "conditioning the market." Conditioning the market involves
releasing a steady stream of relatively unimportant individual news
items to slowly generate excitement about the future release of drugs
by those who might be eligible to use them. Clinical trials milestones,
like hitting recruitment thresholds and study initiation, are often
announced by pharmaceutical companies and by academic research
centers' newsletters in press releases and e-mail blasts. From there,
they are sometimes amplified by technology and science reporters in
both specialty and mainstream news outlets. In the food allergy space,
patient advocacy organizations also amplify company announcements of milestones. This genre of communication is distinct from
the kind of promissory hype that scholars like Nik Brown, Michael
Fortun, and Kaushik Sunder-Rajan previously analyzed in investor-
facing communications.[60] Rather than promising, or not promising,
the achievement of certain spectral financial milestones, conditioning
the market through clinical trials announcements reports on real activities involving physical drugs and actual human bodies. Speeding
up enrollment and other milestones with the help of patient registries
and clinical networks, like those offered by FARE, can increase the frequency of good news, creating an aura of success around companies
developing drugs before their products even hit the market.

The emerging forms of support for pharmaceutical development
offered by food allergy advocacy organizations, like FARE's clinical
network and patient registry systems, tighten the double binds of
food allergy advocacy. Accelerating treatments for food allergy would
appear to be beneficial to food allergic people. However, it provides
a variety of benefits to the companies developing new drugs while
trial participants (who may also be future users) are called on to be
personally responsible for carrying out study protocols and to subsidize company efforts with their own time, money, and bodies. While
disavowing funding from Mylan because of their market dominance,
FARE, via its clinical network and patient registry, is facilitating the
market-building efforts of other companies for other products. Although one company, Mylan, has been excluded from the circuits of
favor that might be expected in return for large donations, a mutually

shared interest in quickly developing new "drugs for life" for people with food allergy is reaffirmed.[61] What is more, because children are the prime target users for many food allergy treatments and a primary group under study in many commercial food allergy immunotherapy studies, the private effort expended to develop new food allergy therapies is also caught up in the heteronormative and reproductive dynamics of caretaking within food allergy families.

In the end, although some of the specifics changed, the power dynamics between people with food allergy, advocacy organizations, and pharmaceutical companies were barely altered after the EpiPen pricing scandal. Advocacy organizations are still in a double bind that makes them reliant on industry funds for operations and specific initiatives. Their headline efforts include projects like patient registries that provide clear value to industry while appearing to serve more scientific and neutral ends than accepting funding for legislative advocacy and branded awareness events. These partnerships help create new markets for upcoming and existing drugs, cementing the legitimacy of for-profit medicine and largely unregulated drug markets as plausible solutions to the personal and financial challenges of food allergic living. Food allergic people can participate as research subjects but have limited control over the relationships between professionalized advocacy organizations and industry actors who seek to make money from treating their condition. In the case of stock epinephrine bills, close relationships were valuable to drug makers because they helped expand an existing market. In the case of patient registries and clinical networks, the offer of more rapid patient recruitment promises cost savings as a service to companies while simultaneously providing an appearance of altruistic concern for easing the suffering of people with food allergies with too few treatment options. In both cases, advocacy is complicit with an industry's profit-seeking and market-expansion activities while claiming to serve the interests of people with food allergy.

WHAT WORLDS CAN ACTIVISTS MAKE?

The EpiPen pricing scandal and the ongoing relations between food allergy advocacy organizations and pharmaceutical companies are indicative of a mode of patient advocacy that works in alignment with industry interests to grow markets for drugs. Advocacy organizations are in a double bind, reliant on pharmaceutical companies for funding and hoping to maintain friendly relations so that some version of patient experience is heard by companies. Meanwhile, those same drug companies make decisions that hurt the financial well-being of the people whom patient organizations represent. Even a mainstream political crisis about the rapidly rising price of the EpiPen was not enough to fundamentally shake the close relationship between patient advocacy groups and the pharmaceutical industry. While the points of emphasis in the relationship may have changed, they ultimately remained exceedingly close. Food allergy advocacy is likely not the only space in which drug companies provide large sums to professionalized nonprofit organizations that claim to speak on behalf of patients, and where patient organizations in turn invest in awareness campaigns and research programs that ease the way for drug companies to expand markets and develop new products.

There are, of course, exceptions to this model of patient advocacy. Second-wave feminist self-help groups in the 1970s, for example, organized around radical feminist anger at the male-dominated health system of the time focused more on DIY solutions and small-scale, networked interventions, at least early in the decade.[62] Biohacking has opened up new possibilities for health activism. Transfeminist biohackers, for example, are committed to justice in health care access, especially for hormone replacement therapies that constitute part of basic health care for transgender people.[63] The anarchist biohacking group Four Thieves Vinegar Collective has gone so far as to provide instructions for crafting an epinephrine auto-injector at home using supplies widely available at grocery and hardware stores, cutting out pharmacy benefit managers, pharmacies, doctors, nurses, hospitals and clinics, pharmaceutical companies, health insurers, and even pharmaceutical device designers all in one fell swoop.[64]

Yet such attempts to bypass industry actors are not without risk and additional work. Hacking together informal alternatives to expensive and exclusionary medical markets means bypassing regulatory checkpoints, which opens up hackers and inventors to potential legal liability for dispensing medical advice outside proper channels or in the event that someone is injured by their interventions. It also does not entirely insulate users of hacked medical technologies from reliance on the medical device and active pharmaceutical ingredient manufacturers. These companies still provide the hormones and syringes that hackers assemble, although it does bypass many of the middlemen in the system who assemble the basic components into more complex devices, give them brand names, and market them. Perhaps most importantly, engaging in biohacking with minimal risk requires an interest in self-education and personal connections to networks of medical, engineering, and other experts who are willing to potentially put themselves on the line legally to share information about how to bypass the traditional gatekeepers of medical knowledge and care. Not everyone with a chronic condition has the time, interest, or connections to do so. It requires yet more care work for oneself, for loved ones, and for community members. As Leah Lakshmi Piepzna-Samarasinha reminds us, care work does not get done on its own. Who will be responsible for doing the work of care in these workaround systems?[65]

In the case of food allergy advocacy, industry capture of nonprofits like FARE, AAN, KFA, and FAACT seems extensive. The horizon of possibility for these organizations includes advocating for federal and state policy changes that expand pharmaceutical companies' markets and doing some of the research and development work for pharmaceutical partners. Even the perception of a national crisis in drug pricing prompted only a momentary pause in strategy and softly critical comments about the systemic complexity of drug pricing that avoided placing blame on any one individual or company. The memory of this crisis seems exceedingly short lived. On June 4 and 5, 2020, FARE, which still does not disclose any support from Mylan on its website, released a blog post and then a press release publicizing the release of a new report advocating for increased communication about OIT to patients.[66] The justification for this move, according to the press release, was that they were advocating for increased communication "anticipating the impact of FDA approval of Palforzia in expanding patient and physician interest in OIT."[67] Palforzia is the name of the commercial peanut allergy OIT treatment marketed by Aimmune Therapeutics and approved by the FDA in January 2020. Aimmune Therapeutics, as discussed earlier in this chapter, is the pharmaceutical company from which FARE reaped a net investment asset windfall of over $47 million in 2015.

This statement, and others like it, suggest that food allergy advocacy is stuck in a loop where the same type of market solutions continually reappear. An illness can be treated with a drug; nonprofit advocacy organizations build a financial relationship with the maker of the drug; organizations advocate for the expansion of the market and supposedly easier access to the drug for users. Meanwhile, the structures of everyday responsibility for care work remain untouched. Children and families persist as emblems for the cause, but the everyday relations within families, within communities, and with medical markets that shape the conditions of possibility for them to thrive change little, if at all.

What of alternative solutions that do not repeat these patterns of promotion of and financial reliance on the for-profit pharmaceutical industry? What if we took the DIY solution proposed by Four Thieves Vinegar Collective seriously and created (infra)structures for such options to coexist alongside finished medical products? Or, more radically, why don't food allergy advocacy organizations support universal, single-payer health care coverage in which the government payer organization has the right to negotiate prices and is insulated from industry conflicts of interest? Or how about obligatory nonprofit status for pharmaceutical companies themselves?[68] Such imaginings are themselves still only reformist (still only what is possible within contemporary legal, regulatory, and tax frameworks afforded by U.S. law and policy today) and not radical—fundamentally committed to remaking structures of expertise, power, and circulation in the distribution and delivery of medical care in the country. Yet they would still represent a distinctly different approach to providing broad and affordable access to a medical tool like the EpiPen than the current focus on market making.

More questions thus emerge. How to do health activism otherwise? How to do it in ways that truly make better futures for all by centering cross-community solidarity? When and where and with whom might this be possible? What structures and bureaucratic forms might enable it? What new reproductive politics are possible if market making was abandoned as a realistic remedy—a politics perhaps focusing less on abstract invocations of children and families and offering more concrete ways to redistribute responsibility for care work? In short, where does health activism go from here?

CONCLUSION

ACTIVIST FUTURES

You have now followed me on a journey from the home to the clinic to the halls of Congress to the pages of the *New York Times* and Bloomberg Business News. As a feminist scholar, the choices I made to tell this particular situated story about food allergy experience and advocacy was structured by the old feminist saw: The personal is political. The personal in the stories you have just read concerns what goes on within the private, and economically privatized, space of the nuclear family. In the contemporary United States, the family is a specific social institution shot through with normative ideas about gender, race, class, and nation. It is a site where the structural and personal collide in consequential ways. What happens within families and households managing food allergy, then, is not isolated from the public politics of the condition. The public and private deeply inform each other.

Seen through a critical feminist STS lens, health advocacy work is reproductive. It sustains the family as a privileged space and family members, particularly mothers, as the proper and natural caretakers of children and people with food allergy. Moreover, advocacy work extends the privatization of care through supporting the expansion of for-profit markets for treatments that are administered following the unwritten rules of normative caretaking practices. In short, this book has sought to (re)integrate the family into the politics of health activism while maintaining a critical feminist perspective on the ideological and practical role of the family in the lives of people managing food allergy.

From the moment of diagnosis with food allergy, the personal experience of managing a deadly disease, as an individual or as a parent, shapes the emergent political sensibilities of food allergy activism in the contemporary United States. Understanding how to use epinephrine, reading scientific literature, and advocating for stock epinephrine laws in the halls of state assemblies and the U.S. Congress are all refracted through personal experience, including experiences of fear, confusion, and finding one's own voice as a woman, parent, patient, and advocate. Experience is a crucible for vetting the veracity of biomedical claims about the condition, as early chapters demonstrated. In later chapters, my examination of a handful of specific advocacy actions show how political solutions pursued through legislative advocacy and public awareness campaigns are tied to the experiences of the individuals—mostly white, middle-class women, as well as professionalized advocacy staff and corporate lobbyists—who position the family as an key object of political concern. Finally, the last chapter showed how flexibly children, schools, and families can be invoked to justify (in)action concerning the rising price of drugs and the expansion of pharmaceutical markets. These social activities support the maintenance and domain expansion of normative structures of race, class, gender, and markets, making them integral to family and private life and reinforcing the family as a site for the reproduction of these differentiating and hierarchizing structures.

IMAGINING OTHERWISE

The importance of other health and disability movements in providing legal, bureaucratic, organizational, and rhetorical frameworks for food allergy activism are extensive, although these links were rarely acknowledged or articulated by participants in my research. The emphasis on treatment activism—raising money, awareness, and political will to support the development and distribution of therapeutic drugs—is particularly notable. Food allergy activists in the 2010s owe much to the successful legacy of "drugs into bodies" as a cornerstone of AIDS treatment activism that succeeded in pushing drug companies and federal agencies to accelerate the development of pharmaceutical therapeutics. Food allergy advocacy is comfortably aligned with this paradigm, for example, in supporting expanded access to epinephrine auto-injectors in alliance with Mylan and the establishment of FARE's clinical network and patient registry. As Lisa Diedrich argues, however, "the phrase and practice ['drugs into bodies'] encapsulates a very particular conjuncture of illness–thought–activism in neoliberal times. We are now living the side effects of the success of treatment activism."[1] These side effects include, as several chapters in this book discussed, complicity with the expansion of lucrative private markets for new and existing drugs, silence on rapidly rising drug prices from organizations claiming to represent patients, and the need to rely on pricy specialty foods and home goods as solutions to food allergy.

But to quote more of the same passage by Diedrich: "Could it have been and be otherwise?" Was it—is it—inevitable that providing safety and health for people with food allergy would rely on patriarchal and market-based understandings of the role of the family and the free market in the maintenance of health? Is it necessary to rely on these structures to prepare food allergic children to pursue the "good life"? Writing this conclusion against the backdrop of the Covid-19 pandemic in the fall of 2020 throws into sharper relief how contingent and unnecessary the cruelty of privatized, family-linked care is in the United States.[2] There have been moments in the pandemic when things became so bad that it seemed as though this system must change. In small and too-limited ways, some things did change. In my home state of New York, for example, an executive order from Governor Andrew Cuomo mandated that health insurers cover the cost of Covid-19 testing. However, in the U.S. Congress, the cross-party belief that families ought to be solely responsible for procuring the conditions for life led to the expiration of the first round of expanded unemployment benefits at the end of July 2020. The incoming Biden administration in January 2021 has done little to protect people with either acute or disabling long Covid-19, other than reopening expensive health insurance marketplaces. Here, in a faster-paced fashion, are the same politics of care that govern food allergy activism. Families and individuals are treated as autonomous economic and moral units that ought to manage themselves. Governmental support operates on the assumption that everyone who counts is able to participate in the relevant markets (like the health insurance and job markets), and the only action that is needed to safeguard health is to tweak the markets in minor ways. In the service of this belief, as of September 25, 2020, over 203,000 people have died, and as many as 25 percent of U.S. children do not have enough to eat.[3] By the final days of March 2021, as I complete revisions to this manuscript, the death toll is on pace to triple before the start of summer, currently standing at 548,867.[4]

For health activism to be done otherwise would require a serious reckoning with the interlocking politics of family and health. Health activism that relies on the figure of the mother as defender of children to get things done both relies on and reproduces the gendered organization of care within the family. It also utterly fails in a situation like the Covid-19 pandemic, where the elderly were the first to be hit hard with high mortality rates. Yet appeals to the claim that mothers are the best advocates for children's health persist because they are effective at interpersonal, local, state, and national levels. The stereotype of mother as selfless hero is sometimes the most expedient tool available to those seeking change, and it is therefore understandable that advocates would turn to it to accomplish their goals. However, reliance on this archetype provides an out for lawmakers, regulators, insurers, and employers; it provides them with a way to avoid taking responsibility for improving care infrastructures through policy and government funding. Rights to health can be addressed selectively or partially by design because there is always a family member—a mother, or, in the case of elder care, a daughter—expected to be available to take up the slack if institutionalized mechanisms of care are incomplete.

Relying on mothering and motherhood as a tool for systemic health care change also risks playing into racist pasts about who could be considered an ideal and worthy mother. As Patricia Hill Collins writes, the "traditional" U.S. family ideal is a "privileged exemplar of intersectionality," where systems including gender, race, class, and nation do not exist "as separate systems of oppression" but rather "mutually construct one another."[5] As Collins also notes, the figure of the family is politically adaptable; it has been conscripted to a variety of political aims that otherwise would seem to be in conflict, such as its use by "the conservative right and Black nationalists alike . . . to advance their political agendas."[6] In every context in which it is enlisted to do ideological or political work, the family inserts logics of hierarchy and domination and portrays them as natural and unmovable social facts. Why, then, should the family be a resource in advocacy and activism, when the point of action is to challenge hierarchies and systems of domination, to change the status quo, and to expand freedom and opportunity for those who have so far been denied them?

A meaningful reckoning with the politics of the family as a mediator of health and care would seek to reform or abolish more social institutions than just health care. Dorothy Roberts's body of work vividly examines how medical racism has often operated via the regulation of biological and social reproduction and, by extension, of family composition.[7] Family composition has in turn been enforced through the manipulation of cash and noncash state benefits, including housing, food benefits, and health care, to poor families, who are also disproportionately families of color.[8] Across her projects, she has linked the maintenance of the family via biomedicine to the profession of social work and to the growing criticism of police violence against Black people. Roberts argues, for example, that police abolition must be accompanied by "abolishing family regulation." Medicine and public health are key levers of the enforcement of the nuclear family ideal, offering both carrots and sticks to support the maintenance of the family.[9] To abolish nonmedical institutions, like the police, in which Black people are subjected to physical and mental harms—to be later fixed, often only temporarily and at great cost to individuals and society at large through the tools of biomedicine—requires an examination of what exactly they are designed to defend. The role played by law enforcement in shoring up the security of some (gender-normative, white) families, by safeguarding the holding and transfer of private wealth and property, while preventing undesirable (Black, Latinx, Indigenous, other nonwhite, queer, and disabled) families from accessing such resources suggests just how fundamental the nuclear family plays in contemporary U.S. society.

A more critical consciousness of the connections between family, health, race, and gender may be brewing among food allergy advocates in the exceptionally catastrophic summer of 2020. As I was finishing this book, I came across an essay from a food allergy parent that addressed the problem of how to advance food allergy activism in light of interlocking forms of power and oppression. Published on the Food Equality Initiative website and signed by Emily Brown, the essay reflects on how to hear and include Black children, adults, and families in food allergy activism. Brown published the essay on June 8, 2020, as Covid-19 sank its teeth deeper into U.S. society, and as the country entered its second wave of daily protests against police violence after the killings of Breonna Taylor and George Floyd. Brown writes:

> For far too long, white-led patient advocacy organizations have been hyper-focused on alleviating the challenges of the privileged and have failed to listen to the needs and priorities of patients who bear the overwhelming burden of the disease.
>
> These failures reinforce health disparities that manifest in limited access to care and treatments, allergen-free foods, and emergency epinephrine.
>
> Black children with food allergies are more likely to die from anaphylaxis than white children with food allergies. These Black Lives Matter!
>
> Our voices, our families, and our health can no longer be ignored. We must take action.[10]

While still centering children and families, Brown begins to unpack questions of whose families and lives are prioritized by food allergy advocacy as it operates today. After being "ignored" by a primarily white organization when she was in need of assistance, she formed her own organization to focus on Black families and children. In her lived experience, appeals to unmarked children and families in food allergy awareness and advocacy efforts were too often synonymous with families who were white and wealthy.

I would go one step further than Brown to argue that decentering the whiteness she identifies in her post requires dismantling the reproductive politics of the family that informs food allergy advocacy work in this country. I am heartened by her critique of the whiteness of food allergy advocacy because dislodging the nuclear family from health research and politics, and the whiteness that unmarked appeals to family typically encode, must be a coalitional project. The genealogies of feminist, AIDS, and radical disability activism that I have cited offer ways to think the body in opposition to capitalism, heteronormativity, and racism—although they each also offer cautionary tales of how advocacy organizations can be co-opted to support these oppressive structures as well. However, no one drug, no single standard for disability benefits, no umbrella expectation for a universal model of "good" care will accommodate every person with food allergy, let alone every person managing a chronic illness or disability. Any such movement must be based on intersectional analysis of how both health and the family operate as social institutions that direct the exercise of interlocking systems of power, like race, gender, wealth, and nationality. As Brown's analysis suggests, the necessity of these expansive demands holds true in the specific case of food allergy activism as much as it does in other aspects of everyday life and at other scales of analysis.

This book has offered one example of how such an analysis might proceed. I have taken a critical view of health activism informed by feminist and disability justice thinkers. I did not take claims about the intent to do good at face value; rather, I investigated how such claims influenced policy and everyday life through actual awareness and legislative campaigns, pricing decisions, and organizational structures. I end this project interested not only in how people involved in health advocacy work manage the everyday challenges of chronic conditions but also what and whom the experiences and platforms of leading activists do not include. Asking who is left out is a crucial gesture of feminist methodology that often exposes uncomfortable truths. With this in the back of my mind, I sought to connect what happens in the private space of the food allergy home to the public stages of advocacy to examine who is left out of the benefits of advocacy if advocates themselves come to their work with a situated experience of the world. Situating, as Donna Haraway had taught feminist scholars, is a necessary tool for telling fuller truths about the world, but any individual's situated truth is still only partial. The account I offer was also shaped by the partial perspectives I encountered in my research—that is, by the fact that the participants involved and organizations examined were primarily white and middle class, and all based in the United States.

The version of health activism I document in this book was also shaped by the fact that the individuals and groups discussed were mostly narrowly focused on how to make potentially life-threatening, everyday struggles a little easier to manage. This "emergency time"[11] frame is a common context for health activism in the United States today, but it does not provide much space for considering how health activism motivated by the experience of a specific condition or illness could be done in a way that prioritizes expansive societal changes over minor tweaks that fail to challenge the status quo. My research participants and the organizations I examined by and large did not ask how to do things otherwise on a grand scale. Rather, most asked what would work if we accept the state of the world as largely unchangeable and focus on these small issues of direct concern to our lives and the lives of people we are directly connected to.

Make no mistake: It is difficult to imagine otherwise, especially in a time of crisis, be it the individual crisis of adapting to life with a deadly disease or the collective crisis of a global pandemic. I write during an urgent moment for health care and families in the United States, and in its wake, the future seems to telescope away, to blend into the vague horizon where we cannot possibly predict what happens next. When we recognize that nothing seems to change despite the best of intentions, it is tempting to feel that we are living in a moment akin to the Dithering in Kim Stanley Robinson's science fiction novel 2312: a time of inaction in the face of obvious and interlocking environmental and social crises.[12] However, in this world, the embodied world, not the world of fiction, we have the resources to imagine—and, certainly, in twenty-first-century United States, to provide—care beyond mothering, concern beyond the immediate family, comfort that does not reify whiteness, medicines available to all, and solidarity among all caretakers. Health activism roots the pursuit of a better life in embodied experience, providing important clues about how to imagine health, bodies, family, and community otherwise. Yet any single community or campaign offers only a specific, partial, and ultimately incomplete map for what comes next. It is in thinking via lived experience, with history, across communities, and with people who have been so far left out, that robust imaginings of better futures have any hope of becoming lived reality.

ACKNOWLEDGMENTS

Whether this research would result in a book was uncertain for long stretches of time. As a piece of scholarship, its fate has twisted and turned with my own path as a worker. Like my academic career, it moved forward in fits and starts when I had small windows of opportunity to work on it. This project began as a doctoral dissertation at Cornell University, but I completed writing in 2015 and 2016 while living in New York City, making rent by teaching at the Brooklyn Institute for Social Research and working with a group of entrepreneurial colleagues involved with biotechnology startups Allovate Therapeutics and Intrommune Therapeutics. Thanks to a fortuitously timed e-mail from a colleague in the summer of 2017, the opportunity to join the Technology, Culture, and Society (TCS) faculty at NYU Tandon School of Engineering presented itself. I jumped at the chance to be an adjunct instructor with a community of incredibly talented and diverse engineering students. In immediate terms, I mainly needed academic library access and my own health insurance, although it turned out to be perhaps the best decision I have made in recent years. Adjuncting doesn't fully pay the bills, so I continued to work through an LLC I created, Implosion Labs, consulting for clients including international corporate design research teams and United States–based nonprofits on research strategy, original research, and white papers. The current chapter of my work life, and the space to finally finish this book, began in September 2019, when, through a series of unlikely events, I joined the NYU Tandon TCS faculty full-time, first temporarily and since 2020 in a renewable, full-time, contract position.

Although I have in many ways now made it by landing a full-time academic job, the conditions of academic labor represented by this path point to an industry in crisis and decline. It was not clear whether I would be able to make any sort of career doing academic work from 2015, when I began applying to post-PhD academic jobs, until March 2020, when I signed my first renewable contract with NYU the day before the Covid-19 pandemic lockdown began and a hiring freeze started on campus. I felt committed to seeing the book project through, so I continued the process of rewriting, revising, and seeking a book contract even when precariously employed.

In the end, I am glad that I worked on this book through precarity. The book would have turned out differently had I won the lottery of a prestigious postdoc or a tenure-track job right after finishing my PhD. My strategies, the timeline for completing the book, and my sense of relevant scholarly communities would have looked very different had I been able to go a more traditional route. It would have been easier, surely, and the book might have been published sooner. Stable academic employment would have saved me both financial anxiety and anxious heartache that something I was good at—being an academic—was something I was preparing to leave behind. Throughout most of the writing process, I was mourning the colleagues, mentors, and students I was afraid I would be forced to part ways with. Yet this book is immeasurably better for my work with academia-skeptical political theorists at the Brooklyn Institute for Social Research; for my many conversations about editorial policies and radical publishing with editors at Verso, who lent the institute space to hold classes; for living in a West Indian neighborhood in New York City not because I had to for a short-term job but because I chose to live near family after growing up mostly around white people as a light-skinned Black woman; for learning about bottom-up political action through my partner's political volunteering work; for working inside the belly of the capitalist beast and finding a way through that allowed me to maintain most of my integrity. It would be a more disciplinary and disciplined text without these experiences. It would be much more boring.

Because this project followed me through so many complicities, institutions, and friendships, I have a long list of thanks. First, I wish to thank many colleagues at Cornell STS and beyond, starting with my dissertation committee members, Michael Lynch, Sara Pritchard, and Marina Welker; my first-year advisor who helped me navigate many confusing situations, Bruce Lewenstein; and reader Stacey Langwick in Cornell's anthropology department. In addition to all the work that a dissertation committee typically does in shaping new scholars and their scholarship, their patience and support transformed several seemingly impossible situations into navigable problems. I owe Stephen Hilgartner a depth of thanks for the opportunity to work with him as a teaching assistant and for his frank mentorship in graduate classes and office hours. Rachel Prentice indelibly shaped my entry into the medical anthropology/STS nexus, and I forever owe her a debt for that. Ronald Kline remains one of the kindest and most generous senior colleagues I have ever met, and I know that I am joined by many of my fellow Cornell STS graduates in extending him gratitude. He created space for me to think beyond my primary areas of scholarship and introduced me to the history of cyborgs and cybernetics—topics that have sustained me both intellectually and financially more times than I can count. I also thank all of my graduate school colleagues and coconspirators, especially my two sets of cohort mates, Judd Anderman, Owen Marshall, Kasia Tolwinski, and Alexis Walker, and Shoan-Yin Cheung and Enongo Lumumba-Kasongo, as well as Cornell graduate school friends and cothinkers beyond my STS cohorts, including Lisa Avron, Charis Boke (a continued and necessary presence in my intellectual life), Mary Beth Deline, Vinny Ialenti, Jess Polk, and Emma Zuroski. Finally, I extend thanks to several other scholars beyond my department whose wise feedback and advice helped advance the project at crucial moments, including Faye Ginsburg, Rayna Rapp, and the rest of the Science Studies Writing Group at NYU circa 2014–15; fellow food allergy researcher Matthew Smith; and Joan Brumberg, for deepening my engagement with history of medicine when I worked as her teaching assistant.

After my PhD, the list gets longer. At the Brooklyn Institute for Social Research, my longest affiliation second only to grad school, I am indebted to Ajay Singh Chaudhaury and Suzy Schneider for creating a truly unique intellectual community that sustains my soul. I also thank my friend of the heart and Brooklyn Institute comrade Rebecca Ariel Porte, poet and literary scholar extraordinaire who makes this world a better place simply by her existence in it; I am on tenterhooks for the end of the pandemic when we can eat soup in Brooklyn together again. I sincerely thank my startup colleagues at Allovate and Intrommune, Erick Berglund, Michael Nelson, Bill Reisacher, and Kate Rochlin, for taking a chance on me and teaching me that thinking strategically is a skill that I am quite good at. I thank fellow medical anthropologist Amber Benezra for thinking to reach out to me about teaching at NYU in 2017, and for the friendship and leadership she embodied while we taught together in STS. My most heartfelt thanks go to my many collaborators, clients, and friends with whom I worked on contract and Implosion Labs projects from 2017 to 2019, especially Liz DeLuca, Daniel Kelley, Jordan Kraemer, Anne Lin. Deep thanks go out as well to my colleagues, current and former, at NYU Tandon in the TCS department, including my department chair and enthusiastic advocate Jonathan Soffer, along with Ahmed Ansari, Tega Brain, Amber Benezra, Luke DuBois, Jean Gallagher, Jim Lewis, Melissa Maldonado-Salcedo, Jim Lewis, and Mona Sloane.

One of the wonderful things about leaving my home university's college town after finishing coursework in my third year was that it pushed me to build a network beyond Cornell and beyond what I was trained to think of as "my field." The many workshop groups, conference panels, and academic society service projects I took on were joyful work that introduced me to colleagues who shaped my life in many meaningful ways. I owe some of the biggest thanks to Nayantara Sheoran Appleton, who inducted me into service work in the Society for Medical Anthropology (SMA) in 2014, and Elizabeth Chin, who brought me into her orbit via the Wakanda University project in 2018. Both Nayantara and Elizabeth taught me how to inhabit the field of anthropology as a woman of color without losing hope or vitality, and they continue to be treasured mentors and and friends. Many thanks to all of my other colleagues over the years in SMA Special Interest Group leadership and the SMA executive board, who also created a home base in the field for me. Thanks go out as well to collaborators on Society for the Social Studies of Science projects, especially Joan Donovan and Christy Spackman, and Kim Fortun for the invitation, even though our project about the marginality of certain groups of scholars fizzled before completion as a result of our own precarity at the time. A long list of people have also, through ongoing friendship or just a well-timed phrase, made it feel like writing an academic book and continuing to do academic research are worthwhile endeavors. These include Sareeta Amrute, Charles Briggs, Dána-Ain Davis, Andrea Dietrich, Laura Forlano (dear friend, mentor, and collaborator on the next book), Adriana Garriga-López (your well-timed assurance that I deserved "dignified work" after a 2017 conference panel sustained me for years), Mar Hicks, Jacklyn Lacey, Sameena Mulla, E. Thorkelson, Meredith Whittaker, and the ever-honest witches of the Anthro Cauldron.

Thanks also to the many readers of and respondents to book chapters and other writing who helped me get to this point over the years. On my way to the PhD, these included the Cornell STS students writing group; all of the participants in the Dietary Innovation and Disease Conference in Venice, Italy, in 2016, which happily introduced me to the ever-inspiring Emily Contois; Eugene Raikhel, as editor of *Somatosphere* as well as a gracious behind-the-scenes champion of many aspects of my work; colleagues I met through NYU's Media, Culture, and Communication department during my dissertation, especially Beza Merid and Tamara Kneese; and the Writing the Body NYU graduate student writing group, especially Emily Lim Rogers. In the years since, I owe gratitude especially to Rob Horning, my editor at Real Life and quietly editor to an entire generation of (mostly digital) STS scholars, much to the advantage of all of our work, and Nathan Jurgenson for creating and sustaining this and other spaces for misfit STSers like me; to my colleagues at the AI Now institute, especially Theodora Dryer, Elizabeth Kaziunas, and Sarah Myers West for creating space to engage with my decidedly non-AI-related work; all of the Rensselaer Polytechnic Institute STS department graduate students circa 2017–21 for both ongoing friendship and direct engagement with my research and writing, especially Hined Rafeh; Theresa MacPhail, for productive, just-post-PhD feedback and brainstorming; Nick Seaver, for both exchanging work over the years and for spicy back channels; and Winifred Tate, for a late-stage gut check that I really was on to something with the trajectory of this book. Thank you as well to the editors and reviewers at *Medicine Anthropology Theory* and *Catalyst: Feminism, Theory, Technoscience* for developing earlier versions of two chapters of this book, especially Banu Subramaniam, who patiently led me through the editorial process for my article at *Catalyst* during a particularly chaotic time in my career.

This research was supported by a variety of internal and external funding. Research travel and materials were made possible by a Doctoral Dissertation Research Improvement Grant from the National Science Foundation (award SES-1430489), a Cornell University Society for the Humanities Graduate Student Humanities Travel Research Grant, and a Cornell University Graduate Research Travel Grant. Generous support for my time at Cornell was provided by a one-year SUNY Diversity Fellowship via the Department of Communication, one year of Sage Fellowship provided by Cornell University via the Department of Science and Technology Studies, a Cornell University Provost Diversity Fellowship, two semesters of support from the Cornell University Knight Institute for Writing in the Disciplines for teaching two first-year writing seminars, and three semesters of teaching assistant support from the Department of Science and Technology Studies.

Finally, my deepest thanks to the folks most directly involved with producing this book. Thank you to my amazing editor at the University of Minnesota Press, Jason Weidemann. What other academic press editor shows up at a conference panel of all graduate students he doesn't know just to learn about fresh work? Since 2014, when he saw my first American Anthropological Association conference presentation less than a year into my research, Jason has believed in this project and encouraged me as a scholar and writer. No one has done more in my career to keep me focused on why my scholarship matters and to provide motivation to keep going. Thank you as well to the rest of the University of Minnesota Press staff, especially Zenyse Miller, who led work on the administrative processes that made this book possible. My thanks to my family, especially my parents, Bianca St. Louis and Ernie Glabau, and baby sis Tiala Glabau, who supported me through the sometimes confounding process of getting a PhD and working in academia. They taught me that I deserve respect from others and kept me grounded in this most ungrounding of professions. Finally, thank you to my partner, Peter Rawlings, with whom I've shared my entire adult life, and who is truly my better half. Any good political instincts I may have I owe to him, the loyalest and kindest of companions. Nothing makes me more excited than becoming parents together in six short weeks.

NOTES

INTRODUCTION

1. U.S. Food and Drug Administration, "January 31, 2020 Approval Letter—PALFORZIA," 1.

2. Blankenship, "Aimmune's Controversial Peanut Allergy Med."

3. Smith, "FDA Approves Aimmune's Palforzia OIT."

4. Kids with Food Allergies, "Breaking News: FDA Approves Palforzia."

5. Children's Hospital of Philadelphia, "CHOP's Food Allergy Research Highlighted Following FDA's Approval of Palforzia," February 7, 2020, https://www.chop.edu/news/chop-s-food-allergy-research-highlighted-following-fda-s-approval-palforzia.

6. Aimmune Therapeutics, "FDA Approves Aimmune's PALFORZIA™ as First Treatment for Peanut Allergy," January 31, 2020, https://ir.aimmune,com/news-releases/news-release-details/fda-approves-aimmunes-palforziatm-first-treatment-peanut-allergy.

7. U.S. Food and Drug Administration, "January 31, 2020 Approval Letter—PALFORZIA," 6–7.

8. Cooper, *Family Values.*

9. Marx and Engels, *Marx–Engels Reader;* Engels, *Origin of the Family;* Firestone, *Dialectic of Sex;* Hochschild and Machung, *Second Shift;* Federici, *Caliban and the Witch.*

10. Federici and Austin, *New York Wages for Housework Committee.*

11. Davis, *Women, Race, and Class;* hooks, *Feminist Theory;* Collins, "Black Women and Motherhood."

12. Roberts, *Shattered Bonds.*

13. Bridges, *Reproducing Race.*

14. Akrich, "From Communities of Practice"; Callon and Rabeharisoa, "Research 'in the Wild'"; Rabeharisoa and Callon, "Involvement of Patients' Associations."

15. Murphy, *Seizing the Means of Reproduction;* Hester, *Xenofeminism.*

16. Epstein, "Construction of Lay Expertise"; Epstein, *Impure Science.*

17. Hewett, "Talkin' 'bout a Revolution."

18. Martin, "The End of the Body?"; Martin, *Flexible Bodies;* Anderson and Mackay, *Intolerant Bodies;* Biss, *On Immunity.*

19. Von Pirquet, trans. and qtd. in Jackson, *Allergy,* 38.

20. Jackson, *Allergy.*

21. Smith, *Another Person's Poison.*

22. Jackson, *Allergy;* Smith, *Another Person's Poison.*

23. Jerschow et al., "Fatal Anaphylaxis."

24. Waggoner, "Parsing the Peanut Panic."

25. Jackson, *Allergy,* 74. The field of allergy and immunology also has a rich literature of internalist histories of allergy and allergy immunotherapy. These histories are passed down informally in medical resident training programs, like one I attended during this research, as well as in conference talks and published papers. Preeminent allergist Robert Wood, for example, opens his 2016 *JAMA* article, "New Horizons in Allergen Immunotherapy," with: "Even though allergen immunotherapy has been studied for more than a century, a great deal remains unknown about this commonly used treatment" (1711). This opening gambit is accompanied by a citation of a 1911 article by Noon, Cantab, and Eng, "Prophylactic Inoculation against Hay Fever."

26. Jones, Burks, and Dupont, "State of the Art."

27. Strathern, *Partial Connections;* Haraway, "Situated Knowledges."

28. Chapter 4 discusses in detail the common frictions between parent-led and disabled people–led disability and health activism. This has been an especially urgent issue in activism led by or about neurodivergent people, like autism activism. For a brief catalog of the differences in activist frames offered by parents and disabled people, see Carey, Block, and Scotch, "Sometimes Allies."

29. Haraway, "Situated Knowledges"; Hartsock, "Feminist Standpoint."

30. Latour, "Why Has Critique Run Out of Steam?" Latour characterizes "matters of concern" as a third way between facts and unrestrained critique of everything, and he suggests that it offers a way to critique scientific knowledge while recognizing its basis in real materials and practices. Studying

matters of concern ought to be, as he writes, "a multifarious inquiry launched with the tools of anthropology, philosophy, metaphysics, history, sociology to detect *how many participants* are gathered in a *thing* to make it exist and to maintain its existence" (246). As a difficult-to-define disease, food allergy figures as a matter of concern both because it is something that is of concern to many and because its meaning, nature, and solutions are contested by a wide range of actors who nonetheless take its facticity—its material existence and its consequential effects on those diagnosed with it—as a given.

31. Callon, "Some Elements"; Law, "On the Methods of Long-Distance Control"; Latour, "Give Me a Laboratory."

32. Petryna, "Biological Citizenship"; Petryna, *Life Exposed;* Nguyen, "Antiretroviral Globalism." See also Biehl, *Vita,* and Biehl, "Activist State," for further elaboration of the idea of biological citizenship, situating the phenomenon more specifically in the neoliberalization of the Brazilian state and its health care system.

33. Epstein, "Construction of Lay Expertise"; Epstein, *Impure Science;* Fortun, *Advocacy after Bhopal.*

34. Martin, "Anthropology and the Cultural Study of Science," 34.

35. Ahmed, *Living a Feminist Life,* 66.

36. Das and Addlakha, "Disability and Domestic Citizenship"; Lock, *Twice Dead;* Kaufman, *Ordinary Medicine;* Kaufman and Fjord, "Medicare, Ethics, and Reflexive Longevity."

37. Hochschild, "Commodity Frontier."

38. In *Breathing Space,* Gregg Mitman observes that one of the practical and ontological challenges posed by respiratory allergy to twentieth-century biomedicine is the fact that disease-triggering agents are pollen proteins made by plants. These proteins exert agency on the human world as a by-product of their own agency as plant materials whose function it is to move easily and be sticky in order to facility plant reproduction. They are difficult to keep out, remove, and eliminate in a way that is different from pathogens like bacteria and viruses, and to do so required the development of new technologies like air-conditioning units with built-in air filtration mechanisms.

39. This book seeks to make its primary theoretical interventions in STS and medical anthropology. For that reason, disability studies scholars may not find that it offers groundbreaking theoretical development for their field. However, STS and anthropology still stand to learn a great deal about agency and theories of bodily difference from disability studies. Anthropology and disability studies in particular have a contentious relationship because anthropologists often theorize disability as a deficit or flaw, one of the main

rhetorical positions that disability studies has fought since its founding. Furthermore, the aspects of disability history that are discussed in this book are selected as a result of their ethnographic relevance rather than from a desire to offer a complete history of disability for my readers. There may be events or pieces of legislation, for example, that may have made sense to include from a disability history perspective but that were not relevant to the ethnographic events or concerns of my participants, so I left them out.

40. Shakespeare, "Disability, Identity, and Difference"; Shakespeare and Watson, "Defending the Social Model"; Garland-Thomson, "Integrating Disability"; Garland-Thomson, "Feminist Disability Studies."

41. Williamson, *Accessible America*, 71.

42. Williamson, *Accessible America*.

43. Hamraie, *Building Access*, 29.

44. Csordas, "Embodiment," 5.

45. Livingston, *Debility.*

46. Ginsburg and Rapp, "Disability Worlds."

47. Hewett, "Talkin' 'bout a Revolution," 34.

48. Reich, *Calling the Shots.*

49. Kirkland, *Vaccine Court.*

50. Kimura, *Radiation Brain Moms.*

51. Fortun, *Advocacy after Bhopal;* Murphy, *Sick Building Syndrome.*

52. Longino, "Can There Be a Feminist Science?"

53. Epidemiological studies are mixed on the question of whether or not there are racial differences in the incidence of food allergy, and if so, which races may have higher incidences of the condition. See Branum and Lukacs, "Food Allergy among U.S. Children"; Greenhawt et al., "Racial and Ethnic Disparity"; and Jerschow et al., "Fatal Anaphylaxis." However, the degrees of difference found in some studies are likely not large enough to produce a racially uniform community of activists even if these differences turn out to exist.

54. Low, "Maintaining Whiteness."

55. Dow, *Mothering while Black;* Collins, "Black Women and Motherhood"; Mattingly, "Moral Perils."

56. Collins, "It's All in the Family."

57. Shange, *Progressive Dystopia.*

58. Haraway, "Situated Knowledges"; Harding, "Feminist Standpoint Epistemology."

59. Merchant, "Scientific Revolution"; Schiebinger, *Nature's Body;* Shapin and Schaffer, *Leviathan and the Air-Pump;* Sismondo, "Scientific Domains"; Longino, "Can There Be a Feminist Science?"

60. Keller, "Gender/Science System"; Haraway, "Biological Enterprise."

61. Ahmed, "Phenomenology of Whiteness"; Hartigan, "Establishing the Fact of Whiteness"; Yancy, *Look, a White!*

62. Yancy, *Look, a White!*, 7.

63. Ahmed, "Phenomenology of Whiteness," 154.

64. Marcus, "Ethnography in/of the World System"; Choy et al., "New Form of Collaboration."

65. In the interest of respecting the privacy of support group participants, that experience was outside the scope of my research. What I learned through that experience is not included in this text. A small number of group members decided to participate separately in oral history–style interviews.

66. Callon, "Some Elements"; Latour, "Give Me a Laboratory."

67. Glabau, "Morality in Action."

68. Ahmed, "Affective Economies."

69. Haraway, *Staying with the Trouble*, 12.

1. THE MORAL LIFE OF EPINEPHRINE

1. Sicherer and Sampson, "Food Allergy."

2. Jackson, Howie, and Akinbami, "Trends in Allergic Conditions."

3. Jackson, *Allergy;* Raffaetà, "Conflicting Sensory Relationships"; Raffaetà, "Allergy Narratives in Italy"; Nettleton et al., "Food Allergy and Food Intolerance"; Nettleton et al., "Experiencing Food Allergy"; Waggoner, "Parsing the Peanut Panic."

4. Appadura, "Commodities and the Politics of Value."

5. Mauss, "Techniques of the Body"; Scheper-Hughes and Lock, "Mindful Body"; Csordas, "Embodiment"; Geurts, *Culture and the Senses.*

6. Dumit, "Digital Image"; Dumit, "Is It Me or My Brain?"; Rapp, *Testing the Woman;* Healy, "Shaping the Intimate"; Biehl and Moran-Thomas, "Symptom."

7. Csordas, "Embodiment," 5.

8. Zigon and Throop, "Moral Experience," 3.

9. Zigon and Throop, "Moral Experience," 8.

10. Laidlaw, *Subject of Virtue.*

11. Mattingly, *Moral Laboratories.*

12. Cooper, *Family Values.*

13. Simons et al., "International Consensus on (ICON) Anaphylaxis."

14. Gupta et al., "Economic Impact."

15. Dumit, *Drugs for Life;* Kaufman, *Ordinary Medicine.*

16. Koons and Langreth, "How Marketing Turned the EpiPen into a Billon-Dollar Business."

17. Sanofi, "Sanofi US Issues Voluntary Nationwide Recall of Auvi-Q Due to Potential Inaccurate Dosage Delivery," Sanofi News, October 18, 2015, http://www.news.sanofi.us/2015-10-28-Sanofi-US-Issues-Voluntary-Nationwide-Recall-of-Auvi-Q-Due-to-Potential-Inaccurate-Dosage-Delivery.

18. Woodrum, "All Auvi-Q Epinephrine Autoinjectors Recalled."

19. For nuclear preparedness, see Jasanoff, "American Exceptionalism"; Gusterson, "Nuclear Futures"; Masco, "Survival Is Your Business." For bioweapons, see Anderson, "Preemption, Precaution, Preparedness," and Lakoff, "Generic Biothreat." For cancer, see Jain, "Living in Prognosis." For high blood pressure, see Dumit, *Drugs for Life*.

20. Timmermans, *Sudden Death*.

21. Some medical practitioners have challenged the use of quick fixes, including within allergy and immunology. The diabetes and atherosclerosis clinics studied by Annemarie Mol in the Netherlands offer an example of an approach to managing chronic conditions that prioritizes the question of how best to live, rather than only how to address an urgent situation. The clinicians she profiles focus on preventing and slowing the progression of disease by guiding patients toward changing their everyday habits instead of advocating heroic biomedical interventions. Mol calls this the logic of care. Mol, *Body Multiple*; Mol, *Logic of Care*.

22. Kaufman, *Ordinary Medicine*.

23. Simons et al., "World Allergy Organization Anaphylaxis Guidelines."

24. In 2020 a new pharmaceutical option came to market to readjust the underlying immune response that causes peanut allergy and thereby reduce the risk of serious reactions for people with peanut allergy. The first product on the market, Palforzia, is marketed by Aimmune Therapeutics. Aimmune announced FDA market clearance for the product on January 31, 2020. U.S. Food and Drug Administration, "FDA Approves First Drug for Treatment of Peanut Allergy for Children," press release, January 31, 2020, https://www.fda.gov/news-events/press-announcements/fda-approves-first-drug-treatment-peanut-allergy-children.

25. Goffman, *Asylums*, 148–50.

26. Goffman, *Asylums*, 134–35.

27. "Mixing up the milks" was a surprisingly common example discussed among food allergy moms or shared with me as an example of how highly specific food allergy planning had to be. I heard versions of this story numerous times over the course of my research.

28. Cornago, "The Life—and Death—of Giovanni Ciprioano (Age 14)."

29. Antico, "Our First Experience."

30. Rutter, "Remembering Those We Have Lost."

31. Dumit, "Illnesses You Have to Fight to Get"; Landzelius, "Incubation of a Social Movement?"; Panofsky, "Generating Sociability"; Rabeharisoa and Callon, "Involvement of Patients' Associations"; Rabeharisoa, "From Representation to Mediation."

32. Antico, "Our First Experience."

2. WHO IS TO BLAME?

1. Du Toit et al., "Randomized Trial of Peanut Consumption."

2. Du Toit et al., "Randomized Trial of Peanut Consumption"; Du Toit et al., "Allergen Specificity."

3. This is much less true for low-income women of color, especially Black women, than it is for the middle-class and upper-middle-class, mostly white women I encountered in my research. As researchers like Dorothy Roberts, in *Shattered Bonds*, and Bridges, in *Reproducing Race*, illustrate in depth, poor women, and especially poor Black women, have their family structures, roles, and activities heavily policed by the state via agencies like child protective service and public health care—sometimes as early as the moment pregnancy is confirmed by a urine test in a doctor's office. The penalties for failing to conform to normative, middle-class, white notions of good parenting is the constant threat of the removal of children from the mother, home, and family, too often for prolonged lengths of time or permanently. For low-income women, parenting is subject to intensive scrutiny from public agencies. As Bridges puts it, this is an economically stratified form of biopolitical management and violence: "It is not all women whose lives are intervened into and regulated in the way mandated by the Medicaid/PCAP apparatus. . . . Rather, it is only poor, uninsured women's lives that are rendered accessible to state intervention, regulation, and management." Bridges, *Reproducing Race*, 68.

4. Brown, *Plutopia*, makes the link between history of technology and history of the family explicit. In the planned "atomic cities" of the post–World War II era she profiles, Brown shows how sites of technological innovation and intensification also served as petri dishes for the emergent ideology of the small, isolated, compulsorily heteronormative and heterosexual family unit. In the United States in particular, "nuclear" families were mobilized explicitly for the purpose of taming unruly laboring men. The nuclear family is thus historically a site of gendered discipline as well as a highly relevant

site to pay attention to for scholars in STS who seek to understand how novel technoscience is transmuted into everyday common sense.

5. Lewis, *Full Surrogacy Now.*

6. In "Competing Responsibilities," Trnka and Trundle offer a useful discussion of responsibilization in an anthropological context.

7. Keirns, "Better than Nature," 513.

8. Keirns, "Better than Nature," 519.

9. Jackson, *Allergy,* 10.

10. Mitman, *Breathing Space.*

11. Keirns, "Better than Nature."

12. Smith, *Another Person's Poison.*

13. Mitman, "Geographies of Hope."

14. Perry et al., "Distribution of Peanut Allergen."

15. This is a twenty-first-century analogy to Bruno Latour's analysis of Louis Pasteur's ability to move microbes from agricultural field to lab to field again as part of his demonstration of the existence of the anthrax bacillus. According to Latour, Pasteur's success was attributable to his ability to draw together human and nonhuman actants in coordinated activity in both laboratory and field demonstrations, then tell a story about the activity that took place in such a way that the two settings were understood by farmers, the press, and the French public to be saying meaningful things, the one about the other. Pasteur, in short, extended his laboratory beyond the laboratory into farmers' fields. In this case, the home is extending into the laboratory, overspilling its bounds and sneaking in beneath the notice of researchers, not the laboratory into the home. Latour, "Give Me a Laboratory."

16. Smith, *Another Person's Poison,* 76.

17. Smith, *Another Person's Poison,* 95.

18. Smith, *Another Person's Poison,* 97.

19. Keirns, "Better than Nature"; Mitman, "Geographies of Hope"; Smith, *Another Person's Poison,* 120.

20. Smith, *Another Person's Poison,* 93–94.

21. Smith, *Another Person's Poison,* 156.

22. For subcutaneous immunotherapy, see Oppenheimer et al., "Treatment of Peanut Allergy," and Nelson et al., "Treatment of Anaphylactic Sensitivity." For treatments delivered by mouth, see Narisety and Keet, "Sublingual vs. Oral Immunotherapy." For epicutaneous delivery, see Senti, Freiburghaus, and Kundig, "Epicutaneous/Transcutaneous Allergen-Specific Immunotherapy."

23. In my research with food allergy parents, Dr. Wood and Dr. Burks were still highly sought-after clinicians for food allergic children. Studies from their laboratories were highly anticipated at conferences. They were sought after interviewees by food allergy bloggers and magazines. Several former collaborators and trainees became widely recognized clinicians and researchers in their own rights during the period of my ethnographic research and since.

24. Strachan, "Hay Fever, Hygiene, and Household Size," 1260.

25. Strachan, "Family Size, Infection, and Atopy."

26. Holbreich et al., "Amish Children."

27. Stein et al., "Innate Immunity and Asthma Risk."

28. Du Toit et al., "Randomized Trial of Peanut Consumption"; Du Toit et al., "Allergen Specificity."

29. Interim results were publicly announced at scientific allergy meetings in 2015 and 2016, with the peer-reviewed paper about the study formally published in *Journal of Allergy and Clinical Immunology: In Practice* in 2018. For the final article, see Bird et al., "Efficacy and Safety of AR101."

30. Sampson et al., "Epicutaneous Immunotherapy."

31. U.S. Food and Drug Administration, "January 31, 2020 Approval Letter—PALFORZIA"; U.S. Food and Drug Administration, "FDA Approves First Drug for Treatment of Peanut Allergy for Children."

32. Marx, *Machine in the Garden.*

33. Raffaetà, "Allergy Narratives in Italy," 136.

34. O'Brien, *Unhealthy Truth*, 1–2.

35. O'Brien, *Unhealthy Truth*, 3.

36. O'Brien, *Unhealthy Truth*, 46.

37. O'Brien, *Unhealthy Truth*; O'Brien, "Science for Sale."

38. James Laidlaw offers a helpful way to think about blame in situations where nonhuman agency is involved. Bringing together actor–network theory and classical anthropological theory, he rereads Evans-Pritchard's discussion about blame and witchcraft among the Azande: "To claim your misfortune as an instance of witchcraft was to declare that it wasn't an accident or coincidence and that it wasn't deserved or unavoidable. It was to see yourself as a victim of an agent who could in principle be held to account, a victim, that is, of a responsible self, connected to you via an unseen agency." In food allergy, the direct agent responsible for developing a sensitivity or experiencing a reaction is nonhuman: pieces of food, immune signaling molecules, and the like. But food allergic individuals and food allergy parents often seek to find an agent to blame that is behind the unruly nonhuman substance,

echoing the structure of witchcraft accusations in this canonical anthropological text. Laidlaw, "Agency and Responsibility," 156.

39. Greer, Sicherer, and Burks, "Effects of Early Nutritional Interventions."

40. In talks about this project, I have almost always fielded a question about whether vaccines are blamed for food allergy. That is why I have at times compared food allergy activism to mothers mobilizing for vaccine safety. I have followed the associations made by both my research and scholarly interlocutors in where to direct my attention and how to contextualize my findings. However, among my participants, the connection to vaccines was infrequent. My participants overwhelmingly saw biomedical experts, like researchers and physicians, as their allies in advocacy fights. However, outside of ethnographic interviews, I often came across internet posts and books that connected allergies and vaccines. When I asked people about these arguments in interviews, they had a lot to say about them, although they typically assured me they did not agree with antivaccine advocates. This link is thus relevant to understanding the wide range of ideas currently circulating in the United States about food allergy etiology, even though it was not typically expressed by my direct interlocutors.

41. Fraser, *Peanut Allergy Epidemic*, 64.

42. Briere et al., "Prevention and Control of *Haemophilus influenzae*."

43. Fraser, *Peanut Allergy Epidemic*, 35.

44. Ryan and Runswick-Cole, "Repositioning Mothers."

45. Blum, "Mother-Blame," 202.

46. Cowan, "Industrial Revolution," 23.

47. Metzl, "Mother's Little Helper."

48. Nelkin and Lindee, *DNA Mystique;* Lovett, *Conceiving the Future.*

49. Rapp, "Gender, Body, Biomedicine"; Blum, "Mother-Blame"; Mattingly, "Moral Perils."

50. Bridges, *Reproducing Race.*

51. Roberts, *Shattered Bonds.*

52. Cant, Marsden, and Kilshaw, "Egg and Cows' Milk Hypersensitivity"; Sorva and Mikinen-Kiljunen, "Immunodeficiency and Other Clinical Immunology Secretion"; Vadas et al., "Detection of Peanut Allergens."

53. Zeiger, "Food Allergen Avoidance."

54. Lack et al., "Factors Associated with the Development of Peanut Allergy."

55. Greer, Sicherer, and Burks, "Effects of Early Nutritional Interventions."

56. Fleischer et al., "Primary Prevention of Allergic Disease," 30.

57. O'Brien, *Unhealthy Truth*, 76.

58. O'Brien, *Unhealthy Truth*, 78.

59. O'Brien, *Unhealthy Truth*, 42.

60. Hewett, "Food Allergies and the Good Enough Mother."

61. Hewett, "Food Allergies and the Good Enough Mother."

62. Charles, "Suspicion and/as Radical (Care)," 89.

63. Latour and Woolgar, *Laboratory Life*; Callon, "Some Elements."

64. Latour, "Give Me a Laboratory."

3. THE HYGIENIC SUBLIME

1. DeLuca and Demo, "Imagining Nature."

2. Mitman, *Breathing Space*.

3. Mitman, "Geographies of Hope"; Mitman, *Breathing Space*.

4. Jackson, *Allergy*.

5. Mitman, *Breathing Space*; Keirns, "Better than Nature."

6. Kline, "Ideology and Social Surveys"; Bijker and Bijsterveld, "Women Walking."

7. Cowan, *More Work for Mother*; Tomes, *Gospel of Germs*.

8. For Martha Stewart, see Bentley, "Martha's Food." For foodie culture, see Cairns, Johnston, and Baumann, "Caring about Food." For Starbucks pumpkin spice lattes, see Powell and Engelhardt, "Perilous Whiteness."

9. Murphy, *Sick Building Syndrome*, 177.

10. Burke, *Philosophical Enquiry*; Stormer, "Addressing the Sublime"; Brunner and Dawson, "Marketing the Recreational Sublime."

11. Peeples, "Toxic Sublime"; Brunner and Dawson, "Marketing the Recreational Sublime"; DeLuca and Demo, "Imaging Nature."

12. Stormer, "Addressing the Sublime."

13. Stormer, "Addressing the Sublime," 214.

14. Stormer, "Addressing the Sublime," 216.

15. Peeples, "Toxic Sublime."

16. Miles, *Gothic Writing*; Stormer, "Addressing the Sublime."

17. Cronon, "Trouble with Wilderness."

18. Nye, *American Technological Sublime*.

19. Anderson, *Colonial Pathologies*.

20. Jasanoff and Kim, "Containing the Atom."

21. Nakamura, *Cybertypes*.

22. Hochschild, "Commodity Frontier," 35.

23. Van Evra, "Kitchens that Cook."

24. Anderson, "Natural Histories"; Valenčius, *Health of the Country.*

25. Leavitt, "'Typhoid Mary' Strikes Back"; Tomes, *Gospel of Germs;* Tomes, "Making of a Germ Panic"; Platt, "Clever Microbes."

26. Mitman, *Breathing Space.*

27. Keirns, "Better than Nature."

28. Keirns, "Better than Nature," 524.

29. I cannot look at or recall this ad now without hearing the frequently spoken words of coconspirator and fellow anthropologist Elizabeth Chin in my head: "Add some color!" This was a frequent mantra in our 2018 and 2019 collaborative exhibition at Wakanda University. Chin's exhortation applies to the white ideological spaces of design education, her day job, as well as the white epistemological spaces of the field of anthropology, her scholarly field of origin. This exclamation is meant to index whiteness at several levels: the plain, simple, and often colorless aesthetic of "good design" sought out by Western elites; the predominance of white people in positions of power in both design and anthropology; and the blandness, and ultimate inefficacy, of institutional responses in the form of "diversity and inclusion" discourses.

30. Cowan, *More Work for Mother;* Tomes, *Gospel of Germs.*

31. Tomes, *Gospel of Germs;* Colgrove, *State of Immunity.*

32. Cowan, *More Work for Mother.*

33. Cowan, *More Work for Mother,* 177.

34. Cowan, *More Work for Mother,* 187.

35. Abel and Nelson, "Circles of Care."

36. Cowan, "Industrial Revolution"; Kline, "Ideology and Social Surveys"; Bijker and Bijsterveld, "Women Walking."

37. Bentley, "Martha's Food."

38. Cairns, Johnston, and Baumann, "Caring about Food"; Parr, "Modern Kitchen."

39. Crenshaw, "Demarginalizing the Intersection of Race and Sex," 149.

40. Branum and Lukacs, "Food Allergy among U.S. Children"; Greenhawt et al., "Racial and Ethnic Disparity"; Jerschow et al., "Fatal Anaphylaxis."

41. Andrea's statement recalls Sara Ahmed's argument that "when you expose a problem you pose a problem." Ahmed, like Andrea, is discussing what happens when women, more specifically feminists of color, call out institutional sexism and racism. Ahmed, *Living a Feminist Life,* 37.

42. Collins, "It's All in the Family."

43. In addition to Donna Haraway's evolving provocation to rethink kinship and kin making, first via the figure of the cyborg, then via dogs, and

most recently via human–endangered species hybrids, Kim TallBear has recently launched a critique of what she has termed "settler sexuality": Western heteropatriarchal serially monogamous sexuality premised on kinship relations as property relations. TallBear and Willey, pushing readers to think beyond restrictive and oppressive settler sexuality, write: "If we are to move beyond the reproduction of the dyadic family's scripting and privileged status, we need to understand nature differently. We need to rethink sex as the central organizing principle of human sociality, the human as the only important unit of relational ethics, and the white supremacist settler and other colonial cultural scripts as ethical measures of belonging through which the naturalized ideal of the family emerged historically. . . . Our ability to imagine nature and relationality differently are deeply enmeshed, and this imaginative work is vital to the re-worlding before us." Haraway, *Staying with the Trouble;* TallBear and Willey, "Introduction," 5.

44. Schwartz, *Birthing a Slave;* hooks, *Feminist Theory.*

45. Haraway, "FemaleMan©_Meets_OncoMouse™."

46. Latour, *We Have Never Been Modern.*

47. Shotwell, *Against Purity,* 6.

48. Reardon and TallBear, "Your DNA Is Our History."

49. Trnka and Trundle, "Competing Responsibilities."

50. Hobart and Kneese, "Radical Care," 4.

4. ACTIVIST POLITICS

1. Solomon, "Obama Signs Bill to Increase EpiPen Availability in Schools."

2. Jarrett, "President Obama Signs New EpiPen Law."

3. New Hampshire Code, "Relative to the Administration of Epinephrine" (passed May 3, 2016).

4. Rabeharisoa and Callon, "Involvement of Patients' Associations"; Callon and Rabeharisoa, "Research 'in the Wild.'"

5. While some readers of this book may find it hard to believe, during my PhD training, none of my medical anthropology mentors or advisors at my primary institution read disability studies; some had not even heard of its existence as a field. I did not begin to meet other STS scholars working on disability until 2015, when a more senior colleague, Nayantara Sheoran Appleton, supported my desire to release a call for papers for a panel bringing together STS, medical anthropology, and disability studies on behalf of the Science, Technology, and Medicine special interest group of the Society for Medical Anthropology. The panel, "Replaceable Parts: Becoming Cyborg,"

happened at the 2015 society for the Social Studies of Science conference in Denver, Colorado.

6. Carey, Block, and Scotch, "Sometimes Allies."

7. This blog post is no longer available online as of the time of writing in September 2020.

8. Mauldin, *Made to Hear.*

9. Mauldin, *Made to Hear,* 14.

10. Ne'eman, "The Future (and the Past) of Autism Advocacy."

11. Rosenblatt, "Autism, Advocacy Organizations, and Past Injustice."

12. Bumiller, "Quirky Citizens."

13. Cascio, "Neurodiversity."

14. Stevenson, Harp, and Gernsbacher, "Infantilizing Autism."

15. Carey, Block, and Scotch, "Sometimes Allies."

16. Ne'eman, "The Future (and the Past) of Autism Advocacy"; Piepzna-Samarasinha, *Care Work.*

17. Piepzna-Samarasinha, *Care Work,* 23.

18. Piepzna-Samarasinha, *Care Work,* 46

19. Epstein, "Construction of Lay Expertise"; Epstein, *Impure Science;* Kirkland, *Vaccine Court;* Reich, *Calling the Shots.*

20. Hamraie, *Buliding Access,* 95.

21. Hewett, "Talkin' 'bout a Revolution."

22. Reich, *Calling the Shots,* 73.

23. According to Melinda Cooper, the privatization of care for sick and disabled people and the expansion and strengthening of market mechanisms into life-sustaining domains, like housing and health care, are complementary aspects of how neoliberalism increased reliance on the nuclear family in the second half of the twentieth century. In Cooper's view, the nuclear family took up the slack in social services created in the wake of the Volker shock in the late 1970s and the Reagan administration's defunding of social services starting in the 1980s. While the market was supposed to more efficiently regulate the distribution of necessary goods and services, like health care, what in fact happened was that it created greater scarcity for the poor and marginalized, with family members assumed to step in to sustain life and livelihoods whenever necessary. In short, neoliberalism as a public, fiscal policy made the nuclear family more central to the day-to-day operations of the U.S. state. Cooper, *Family Values.*

24. Douglas, "As If You Have a Choice," 167.

25. Section 504, Rehabilitation Act of 1973, 29 U.S.C. § 701; U.S. Department of Justice, "Americans with Disabilities Act of 1990 and Revised ADA

Regulations Implementing Title II and Title III," Pub. L. No. 110–325 (2014), https://www.ada.gov/2010_regs.htm.

26. Francoeur, "Food Allergy School Health Plans."

27. U.S. Department of Justice, "Americans with Disabilities Act of 1990."

28. Waggoner, "Parsing the Peanut Panic."

29. U.S. Centers for Disease Control and Prevention, "Voluntary Guidelines for Managing Food Allergies in Schools and Early Care and Education Programs," 2013, https://www.cdc.gov/healthyschools/foodallergies/pdf/20_316712-A_FA_guide_508tag.pdf.

30. Verbatim comment to Spohr, "No Sandwich Is More Important than a Child's Life."

31. "Emotional labor" is a term originally coined by Arlie Russell Hochschild in *Managed Heart*, first published in 1983. Hochschild argues that a new kind of labor has become increasingly prevalent in the U.S. economy, a kind of labor focused on managing the emotional status of clients rather than making things or providing life-sustaining services. This work is called emotional labor. In Hochschild, it is exemplified by the labor of flight attendants, whose training she studies ethnographically. Emotional labor is often not recognized as labor but rather as an extension of supposedly natural feminine tendencies, so it is consequently undervalued and underpaid. In the context of mothers' involvement with children's schooling, Maeve O'Brien uses the term "emotional capital" to designate the capacity for emotional labor: "a resource that facilitates mothers in the transmission of social and cultural capital to their children, one that includes skills, love, affection and a willingness to spend time and energy on their education." Hochschild, *Managed Heart;* O'Brien, "Gendered Capital," 139.

32. While Giorgio Agamben has often been invoked to discuss the "sacrificial" nature of certain groups and individuals in contemporary contexts of care and life-risking/lifesaving administrative structures, tort law and disaster framing are more relevant to the specific issues at play with stock epinephrine legislation. Therefore, I focus on these concepts in this section. Agamben, *Homo Sacer.*

33. Jain, *Injury.* Anna Kirkland argues that so-called vaccine courts, which operate outside both administrative and tort law processes, are an ideal compromise for awarding damages when modern medicine causes injury that does not overwhelm the ordinary court system and feed into antivaccination conspiracy theories. Vaccine courts are a special case that removes vaccine injuries from adjudication via the more common framework for assessing harms to individuals caused by modern medicine, medical

malpractice. Epinephrine auto-injector injuries would not be subject to the vaccine court system but rather to tort or medical malpractice frameworks. Kirkland, *Vaccine Court*.

34. Gonzalez, "When Tort Falls Short."

35. Naomi Klein offers the concept of disaster capitalism as a way to comprehend how policy makers and corporations have come to see natural, health, and political disasters as opportunities for financial growth. Klein positions disaster capitalism as a consequence of the "shock doctrine" promulgated by neoliberal economists like Milton Friedman starting in the 1970s. Klein, *Shock Doctrine*, 7. No good disaster goes to waste in this worldview; any crisis can be seized on by economists and businesses as a way to increase profits and privatize previously public services. Anthropologist Vincanne Adams also adopts the term disaster capitalism to discuss the financial opportunities seized by relief organizations and companies providing supplies for rebuilding New Orleans after Hurricane Katrina in 2005. While the disasters in question in food allergy activism tend to be personal or familial in nature, they affect a huge number of people—tens of millions in the United States alone. At this scale, even such distributed disasters create a tempting market for the introduction of technocratic, privatized solutions. Klein, *Shock Doctrine;* Adams, *Markets of Sorrow*.

36. Carey, Bock, and Scotch, "Sometimes Allies"; Ne'eman, "The Future (and the Past) of Autism Advocacy."

37. Dumit, *Drugs for Life*.

38. Lakoff, "Generic Biothreat"; Adams, Murphy, and Clarke, "Anticipation"; Anderson, "Preemption, Precaution, Preparedness."

39. Barnes, "Understanding the Social Model"; Shakespeare, "Disability, Identity and Difference."

40. Asthma and Allergy Foundation of America, "The Asthma and Allergy Foundation of America (AAFA) Statement in Support of Stocking Epinephrine Auto-injectors in Schools," 2013.

41. This positioning expands a proposed solution designed with the concern of one group in mind to a potentially universally helpful solution, in consonance with inclusivity and universal design discourses from the wider field of disability activism. However, as Hamraie discusses in *Building Access*, such universal inclusivity may ultimately miss the mark by flattening all forms of difference and excluding the consideration of things like gender and class from the frame of disability activism.

42. FARE, "School Access to Epinephrine Map," Programs and Advocacy, http://www.foodallergy.org/advocacy/epinephrine/map.

43. California Advocates for Food Allergies (@CaAdvocatesFA), Twitter post, May 14, 2014, https://twitter.com/CAFoodAllergy/media.

44. California Advocates for Food Allergies (@CaAdvocatesFA), Twitter post, May 20, 2014, https://twitter.com/CAFoodAllergy/media.

45. Murphy, "Immodest Witnessing"; Murphy, *Sick Buliding Syndrome;* Murphy, *Seizing the Means of Reproduction;* Klawiter, *Biopolitics of Breast Cancer;* Jain, *Malignant.*

46. In a study of 1970s U.S. radical women's health activists, Michelle Murphy draws on Joan Scott's argument concerning the limited feminist political possibilities of the "evidence of experience." Scott's original concern is about how first-person experiences of identity in historical archives are often naturalized and unchallenged by historians when they should be explored in more depth as the result of or contributors to ongoing social processes. Here I am interested in how activists, not professional historians, leverage (gendered and classed) experience as a form of evidence in activism that is recognized as a legitimate form of evidence when presented alongside biomedical evidence about food allergy. Yet I take up Scott's and Murphy's concerns about naively accepting experience as authoritative evidence throughout the current project by interrogating whose experience counts as evidence, and how history has set up the experience of some—but not others—as potentially authoritative in politics and biomedicine. Murphy, "Immodest Witnessing"; Murphy, *Seizing the Means of Reproduction;* Scott, "Evidence of Experience."

47. Murphy, "Immodest Witnessing"; Murphy, *Seizing the Means of Reproduction.*

48. Murphy, *Seizing the Means of Reproduction.*

49. Roberts, *Killing the Black Body.*

50. Manjari Mahajan offers a useful model for understanding the ways that preformulated models for health policy circulate and are validated. Public health response models coordinated by global health organizations or transnational networks of experts often circulate foreknowledge of health crises, or models that propose that solutions to newly emerging health crises already exist. For example, "solutions" were proposed by transposing public health responses to AIDS from sub-Saharan African nations to India in the 1990s. Such transpositions, she argues, excessively simplify the local cultural, economic, and political aspects of health crises by ignoring local conditions. Similarly, Mylan's one-size-fits-all bill faced serious critique from activists because it did not account for the variety of state regulations for drug prescriptions and liability law. In this case, activists and lawmakers intervened to modify the law before implementation. Mahajan, "Designing Epidemics."

51. A "sweet" and "professional" demeanor is but one enactment of normative femininity that helps parent advocates press their case. Another is that of the "feminine warrior" that P. N. Douglas documents in autism parent advocacy. Douglas explains that the feminine warrior is one figure through which "seemingly natural ties come into being over and over again in ordinary acts of everyday interpretive consciousness." Similar to what I claim about the role of mothers in food allergy advocacy, Douglas suggests that it is the enactment of the feminine warrior persona that helps to make the connection between mothering and advocacy seem natural, inevitable, and unstoppable, even though "there is nothing 'natural' about the meanings we make of autism, and autism mothers." Douglas, "As If You Have a Choice," 172.

52. Low, "Maintaining Whiteness."

53. Mattingly, "Moral Perils."

54. Douglas, "As If You Have a Choice."

55. Piepzna-Samarasinha, *Care Work.*

56. Rosenblatt, "Autism, Advocacy Organizations, and Past Injustice."

57. Kimura, *Radiation Brain Moms;* Kirkland, *Vaccine Court.*

5. THE EPIPEN PRICING SCANDAL AND THE FUTURE OF FOOD ALLERGY ADVOCACY

1. CSPAN, "EpiPen Price Increases."

2. Koons and Langreth, "How Marketing Turned the EpiPen into a Billion-Dollar Business"; Koons, Keller, and Langreth, "How EpiPen's Price Rose and Rose"; Morgenson, "EpiPen Price Rises"; Parker-Pope, "How Parents Harnessed the Power of Social Media"; Parker-Pope and Peachman, "EpiPen Price Rise Sparks Concern."

3. Pollack, "Drug Goes from $13.50 a Tablet to $750, Overnight"; Bloomberg Business, "Drug Goes from $13.50 to $750 Overnight."

4. Parker-Pope, "How Parents Harnessed the Power of Social Media"; Parker-Pope and Peachman, "EpiPen Price Rise Sparks Concern."

5. Rabeharisoa, Moreira, and Akrich, "Evidence-Based Activism."

6. Akrich, "From Communities of Practice"; Martin, *Bipolar Expeditions.*

7. Steven Epstein's study of AIDS activism in the 1980s and 1990s, *Impure Science,* has investigated how claims of credibility helped to position some AIDS activists as legitimate spokespeople for people with AIDS. Another solution to this problem, and the one that seems to be most prevalent in food allergy advocacy, is to trust the word of organizations with professional, full-time staff of recognized nonprofit organizations. I have found in my research that most such professionals also have institutionally legible

credentials, such as past leadership in for-profit health care organizations or advanced degrees in science, medicine, or business.

8. Rabinow, "Artificiality and Enlightenment," 241.

9. American Cancer Society, "2018 Annual Report," https://www.cancer.org/content/dam/cancer-org/online-documents/en/pdf/reports/2018-annual-report.pdf.

10. FARE, "FARE at Work, 2016," https://www.foodallergy.org/media/290/download.

11. FARE, "Return of Organization Exempt from Income Tax, Form 990, 2016, Public Inspection Copy," 2016, https://www.foodallergy.org/media/254/download.

12. Welker, "Corporate Security"; Shever, "Engendering the Corporation"; Dietrich, *Drug Company Next Door*.

13. Greene, "Attention to 'Details'"; Oldani, "Thick Prescriptions."

14. Oldani, "Thick Prescriptions."

15. Mylan, "Social Responsibility at Mylan: 2015 Overview," http://www.mylan.com/-/media/mylancom/files/news/socialresponsibilityatmylan2015overview.pdf, 40.

16. Mylan, "Social Responsibility," 42.

17. Fortun, *Advocacy after Bhopal*, 11.

18. Abraham and Ballinger, "Science, Politics, and Health"; Slayton and Clark-Ginsberg, "Beyond Regulatory Capture."

19. Abraham and Ballinger, "Science, Politics, and Health," 1434.

20. Koons and Langreth, "How Marketing Turned the EpiPen into a Billion-Dollar Business."

21. Parker-Pope, "How Parents Harnessed the Power of Social Media."

22. Parker-Pope and Peachman, "EpiPen Price Rise Sparks Concern."

23. Mylan, "Mylan Taking Immediate Action to Further Enhance Access to EpiPen® (Epinephrine Injection, USP) Auto-injector," press release, August 25, 2016, http://newsroom.mylan.com/2016-08-25-Mylan-Taking-Immediate-Action-to-Further-Enhance-Access-to-EpiPen-Epinephrine-Injection-USP-Auto-Injector#:~:text=25%2C2016%2FPRNewswire%2F-,out-of-pocketcosts.

24. Mylan, "Mylan Taking Immediate Action."

25. Moassessi, "Affordable EpiPens! Really."

26. Moassessi, "Auvi-Q Goes Zero Co-pay Too."

27. Moassessi, "Wahoooo! EpiPen $0 Co-pay Extended!"; Moassessi, "Best Prices for EpiPen and Auvi-Q."

28. Bresch, "Watch the Complete Interview."

29. Bresch, "Watch the Complete Interview."

30. Collins, "It's All in the Family."

31. Mylan, "Mylan to Launch First Generic to EpiPen® Auto-Injector at a List Price of $300 per Two-Pack Carton, a More than 50% Discount to the Brand Product," press release, August 29, 2016, http://newsroom.mylan .com/2016-08-29-Mylan-to-Launch-First-Generic-to-EpiPen-Auto-Injector -at-a-List-Price-of-300-per-Two-Pack-Carton-a-More-than-50-Discount -to-the-Brand-Product.

32. CSPAN, "EpiPen Price Increases."

33. CSPAN, "EpiPen Price Increases."

34. CSPAN, "EpiPen Price Increases."

35. Kyriakides, "Tactics as Empirical and Conceptual Objects," 14.

36. FARE, National Food Allergy Conference, June 21–22, 2014, Rosemont, Illinois.

37. Sanofi markets a variety of asthma medications and briefly marketed a U.S. EpiPen competitor, Auvi-Q, from 2012 to 2016, before Kaléo took back marketing rights and relaunched it under their company's brand.

38. Food Allergy Bloggers Conference, "Our Sponsors, 2013," https:// foodallergybloggerconference.wordpress.com/our-sponsors/.

39. Aimmune Therapeutics, "Allergen Research Corporation Announces $17 Million Series A Financing," 2013, https://ir.aimmune.com/news-re leases/news-release-details/allergen-research-corporation-announces -17-million-series.

40. Aimmune Therapeutics, "Allergen Research Corporation Initiates Phase 2b Clinical Trial for Peanut Allergy Oral Immunotherapy (OIT)," February 27, 2014, https://ir.aimmune.com/news-releases/news-release-details/ allergen-research-corporation-initiates-phase-2b-clinical-trial.

41. Aimmune Therapeutics, "Aimmune Therapeutics Announces Second Quarter 2016 Financial Results," August 10, 2016, https://ir.aimmune.com/ news-releases/news-release-details/aimmune-therapeutics-announces -second-quarter-2016-financial.

42. Aimmune Therapeutics, "Aimmune Therapeutics Reports Second Quarter 2015 Financial Results," August 31, 2015, https://ir.aimmune.com/ news-releases/news-release-details/aimmune-therapeutics-reports-second -quarter-2015-financial; FARE, "Audited Financial Statements: Food Allergy Research and Education, Inc.," 2015, https://www.foodallergy.org/media /249/download.

43. FARE, "FARE at Work, 2015," https://www.foodallergy.org/ media/291/download.

44. Sometime between August 2016 and June 2020, this statement was

removed from the internet. Links to the no-longer-accessible page are still available through social media accounts. FARE, "FARE Statement on Epinephrine Access and Price," August 24, 2016, https://www.foodallergy.org/press-room/fare-statements/082416.

45. This was also removed from the internet by the second half of 2020. FARE, "A Statement from the CEO of FARE," September 7, 2016.

46. Lipton and Abrams, "EpiPen Maker Lobbies to Shift High Costs to Others."

47. FARE, "Corporate Partners," 2020, https://www.foodallergy.org/corporate-partners.

48. FAACT, "2020 FAACT Partners," https://www.foodallergyawareness.org/about/corporate-partners/.

49. Asthma and Allergy Network, "Allergy & Asthma Day on Capitol Hill," 2020, https://allergyasthmanetwork.org/advocacy/allergy-and-asthma-day-on-capitol-hill-aadch/.

50. Rabeharisoa and Callon, "Involvement of Patients' Associations"; Rabeharisoa, Moreira, and Akrich, "Evidence-Based Activism."

51. FARE, "FARE Clinical Network," 2020, https://www.foodallergy.org/research-innovation/elevating-research/fare-clinical-network.

52. FARE, "FARE Clinical Network Celebrates Five Years with Expansion, Further Enhancing State-of-the-Art Patient Care," June 2, 2020, https://www.foodallergy.org/media-room/fare-clinical-network-celebrates-five-years-expansion-further-enhancing-state-art.

53. FARE, "FARE Clinical Network," 2020.

54. FARE, "FARE Patient Registry," 2020, https://www.foodallergypatientregistry.org/.

55. The difficulty of speedy participant enrollment to clinical trials has been highlighted by the initiation of trials for Covid-19 vaccines and therapies in summer 2020. News reports about the slow pace and difficulty of recruiting overall have surfaced. There has also been extensive reporting about the difficulties in recruiting people of color for the trials. Thomas, "Clinical Trials of Coronavirus Drugs"; Farmer, "Covid Vaccine Trials."

56. Petryna, "Ethical Variability"; Petryna, *When Experiments Travel*; Cohen, "Where It Hurts."

57. Fisher, *Adverse Events*.

58. Couzin-Frankel, "First Peanut Allergy Treatment."

59. Fleischer et al., "Effect of Epicutaneous Immunotherapy."

60. Brown, "Hope against Hype"; Fortun, "Mediated Speculations"; Sunder Rajan, *Biocapital*.

61. Dumit, *Drugs for Life*.

62. Murphy, *Seizing the Means of Reproduction*.

63. Hester, *Xenofeminism*.

64. Laufer, "Introducing the EpiPencil."

65. Piepzna-Samarasinha, *Care Work*.

66. FARE, "New Publication Supports Shared Discussions between Doctors and Patients around Oral Immunotherapy," June 4, 2020, https://www.foodallergy.org/fare-blog/new-publication-supports-shared-discussions-between-doctors-and-patients-around-oit; and FARE, "FARE-Led Panel Seeks to Expand Awareness of and Access to Oral Immunotherapy (OIT)," June 5, 2020, https://www.foodallergy.org/media-room/fare-led-panel-seeks-expand-awareness-and-access-oral-immunotherapy-oit.

67. FARE, "FARE-Led Panel."

68. Nonprofit pharmaceutical status for pharmaceutical companies is an idea that has been closely examined over the past decade. Perhaps the highest-profile example is Civica, founded in 2018. The company seeks memberships with health care systems and partnerships with existing industry players to provide drugs without generating a profit for itself. Its first delivery of drugs was the antibiotic vancomycin, delivered to Riverton Hospital in Utah in October 2019. Hale, Woo, and Lipton, "Oxymoron No More"; Harrison, "The Not-for-Profit Civica Rx Will Disrupt the Generic Drug Industry"; Civica Rx, "Patients Are Now Being Treated with a Civica Rx Medication," 2019, https://mk0sakunexoeoby9gsa0.kinstacdn.com/wp-content/uploads/2020/02/Civica-Rx-First-Deliveries.pdf.

CONCLUSION

1. Diedrich, *Indirect Action*, 16.

2. I have discussed the resonances between the ongoing crisis of care for food allergy families and the acute crisis triggered by the Covid-19 pandemic elsewhere. Glabau, "Covid-19 and the Politics of Care."

3. Figure from data available September 25, 2020, from *New York Times*, "Covid in the U.S.: Latest Map and Case Count," https://www.nytimes.com/interactive/2020/us/coronavirus-us-cases.html; Feeding America, "The Impact of Coronavirus on Food Insecurity," 2020, https://www.feedingamerica.org/research/coronavirus-hunger-research.

4. Figure from data available March 29, 2021, from *New York Times*, "Covid in the U.S.," https://www.nytimes.com/interactive/2021/us/coronavirus-us-cases.html.

5. Collins, "It's All in the Family," 63.

6. Collins, "It's All in the Family," 63.

7. Roberts, *Killing the Black Body.*

8. Roberts, *Shattered Bonds.*

9. Roberts, "Abolishing Policing."

10. Brown, "Open Letter."

11. Diedrich, *Indirect Action,* 208.

12. Robinson, *2312;* Donna Haraway adopts "the Dithering" to name the delays around addressing global warming and radically unmaking nuclear family–based kinship in the twenty-first century in "The Camille Stories," in *Staying with the Trouble.*

BIBLIOGRAPHY

Abel, Emily K., and Margaret K. Nelson. "Circles of Care: An Introductory Essay." In *Circles of Care: Work and Identity in Women's Lives,* edited by Emily K. Abel and Margaret K. Nelson, 4–34. Albany: State University of New York Press, 1990.

Abraham, John, and Rachel Ballinger. "Science, Politics, and Health in the Brave New World of Pharmaceutical Carcinogenic Risk Assessment: Technical Progress or Cycle of Regulatory Capture?" *Social Science and Medicine* 75, no. 8 (2012): 1433–40. https://doi.org/10.1016/j.socscimed.2012.04.043.

Adams, Vincanne. *Markets of Sorrow, Labors of Faith: New Orleans in the Wake of Katrina.* Durham, N.C.: Duke University Press, 2013.

Adams, Vincanne, Michelle Murphy, and Adele E. Clarke. "Anticipation: Technoscience, Life, Affect, Temporality." *Subjectivity* 28, no. 1 (2009): 246–65. https://doi.org/10.1057/sub.2009.18.

Agamben, Giorgio. *Homo Sacer: Sovereign Power and Bare Life.* Stanford, Calif.: Stanford University Press, 1998.

Ahmed, Sara. "Affective Economies." *Social Text* 22, no. 2 (2004): 117–39. https://doi.org/10.1215/01642472-22-2_79-117.

Ahmed, Sara. *Living a Feminist Life.* Durham, N.C.: Duke University Press, 2017.

Ahmed, Sara. "A Phenomenology of Whiteness." *Feminist Theory* 8, no. 2 (2007): 149–68. https://doi.org/10.1177/1464700107078139.

Akrich, Madeleine. "From Communities of Practice to Epistemic Communities: Health Mobilizations on the Internet." *Sociological Research Online* 15, no. 2 (2011): 1–17. https://doi.org/10.5153/sro.2152.

Anderson, Ben. "Preemption, Precaution, Preparedness: Anticipatory Action and Future Geographies." *Progress in Human Geography* 34, no. 6 (2010): 777–98. https://doi.org/10.1177/0309132510362600.

Anderson, Warwick. *Colonial Pathologies: American Tropical Medicine, Race, and Hygiene in the Philippines.* Durham, N.C.: Duke University Press, 2006.

Anderson, Warwick. "Natural Histories of Infectious Disease: Ecological Vision in Twentieth-Century Biomedical Science." *Osiris* 19 (2004): 39–61. https://doi.org/10.1086/649393.

Anderson, Warwick, and Ian R. Mackay. *Intolerant Bodies: A Short History of Autoimmunity.* Baltimore, Md.: Johns Hopkins University Press, 2014.

Antico, Paul. "Our First Experience with the Epi—All the Details and 16 Lessons to Take Away." *Allergy Eats!* (blog), May 21, 2014. http://www.allergy eats.com/blog/index.php/our-first-experience-with-the-epi-all-the-de tails-and-16-lessons-to-take-away/.

Appadurai, Arjun. "Introduction: Commodities and the Politics of Value." In *The Social Life of Things: Commodities in Cultural Perspective*, edited by Arjun Appadurai, 3–63. Cambridge: Cambridge University Press, 1986.

Barnes, Colin. "Understanding the Social Model of Disability: Past, Present and Future." In *Routledge Handbook of Disability Studies*, edited by Carol Thomas, Nick Watson, and Alan Roulstone, 12–29. New York: Routledge, 2012.

Bentley, Amy. "Martha's Food: Whiteness of a Certain Kind." *American Studies* 42, no. 2 (2001): 89–100.

Biehl, João Guilherme. "The Activist State: Global Pharmaceuticals, AIDS, and Citizenship in Brazil." *Social Text* 22, no. 3 (2004): 105–32.

Biehl, João. *Vita: Life in a Zone of Social Abandonment.* Berkeley: University of California Press, 2005.

Biehl, João, and Amy Moran-Thomas. "Symptom: Subjectivities, Social Ills, Technologies." *Annual Review of Anthropology* 38, no. 1 (2009): 267–88. https://doi.org/10.1146/annurev-anthro-091908-164420.

Bijker, Wiebe E., and Karin Bijsterveld. "Women Walking through Plans: Technology, Democracy and Gender Identity." *Technology and Culture* 41, no. 3 (2000): 485–515.

Bird, J. Andrew, Jonathan M. Spergel, Stacie M. Jones, Rima Rachid, Amal H. Assa'ad, Julie Wang, et al. "Efficacy and Safety of AR101 in Oral Immunotherapy for Peanut Allergy: Results of ARC001, a Randomized,

Double-Blind, Placebo-Controlled Phase 2 Clinical Trial." *Journal of Allergy and Clinical Immunology: In Practice* 6, no. 2 (2018): 476–85.e3. https://doi .org/10.1016/j.jaip.2017.09.016.

Biss, Eula. *On Immunity: An Inoculation.* Minneapolis, Minn.: Graywolf Press, 2014.

Blankenship, Kyle. "Aimmune's Controversial Peanut Allergy Med Has Its FDA Nod. Will It Sell?" Fierce Pharma, February 3, 2020. https://www .fiercepharma.com/pharma/aimmune-scores-fda-nod-for-controversial -peanut-allergy-med-palforzia.

Bloomberg Business. "Drug Goes from $13.50 to $750 Overnight." September 21, 2015. https://www.bloomberg.com/.

Blum, L. M. "Mother-Blame in the Prozac Nation: Raising Kids with Invisible Disabilities." *Gender and Society* 21, no. 2 (2007): 202–26. https://doi .org/10.1177/0891243206298178.

Branum, Amy M., and Susan L. Lukacs. "Food Allergy among U.S. Children: Trends in Prevalence and Hospitalizations." *NCHS Data Brief,* no. 10 (2008): 1–8.

Bresch, Heather. "Watch the Complete Interview with Embattled Mylan CEO Bresch." Squawk Box, CNBC, August 25, 2016. https://www.cnbc.com/ video/2016/08/25/watch-the-complete-interview-with-embattled-mylan -ceo-bresch.html.

Bridges, Khiara M. *Reproducing Race: An Ethnography of Pregnancy as a Site of Racialization.* Berkeley: University of California Press, 2011.

Briere, Elizabeth C., Lorry Rubin, Pedro L. Moro, Amanda Cohn, Thomas Clark, and Nancy Messonnier. "Prevention and Control of *Haemophilus influenzae* Type B Disease: Recommendations of the Advisory Committee on Immunization Practices (ACIP)." *MMWR Recommendations and Reports* 63, no. RR-01 (2014): 1–14.

Brown, Emily. "Open Letter to the Food Allergy Community." Food Equality Initiative, n.d. Accessed August 13, 2021. https://foodequalityinitiative .org/open-letter-to-the-food-allergy-community/.

Brown, Kate. *Plutopia: Nuclear Families, Atomic Cities, and the Great Soviet and American Plutonium Disasters.* Oxford: Oxford University Press, 2013.

Brown, Nik. "Hope against Hype: Accountability in Biopasts, Presents and Futures." *Science Studies* 16, no. 2 (2003): 3–21.

Brunner, Elizabeth A., and Veronica R. Dawson. "Marketing the Recreational Sublime: Jumbo Wild and the Rhetorics of Humans in Nature." *Critical Studies in Media Communication* 34, no. 4 (2017): 386–99. https://doi.org/10 .1080/15295036.2017.1322706.

Bumiller, Kristin. "Quirky Citizens: Autism, Gender, and Reimagining Disability." *Signs* 33, no. 4 (2008): 967–91. https://doi.org/10.1086/528848.

Burke, Edmund. *A Philosophical Enquiry in the Origin of Our Ideas of the Sublime and Beautiful. With an Introductory Discourse Concerning Taste, and Several Other Additions.* N.p.: D. Buchanan, 1803.

Cairns, Kate, Josée Johnston, and Shyon Baumann. "Caring about Food: Doing Gender in the Foodie Kitchen." *Gender and Society* 24, no. 5 (2010): 591–615. https://doi.org/10.1177/0891243210383419.

Callon, Michael. "Some Elements of a Sociology of Translation: Domestication of the Scallops and the Fishermen of St. Brieuc Bay." In *Power, Action and Belief: A New Sociology of Knowledge?*, edited by John Law, 196–233. London: Routledge, 1986.

Callon, Michael, and Vololona Rabeharisoa. "Research 'in the Wild' and the Shaping of New Social Identities." *Technology in Society* 25, no. 2 (2003): 193–204. https://doi.org/10.1016/S0160-791X(03)00021-6.

Cant, Andrew, R. A. Marsden, and P. J. Kilshaw. "Egg and Cows' Milk Hypersensitivity in Exclusively Breast Fed Infants with Eczema, and Detection of Egg Protein in Breast Milk." *British Medical Journal* 291 (1985): 932–35. https://doi.org/10.1136/bmj.291.6500.932.

Carey, Allison C., Pamela Block, and Richard K. Scotch. "Sometimes Allies: Parent-Led Disability Organizations and Social Movements." *Disability Studies Quarterly* 39, no. 1 (2019). https://doi.org/10.18061/dsq.v39i1.6281.

Cascio, M. Ariel. "Neurodiversity: Autism Pride among Mothers of Children with Autism Spectrum Disorders." *Intellectual and Developmental Disabilities* 50, no. 3 (2012): 273–83. https://doi.org/10.1352/1934-9556-50.3.273.

Charles, Nicole. "Suspicion and/as Radical (Care): Looking Closer at Vaccine Hesitancy in Postcolonial Barbados." *Social Text* 38, no. 1 (2020): 89–107. https://doi.org/10.1215/01642472-7971115.

Choy, Timothy K., Lieba Faier, Michael J. Hathaway, Miyako Inoue, Shiho Satsuka, and Anna Tsing. "A New Form of Collaboration in Cultural Anthropology: Matsutake Worlds." *American Ethnologist* 36, no. 2 (2009): 380–403. https://doi.org/10.1111/j.1548-1425.2009.01141.x.

Cohen, Lawrence. "Where It Hurts: Indian Material for an Ethics of Transplantation." *Daedalus* 128, no. 4 (1999): 135–65.

Colgrove, James. *State of Immunity: The Politics of Vaccination in Twentieth-Century America.* Berkeley: University of California Press, 2006.

Collins, Patricia Hill. "Black Women and Motherhood." In *Motherhood and Space: Configurations of the Maternal through Politics, Home, and the Body,* edited by Sarah Hardy and Caroline Wiedmer, 149–59. New York: Palgrave Macmillan, 2005.

Collins, Patricia Hill. "It's All in the Family: Intersections of Gender, Race, and Nation." *Hypatia* 13, no. 3 (1998): 62–82.

Cooper, Melinda. *Family Values: Between Neoliberalism and the New Social Conservatism.* Cambridge, Mass.: MIT Press, 2017.

Cornago, Georgina. "The Life—and Death—of Giovanni Ciprioano (Age 14): As Told by His Mother, Georgina Cornago." Food Allergy and Anaphylaxis Connection Team, Food Allergy Awareness. Accessed December 5, 2014. http://www.foodallergyawareness.org/about/in_memory_of_giovanni_cipriano-8/.

Couzin-Frankel, Jennifer. "First Peanut Allergy Treatment Gains Backing from FDA Advisory Panel." *Science Magazine,* September 13, 2019. https://www.sciencemag.org/news/2019/09/first-peanut-allergy-treatment-gains-backing-fda-advisory-panel.

Cowan, Ruth Schwartz. "The 'Industrial Revolution' in the Home: Household Technology and Social Change in the 20th Century." *Technology and Culture* 17, no. 1 (1976): 1–23.

Cowan, Ruth Schwartz. *More Work for Mother: The Ironies of Household Technology from the Open Hearth to the Microwave.* New York: Basic, 1983.

Crenshaw, Kimberlé. "Demarginalizing the Intersection of Race and Sex: A Black Feminist Critique of Antidiscrimination Doctrine, Feminist Theory and Antiracist Politics." *University of Chicago Legal Forum* 1989, no. 1 (1989): 139–67.

Cronon, William. "The Trouble with Wilderness; or, Getting Back to the Wrong Nature." In *Uncommon Ground: Rethinking the Human Place in Nature,* 69–90. New York: Norton, 1995.

Csordas, Thomas. "Embodiment as a Paradigm for Anthropology." *Ethos* 18, no. 1 (1990): 5–47. https://doi.org/10.1525/eth.1990.18.1.02a00010.

CSPAN. "EpiPen Price Increases." September 21, 2016. Video, 3:46:15. https://www.c-span.org/video/?415549-1/mylan-inc-ceo-heather-bresch-testifies-epipen-price-increases.

Das, Veena, and Renu Addlakha. "Disability and Domestic Citizenship: Voice, Gender, and the Making of the Subject." *Public Culture* 13, no. 3 (2001): 511–32. https://doi.org/10.1215/08992363-13-3-511.

Davis, Angela. *Women, Race, and Class.* New York: Vintage, 1981.

DeLuca, Kevin Michael, and Anne Teresa Demo. "Imaging Nature: Watkins, Yosemite, and the Birth of Environmentalism." *Critical Studies in Media Communication* 17, no. 3 (2000): 241–60. https://doi.org/10.1080/15295030009388395.

Diedrich, Lisa. *Indirect Action: Schizophrenia, Epilepsy, AIDS, and the Course of Health Activism.* Minneapolis: University of Minnesota Press, 2016.

Dietrich, Alexa S. *The Drug Company Next Door: Pollution, Jobs, and Community Health in Puerto Rico.* New York: New York University Press, 2013.

Douglas, P. N. "As If You Have a Choice: Autism Mothers and the Remaking of the Human." *Health, Culture and Society* 5, no. 1 (2013): 167–81. https://doi.org/10.5195/hcs.2013.137.

Dow, Dawn Marie. *Mothering while Black: Boundaries and Burdens of Middle-Class Parenthood.* Berkeley: University of California Press, 2019.

Du Toit, George, Graham Roberts, Peter H. Sayre, Henry T. Bahnson, Suzana Radulovic, Alexandra F. Santos, et al. "Randomized Trial of Peanut Consumption in Infants at Risk for Peanut Allergy." *New England Journal of Medicine* 372 (2015): 803–13. https://doi.org/10.1056/NEJMoa1414850.

Du Toit, George, Peter H. Sayre, Graham Roberts, Kaitie Lawson, Michelle L. Sever, Henry T. Bahnson, et al. "Allergen Specificity of Early Peanut Consumption and Effect on Development of Allergic Disease in the Learning Early about Peanut Allergy Study Cohort." *Journal of Allergy and Clinical Immunology* 141, no. 4 (2016): 1343–53. https://doi.org/10.1016/j.jaci.2017.09.034.

Dumit, Joseph. "A Digital Image of the Category of the Person: PET Scanning and Objective Self-Fashioning." In *Cyborgs and Citadels: Anthropological Interventions in Emerging Sciences and Technologies,* edited by Gary Lee Downey and Joseph Dumit, 83–102. Santa Fe, N.M.: School of American Research Press, 1997.

Dumit, Joseph. *Drugs for Life: How Pharmaceutical Companies Define Our Health.* Durham, N.C.: Duke University Press, 2012.

Dumit, Joseph. "Illnesses You Have to Fight to Get: Facts as Forces in Uncertain, Emergent Illnesses." *Social Science and Medicine* 62, no. 3 (2006): 577–90. https://doi.org/10.1016/j.socscimed.2005.06.018.

Dumit, Joseph. "Is It Me or My Brain? Depression and Neuroscientific Facts." *Journal of Medical Humanities* 24, no. 1/2 (2003): 35–47. https://doi.org/10.1023/A:1021353631347.

Engels, Friedrich. *The Origin of the Family, Private Property, and the State.* New York: Penguin Classics, 2010.

Epstein, Steven. "The Construction of Lay Expertise: AIDS Activism and the Forging of Credibility in the Reform of Clinical Trials." *Science, Technology, and Human Values* 20, no. 4 (1995): 408–37. https://doi.org/10.1177/016224399502000402.

Epstein, Steven. *Impure Science: AIDS, Activism, and the Politics of Knowledge.* Berkeley: University of California Press, 1996.

Farmer, Blake. "Covid Vaccine Trials Move at Warp Speed, but Recruiting

Black Volunteers Takes Time." KHN, September 16, 2020. https://khn.org/news/covid-vaccine-trials-move-at-warp-speed-but-recruiting-black-volunteers-takes-time/.

Federici, Silvia. *Caliban and the Witch: Women, the Body and Primitive Accumulation*. Brooklyn, N.Y.: Autonomedia, 2004.

Federici, Silvia, and Arlen Austin. *The New York Wages for Housework Committee: History, Theory, Documents*. Brooklyn, N.Y.: Autonomedia, 2018.

Firestone, Shulamith. *The Dialectic of Sex: The Case for Feminist Revolution*. New York: Bantam, 1970.

Fisher, Jill A. *Adverse Events: Race, Inequality, and the Testing of New Pharmaceuticals*. New York: New York University Press, 2020.

Fleischer, David M., Matthew Greenhawt, Gordon Sussman, Philippe Bégin, Anna Nowak-Wegrzyn, Daniel Petroni, et al. "Effect of Epicutaneous Immunotherapy vs. Placebo on Reaction to Peanut Protein Ingestion among Children with Peanut Allergy: The PEPITES Randomized Clinical Trial." *JAMA* 321, no. 10 (2019): 946–55. https://doi.org/10.1001/jama.2019.1113.

Fleischer, David M., Jonathan M. Spergel, Amal H. Assa'ad, and Jacqueline A. Pongracic. "Primary Prevention of Allergic Disease through Nutritional Interventions." *Journal of Allergy and Clinical Immunology: In Practice* 1, no. 1 (2013): 29–36. https://doi.org/10.1016/j.jaip.2012.09.003.

Fortun, Kim. *Advocacy after Bhopal: Environmentalism, Disaster, New Global Orders*. Chicago: University of Chicago Press, 2001.

Fortun, Michael. "Mediated Speculations in the Genomics Futures Markets." *New Genetics and Society* 20, no. 2 (2001): 139–56. https://doi.org/10.1080/14636770120070240.

Francoeur, Laurel. "Food Allergy School Health Plans: 504 vs. IHCP (Video and Resources)." Kids with Food Allergies Webinars, 2014. http://community.kidswithfoodallergies.org/blog/food-allergy-school-health-plans-504-vs-ihcp-video-and-resources.

Fraser, Heather. *The Peanut Allergy Epidemic: What's Causing It and How to Stop It*. New York: Sky Horse, 2011.

Garland-Thomson, Rosemarie. "Feminist Disability Studies." *Signs* 30, no. 2 (2005): 1557–87.

Garland-Thomson, Rosemarie. "Integrating Disability, Transforming Feminist Theory." *National Women's Studies Association Journal* 14, no. 3 (2002): 1–32. https://doi.org/10.2979/NWS.2002.14.3.1.

Geurts, Kathryn Linn. *Culture and the Senses: Bodily Ways of Knowing in an African Community*. Berkeley: University of California Press, 2002.

Ginsburg, Faye, and Rayna Rapp. "Disability Worlds." *Annual Review of*

Anthropology 42, no. 1 (2013): 53–68. https://doi.org/10.1146/annurev-anthro-092412-155502.

Glabau, Danya. "Covid-19 and the Politics of Care." Items: Insights from the Social Sciences, SSRC.org, 2021. https://items.ssrc.org/covid-19-and-the-social-sciences/disaster-studies/covid-19-and-the-politics-of-care/.

Glabau, Danya. "Morality in Action: Risking Death and Caring for Life in American Food Allergy Worlds." PhD diss., Cornell University, 2016.

Goffman, Erving. *Asylums: Essays on the Social Situation of Mental Patients and Other Inmates.* New York: Anchor, 1961.

Gonzalez, Baldemar. "When Tort Falls Short: Crisis, Malpractice Liability, and Women's Healthcare Access." *Columbia Law Review* 119, no. 4 (2019): 1099–132.

Greene, Jeremy A. "Attention to 'Details': Etiquette and the Pharmaceutical Salesman in Postwar American." *Social Studies of Science* 34, no. 2 (2004): 271–92. https://doi.org/10.1177/0306312704043029.

Greenhawt, Matthew, Christopher Weiss, Marisa L. Conte, Marlie Doucet, Amy Engler, and Carlos A. Camargo. "Racial and Ethnic Disparity in Food Allergy in the United States: A Systematic Review." *Journal of Allergy and Clinical Immunology: In Practice* 1, no. 2 (2013): 378–86. https://doi.org/10.1016/j.jaip.2013.04.009.

Greer, Frank R., Scott H. Sicherer, and A. Wesley Burks. "Effects of Early Nutritional Interventions on the Development of Atopic Disease in Infants and Children: The Role of Maternal Dietary Restriction, Breastfeeding, Timing of Introduction of Complementary Foods, and Hydrolyzed Formulas." *Pediatrics* 121, no. 1 (2008): 183–91. https://doi.org/10.1542/peds.2007-3022.

Gupta, Ruchi, David Holdford, Lucy Bilaver, Ashley Dyer, Jane L. Holl, and David Meltzer. "The Economic Impact of Childhood Food Allergy in the United States." *JAMA Pediatrics* 167, no. 11 (2013): 1026–31. https://doi.org/10.1001/jamapediatrics.2013.2376.

Gusterson, Hugh. "Nuclear Futures: Anticipatory Knowledge, Expert Judgment, and the Lack that Cannot Be Filled." *Science and Public Policy* 35, no. 8 (2008): 551–60. https://doi.org/10.3152/030234208X370639.

Hale, Victoria G., Katherine Woo, and Helene Levens Lipton. "Oxymoron No More: The Potential of Nonprofit Drug Companies to Deliver on the Promise of Medicines for the Developing World." *Health Affairs* 24, no. 4 (2005): 1057–63. https://doi.org/10.1377/hlthaff.24.4.1057.

Hamraie, Aimi. *Building Access: Universal Design and the Politics of Disability.* Minneapolis: University of Minnesota Press, 2017.

Haraway, Donna. "The Biological Enterprise: Sex, Mind, and Profit from Human Engineering to Sociobiology." In *Simians, Cyborgs, and Women: The Reinvention of Nature,* 43–68. New York: Routledge, 1991.

Haraway, Donna. "FemaleMan©_Meets_OncoMouse™. Mice into Wormholes: A Technoscience Fugue in Two Parts." In *Modest_Witness@Second_Millennium.FemaleMan©_Meets_OncoMouse™,* 49–118. New York: Routledge, 1997.

Haraway, Donna. "Situated Knowledges: The Science Question in Feminism and the Privilege of Partial Perspective." *Feminist Studies* 14, no. 3 (1988): 575–99. https://doi.org/10.2307/3178066.

Haraway, Donna. *Staying with the Trouble: Making Kin in the Chthulucene.* Durham, N.C.: Duke University Press, 2016.

Harding, Sandra. "Feminist Standpoint Epistemology." In *The Gender and Science Reader,* edited by Muriel Lederman and Ingrid Bartsch, 145–68. New York: Routledge, 2001.

Harrison, Marc. "The Not-for-Profit Civica Rx Will Disrupt the Generic Drug Industry." Stat News, March 14, 2019. https://www.statnews.com/2019/03/14/how-civica-rx-will-disrupt-generic-drug-industry/.

Hartigan, J. "Establishing the Fact of Whiteness." *American Anthropologist* 99, no. 3 (1997): 495–505. https://doi.org/10.1525/aa.1997.99.3.495.

Hartsock, Nancy C. M. "The Feminist Standpoint: Developing the Ground for a Specifically Feminist Historical Materialism." In *Discovering Reality,* edited by Sandra Harding and Merrill B. Hintikka, 283–310. Dordrecht: D. Reidel, 1983.

Healy, David. "Shaping the Intimate: Influences on the Experience of Everyday Nerves." *Social Studies of Science* 34, no. 2 (2004): 219–45. https://doi.org/10.1177/0306312704042620.

Hester, Helen. *Xenofeminism.* Medford, Mass.: Polity, 2018.

Hewett, Heather. "Food Allergies and the Good Enough Mother." *Allergic Living,* October 2014.

Hewett, Heather. "Talkin' 'bout a Revolution: Building a Mothers' Movement in the Third Wave." *Journal of the Association for Research on Mothering* 8 (2006): 34–54.

Hobart, Hi'ilei Julia Kawehipuaakahaopulani, and Tamara Kneese. "Radical Care: Survival Strategies for Uncertain Times." *Social Text* 38, no. 1 (2020): 1–16. https://doi.org/10.1215/01642472-7971067.

Hochschild, Arlie Russell. "The Commodity Frontier." In *The Commercialization of Intimate Life: Notes from Home and Work,* 30–44. Berkeley: University of California Press, 2003.

Hochschild, Arlie Russell. *The Managed Heart: Commercialization of Human Feeling*. 2nd ed. Berkeley: University of California Press, 2003.

Hochschild, Arlie Russell, and Anne Machung. *The Second Shift: Working Families and the Revolution at Home*. 3rd ed. New York: Penguin, 2012.

Holbreich, Mark, Jon Genuneit, Juliane Weber, Charlotte Braun-Fahrländer, Marco Waser, and Erika Von Mutius. "Amish Children Living in Northern Indiana Have a Very Low Prevalence of Allergic Sensitization." *Journal of Allergy and Clinical Immunology* 129, no. 6 (2012): 1671–73. https://doi.org/10.1016/j.jaci.2012.03.016.

hooks, bell. *Feminist Theory: From Margin to Center*. Boston, Mass.: South End Press, 1984.

Jackson, Kristen D., LaJeana D. Howie, and Lara J. Akinbami. "Trends in Allergic Conditions among Children: United States, 1997–2011." NCHS Data Brief No. 121. National Center for Health Statistics, May 2013. https://www.cdc.gov/nchs/data/databriefs/db121.pdf.

Jackson, Mark. *Allergy: The History of a Modern Malady*. London: Reaktion, 2006.

Jain, Sarah Lochlann. *Injury: The Politics of Product Design and Safety Law in the United States*. Princeton, N.J.: Princeton University Press, 2006.

Jain, Sarah Lochlann. "Living in Prognosis: Toward an Elegiac Politics." *Representations* 98 (2007): 77–92. https://doi.org/10.1525/rep.2007.98.1.77.

Jain, Sarah Lochlann. *Malignant: How Cancer Becomes Us*. Berkeley: University of California Press, 2013.

Jarrett, Valerie. "President Obama Signs New EpiPen Law to Protect Children with Asthma and Severe Allergies, and Help Their Families to Breathe Easier." White House Blog, November 13, 2013. https://www.whitehouse.gov/blog/2013/11/13/president-obama-signs-new-epipen-law-protect-children-asthma-and-severe-allergies-an.

Jasanoff, Sheila. "American Exceptionalism and the Political Acknowledgment of Risk." *Daedalus* 119, no. 4 (1990): 61–81.

Jasanoff, Sheila, and Sang-Hyun Kim. "Containing the Atom: Sociotechnical Imaginaries and Nuclear Power in the United States and South Korea." *Minerva* 47, no. 2 (2009): 119–46. https://doi.org/10.1007/s11024-009-9124-4.

Jerschow, Elina, Robert Y. Lin, Moira M. Scaperotti, and Aileen P. McGinn. "Fatal Anaphylaxis in the United States, 1999–2010: Temporal Patterns and Demographic Associations." *Journal of Allergy and Clinical Immunology* 134, no. 6 (2014): 1318–28.e7. https://doi.org/10.1016/j.jaci.2014.08.018.

Jones, Stacie M., A. Wesley Burks, and Christophe Dupont. "State of the Art on Food Allergen Immunotherapy: Oral, Sublingual, and Epicutaneous."

Journal of Allergy and Clinical Immunology 133, no. 2 (2014): 318–23. https://doi.org/10.1016/j.jaci.2013.12.1040.

Kaufman, Sharon. *Ordinary Medicine: Extraordinary Treatments, Longer Lives, and Where to Draw the Line*. Durham, N.C.: Duke University Press, 2015.

Kaufman, Sharon, and Laksmi Fjord. "Medicare, Ethics, and Reflexive Longevity: Governing Time and Treatment in an Aging Society." *Medical Anthropology Quarterly* 25, no. 2 (2011): 209–31.

Keirns, Carla C. "Better than Nature: The Changing Treatment of Asthma and Hay Fever in the United States, 1910–1945." *Studies in History and Philosophy of Science, Part C: Studies in History and Philosophy of Biological and Biomedical Sciences* 34, no. 3 (2003): 511–31. https://doi.org/10.1016/S1369-8486(03)00048-7.

Keller, Evelyn Fox. "The Gender/Science System, or Is Sex to Gender as Nature Is to Science?" *Hypatia* 2, no. 3 (1987): 37–49. https://doi.org/10.1111/j.1527-2001.1987.tb01340.x.

Kids with Food Allergies. "Breaking News: FDA Approves Palforzia, a Ground-Breaking Peanut Allergy Oral Immunotherapy Treatment." January 31, 2020. https://community.kidswithfoodallergies.org/blog/breaking-news-fda-approves-palforzia-a-ground-breaking-peanut-allergy-oral-immunotherapy-treatment.

Kimura, Aya Hirata. *Radiation Brain Moms and Citizen Scientists: The Gender Politics of Food Contamination after Fukushima*. Durham, N.C.: Duke University Press, 2016.

Kirkland, Anna. *Vaccine Court: The Law and Politics of Injury*. New York: New York University Press, 2016.

Klawiter, Maren. *The Biopolitics of Breast Cancer: Changing Cultures of Disease and Activism*. Minneapolis: University of Minnesota Press, 2008.

Klein, Naomi. *The Shock Doctrine: The Rise of Disaster Capitalism*. New York: Picador, 2007.

Kline, Ronald. "Ideology and Social Surveys: Reinterpreting the Effects of 'Laborsaving' Technology on American Farm Women." *Technology and Culture* 38, no. 2 (1997): 355–85.

Koons, Cynthia, Michael Keller, and Robert Langreth. "How EpiPen's Price Rose and Rose." Bloomberg Business, September 1, 2016. https://www.bloomberg.com/.

Koons, Cynthia, and Roberg Langreth. "How Marketing Turned the EpiPen into a Billion-Dollar Business." Bloomberg Business, September 23, 2015. http://www.bloomberg.com/news/articles/2015-09-23/how-marketing-turned-the-epipen-into-a-billion-dollar-business.

Kyriakides, Theodoros. "Tactics as Empirical and Conceptual Objects: Patient Activism and the Politics of Thalassaemia in Cyprus." *Engaging Science, Technology, and Society* 2 (2016): 14. https://doi.org/10.17351/ests2016.48.

Lack, Gideon, Deborah Fox, Kate Northstone, and Jean Golding. "Factors Associated with the Development of Peanut Allergy in Childhood." *New England Journal of Medicine* 348, no. 11 (2003): 977–85. https://doi.org/10.1056/NEJMp1415160.

Laidlaw, James. "Agency and Responsibility: Perhaps You Can Have Too Much of a Good Thing." In *Ordinary Ethics: Anthropology, Language, and Action*, edited by M. Lambek, 143–64. New York: Fordham University Press, 2010.

Laidlaw, James. *The Subject of Virtue: An Anthropology of Ethics and Freedom.* Cambridge: Cambridge University Press, 2014.

Lakoff, Andrew. "The Generic Biothreat, or How We Became Unprepared." *Cultural Anthropology* 23, no. 3 (2008): 399–428. https://doi.org/10.1111/j.1548-1360.2008.00013.x.

Landzelius, Kyra. "The Incubation of a Social Movement? Preterm Babies, Parent Activists, and Neonatal Productions in the U.S. Context." *Social Science and Medicine* 62, no. 3 (2006): 668–82. https://doi.org/10.1016/j.socscimed.2005.06.024.

Latour, Bruno. "Give Me a Laboratory and I Will Raise the World." In *Science Observed: Perspectives on the Social Study of Science*, edited by K. Knorr and M. Mulkay, 141–70. London: Sage, 1983.

Latour, Bruno. *We Have Never Been Modern.* Edited and translated by Catherine Porter. Cambridge, Mass.: Harvard University Press, 1993.

Latour, Bruno. "Why Has Critique Run Out of Steam? From Matters of Fact to Matters of Concern." *Critical Inquiry* 30 (2004): 225–49.

Latour, Bruno, and Steve Woolgar. *Laboratory Life: The Construction of Scientific Facts.* 2nd ed. Princeton, N.J.: Princeton University Press, 1986.

Laufer, Mixæl S. "Introducing the EpiPencil." Four Thieves Vinegar Collective, September 19, 2016. https://web.archive.org/web/20201108102513/https://fourthievesvinegar.org/blog/2016/09/introducing-the-epipencil.

Law, John. "On the Methods of Long-Distance Control: Vessel, Navigation and the Portuguese Route to India." In *Power, Action and Belief: A New Sociology of Knowledge?*, edited by John Law, 234–63. London: Routledge and Kegan Paul, 1986.

Leavitt, Judith Malzer. "'Typhoid Mary' Strikes Back: Bacteriological Theory and Practice in Early Twentieth-Century Public Health." *Isis* 83, no. 4 (1992): 608–29.

Lewis, Sophie. *Full Surrogacy Now: Feminism against Family.* New York: Verso, 2019.

Lipton, Eric, and Rachel Abrams. "EpiPen Maker Lobbies to Shift High Costs to Others." *New York Times*, September 16, 2016. https://www.nytimes.com/.

Livingston, Julie. *Debility and the Moral Imagination in Botswana: Disability, Chronic Illness, and Aging*. Bloomington: Indiana University Press, 2005.

Lock, Margaret. *Twice Dead: Organ Transplants and the Reinvention of Death*. Berkeley: University of California Press, 2002.

Longino, Helen. "Can There Be a Feminist Science?" In *Women, Knowledge, and Reality*, edited by Ann Garry and Marilyn Pearsall, 251–63. New York: Routledge, 1996.

Lovett, Laura L. *Conceiving the Future: Pronatalism, Reproduction, and the Family in the United States, 1890–1938*. Durham, N.C.: University of North Carolina Press, 2007.

Low, Setha. "Maintaining Whiteness: The Fear of Others and Niceness." *Transforming Anthropology* 17, no. 2 (2009): 79–92. https://doi.org/10.1111/j.1548-7466.2009.01047.x.79.

Mahajan, Manjari. "Designing Epidemics: Models, Policy-Making, and Global Foreknowledge in India's AIDS Epidemic." *Science and Public Policy* 35, no. 8 (2008): 585–96. https://doi.org/10.3152/030234208X377227.

Marcus, George E. "Ethnography in/of the World System: The Emergence of Multi-sited Ethnography." *Annual Review of Anthropology* 24 (1995): 95–117.

Martin, Emily. "Anthropology and the Cultural Study of Science." *Science, Technology, and Human Values* 23, no. 1 (1998): 24–44.

Martin, Emily. *Bipolar Expeditions: Mania and Depression in American Culture*. Princeton, N.J.: Princeton University Press, 2007.

Martin, Emily. "The End of the Body?" *American Ethnologist* 19, no. 1 (1992): 121–40.

Martin, Emily. *Flexible Bodies: Tracking Immunity in American Culture from the Days of Polio to the Age of AIDS*. New York: Beacon, 1994.

Marx, Karl, and Friedrich Engels. *The Marx–Engels Reader*. Edited by Robert C. Tucker. 2nd ed. New York: Norton, 1978.

Marx, Leo. *The Machine in the Garden: Technology and the Pastoral Ideal in America*. Oxford: Oxford University Press, 2000.

Masco, Joseph. "'Survival Is Your Business': Engineering Ruins and Affect in Nuclear America." *Cultural Anthropology* 23, no. 2 (2008): 361–98. https://doi.org/10.1111/j.1548-1360.2008.00012.x.

Mattingly, Cheryl. *Moral Laboratories: Family Peril and the Struggle for a Good Life*. Berkeley: University of California Press, 2014.

Mattingly, Cheryl. "The Moral Perils of a Superstrong Black Mother." *Ethos* 42, no. 1 (2014): 119–38. https://doi.org/10.1111/etho.12042.

Mauldin, Laura. *Made to Hear: Cochlear Implants and Raising Deaf Children.* Minneapolis: University of Minnesota Press, 2016.

Mauss, Marcel. "Techniques of the Body." *Economy and Society* 2, no. 1 (1973): 70–88. https://doi.org/10.1080/03085147300000003.

Merchant, Carolyn. "The Scientific Revolution and the Death of Nature." *Isis* 97 (2006): 513–33. https://doi.org/10.1086/508090.

Metzl, Jonathan M. "'Mother's Little Helper': The Crisis of Psychoanalysis and the Miltown Resolution." *Gender and History* 15, no. 2 (2003): 240–67. https://doi.org/10.1111/1468-0424.00300.

Miles, Robert. *Gothic Writing, 1750–1820: A Genealogy.* New York: Routledge, 1992.

Mitman, Gregg. *Breathing Space: How Allergies Shape Our Lives and Landscapes.* Princeton, N.J.: Princeton University Press, 2007.

Mitman, Gregg. "Geographies of Hope: Mining the Frontiers of Health in Denver and Beyond, 1870–1965." *Osiris* 19 (2004): 93–111.

Moassessi, Caroline. "Affordable EpiPens! Really." Grateful Foodie (blog), February 21, 2013. https://www.gratefulfoodie.com/affordable-epi-pens -really/.

Moassessi, Caroline. "Auvi-Q Goes Zero Co-pay Too." Grateful Foodie (blog), July 26, 2013. https://www.gratefulfoodie.com/auvi-q-goes-zero-co-pay-too/.

Moassessi, Caroline. "Best Prices for EpiPen and Auvi-Q." Grateful Foodie (blog), June 19, 2015. https://www.gratefulfoodie.com/best-prices-for -epipen-and-auvi-q/.

Moassessi, Caroline. "Wahoooo! EpiPen $0 Co-pay Extended!" Grateful Foodie (blog), January 5, 2015. https://www.gratefulfoodie.com/ wahoooo-epipen-0-co-pay-extended/.

Mol, Annemarie. *The Body Multiple: Ontology in Medical Practice.* Durham, N.C.: Duke University Press, 2002.

Mol, Annemarie. *The Logic of Care: Health and the Problem of Patient Choice.* New York: Routledge, 2008.

Morgenson, Gretchen. "EpiPen Price Rises Could Mean More Riches for Mylan Executives." *New York Times,* September 4, 2016. https://www.nytimes .com/.

Murphy, Michelle. "Immodest Witnessing: The Epistemology of Vaginal Self-Examination in the U.S. Feminist Self-Help Movement." *Feminist Studies* 30, no. 1 (2004): 115–47.

Murphy, Michelle. *Seizing the Means of Reproduction: Entanglements of Feminism, Health, and Technoscience.* Durham, N.C.: Duke University Press, 2012.

Murphy, Michelle. *Sick Building Syndrome and the Problem of Uncertainty: Envi-*

ronmental Politics, Technoscience, and Women Workers. Durham, N.C.: Duke University Press, 2006.

Nakamura, Lisa. *Cybertypes: Race, Ethnicity, and Identity on the Internet.* New York: Routledge, 2002.

Narisety, Satya D., and Corinne A. Keet. "Sublingual vs. Oral Immunotherapy for Food Allergy: Identifying the Right Approach." *Drugs* 72, no. 15 (2012): 1977–89. https://doi.org/10.2165/11640800-000000000-00000.

Ne'eman, Ari. "The Future (and the Past) of Autism Advocacy, or Why the ASA's Magazine, *The Advocate*, Wouldn't Publish This Piece." *Disability Studies Quarterly* 30, no. 1 (2010). https://doi.org/10.18061/dsq.v30i1.1059.

Nelkin, Dorothy, and M. Susan Lindee. *The DNA Mystique: The Gene as a Cultural Icon.* Ann Arbor: University of Michigan Press, 2004.

Nelson, Henry Harold S., Jenny Lahr, R. Rule, Allan Bock, and Donald Y. M. Leung. "Treatment of Anaphylactic Sensitivity to Peanuts by Immunotherapy with Injections of Aqueous Peanut Extract." *Journal of Allergy and Clinical Immunology* 99, no. 6, pt. 1 (1997): 744–51. https://doi.org/10.1016/s0091-6749(97)80006-1.

Nettleton, Sarah, Brian Woods, Roger Burrows, and Anne Kerr. "Experiencing Food Allergy and Food Intolerance: An Analysis of Lay Accounts." *Sociology* 44, no. 2 (2010): 289–305. https://doi.org/10.1177/0038038509357208.

Nettleton, Sarah, Brian Woods, Roger Burrows, and Anne Kerr. "Food Allergy and Food Intolerance: Towards a Sociological Agenda." *Health (London)* 13, no. 6 (2009): 647–64. https://doi.org/10.1177/1363459308341433.

Nguyen, Vinh Kim. "Antiretroviral Globalism, Biopolitics, and Therapeutic Citizenship." In *Global Assemblages: Technology, Politics, and Ethics as Anthropological Problems*, 124–44. London: Blackwell, 2007. https://doi.org/10.1002/9780470696569.ch8.

Noon, L., B. C. Cantab, and F. R. C. S. Eng. "Prophylactic Inoculation against Hay Fever." *Lancet* 177, no. 4580 (1911): 1572–73. https://doi.org/10.1016/S0140-6736(00)78276-6.

Nye, D. *American Technological Sublime.* Cambridge, Mass.: MIT Press, 1994.

O'Brien, Maeve. "Gendered Capital: Emotional Capital and Mothers' Care Work in Education." *British Journal of Sociology of Education* 29, no. 2 (2008): 137–48. https://doi.org/10.1080/01425690701837505.

O'Brien, Robyn. "Science for Sale: The Funding behind the Latest Study on Peanut Allergy." Robyn O'Brien (blog), March 9, 2015. https://robynobrien.com/science-for-sale-the-funding-behind-the-latest-study-on-peanut-allergy/.

O'Brien, Robyn. *The Unhealthy Truth: One Mother's Shocking Investigation into the*

Dangers of America's Food Supply—And What Every Family Can Do to Protect It-self. New York: Broadway, 2009.

Oldani, Michael J. "Thick Prescriptions: Toward an Interpretation of Pharmaceutical Sales Practices." *Medical Anthropology Quarterly* 18, no. 3 (2004): 325–56.

Oppenheimer, John J., Harold S. Nelson, S. Allan Bock, Fran Christensen, and Donald Y. M. Leung. "Treatment of Peanut Allergy with Rush Immunotherapy." *Journal of Allergy and Clinical Immunology* 90, no. 2 (1992): 256–62. https://doi.org/10.1016/0091-6749(92)90080-l.

Panofsky, Aaron. "Generating Sociability to Drive Science: Patient Advocacy Organizations and Genetics Research." *Social Studies of Science* 41, no. 1 (2011): 31–57. https://doi.org/10.1177/0306312710385852.

Parker-Pope, Tara. "How Parents Harnessed the Power of Social Media to Challenge EpiPen Prices." *New York Times*, August 25, 2016. https://www.nytimes.com/.

Parker-Pope, Tara, and Rachel Rabkin Peachman. "EpiPen Price Rise Sparks Concern for Allergy Sufferers." *New York Times*, August 27, 2016. https://www.nytimes.com/.

Parr, Joy. "Modern Kitchen, Good Home, Strong Nation." *Technology and Culture* 43, no. 4 (2002): 657–67.

Peeples, Jennifer. "Toxic Sublime: Imaging Contaminated Landscapes." *Environmental Communication* 5, no. 4 (2011): 373–92. https://doi.org/10.1080/17524032.2011.616516.

Perry, Tamara T., Mary Kay Conover-Walker, Anna Pomes, Martin D. Chapman, and Robert A. Wood. "Distribution of Peanut Allergen in the Environment." *Journal of Allergy and Clinical Immunology* 113, no. 5 (2004): 973–76. https://doi.org/10.1016/j.jaci.2004.02.035.

Petryna, Adriana. "Biological Citizenship: The Science and Politics of Chernobyl-Exposed Populations." *Osiris* 19 (2004): 250–65.

Petryna, Adriana. "Ethical Variability: Drug Development and Globalizing Clinical Trials." *American Ethnologist* 66, no. 19 (2005): 184–97. https://doi.org/10.1525/ae.2005.32.2.183.

Petryna, Adriana. *Life Exposed: Biological Citizenship after Chernobyl.* Princeton, N.J.: Princeton University Press, 2002.

Petryna, Adriana. *When Experiments Travel: Clinical Trials and the Global Search for Human Subjects.* Princeton, N.J.: Princeton University Press, 2009.

Piepzna-Samarasinha, Leah Lakshmi. *Care Work: Dreaming Disability Justice.* Vancouver: Arsenal Pulp Press, 2018.

Platt, Harold L. "'Clever Microbes': Bacteriology and Sanitary Technology in Manchester and Chicago during the Progressive Age." *Osiris* 19 (2004): 149–66.

Pollack, Andrew. "Drug Goes from $13.50 a Tablet to $750, Overnight." *New York Times*, September 20, 2015. https://www.nytimes.com/.

Powell, Lisa Jordan, and Elizabeth S. D. Engelhardt. "The Perilous Whiteness of Pumpkins." *GeoHumanities* 1, no. 2 (2015): 414–32. https://doi.org/10.108 0/2373566x.2015.1099421.

Rabeharisoa, Vololona. "From Representation to Mediation: The Shaping of Collective Mobilization on Muscular Dystrophy in France." *Social Science and Medicine* 62, no. 3 (2006): 564–76. https://doi.org/10.1016/j.soc scimed.2005.06.036.

Rabeharisoa, Vololona, and Michel Callon. "The Involvement of Patients' Associations in Research." *International Social Science Journal* 54, no. 171 (2002): 57–63. https://doi.org/10.1111/1468-2451.00359.

Rabeharisoa, Vololona, Tiago Moreira, and Madeleine Akrich. "Evidence-Based Activism: Patients', Users' and Activists' Groups in Knowledge Society." *BioSocieties* 9, no. 2 (2014): 111–28. https://doi.org/10.1057/biosoc .2014.2.

Rabinow, Paul. "Artificiality and Enlightenment: From Sociobiology to Biosociality." In *Incorporations*, edited by Crary and Kwinter, 234–53. New York: Zone, 1992.

Raffaetà, Roberta. "Allergy Narratives in Italy: 'Naturalness' in the Social Construction of Medical Pluralism." *Medical Anthropology* 32, no. 2 (2013): 126–44. https://doi.org/10.1080/01459740.2012.732632.

Raffaetà, Roberta. "Conflicting Sensory Relationships: Encounters with Allergic People." *Anthropology and Medicine* 19, no. 3 (2012): 339–50. https:// doi.org/10.1080/13648470.2012.692359.

Rapp, Rayna. "Gender, Body, Biomedicine: How Some Feminist Concerns Dragged Reproduction to the Center of Social Theory." *Medical Anthropology Quarterly* 15, no. 4 (2001): 466–77.

Rapp, Rayna. *Testing the Woman, Testing the Fetus: The Social Impact of Amniocentesis in America*. New York: Routledge, 1999.

Reardon, Jenny, and Kim TallBear. "'Your DNA Is Our History': Genomics, Anthropology, and the Construction of Whiteness as Property." *Current Anthropology* 53, suppl. 5 (2012): S233–45. https://doi.org/10.1086/662629.

Reich, Jennifer A. *Calling the Shots: Why Parents Reject Vaccines*. New York: New York University Press, 2016.

Roberts, Dorothy. "Abolishing Policing Also Means Abolishing Family Regulation." *The Imprint*, June 16, 2020. https://imprintnews.org/child-wel fare-2/abolishing-policing-also-means-abolishing-family-regulation/ 44480.

Roberts, Dorothy. *Killing the Black Body: Race, Reproduction, and the Meaning of Liberty*. New York: Vintage, 1998.

Roberts, Dorothy. *Shattered Bonds: The Color of Child Welfare*. New York: Basic Civitas, 2002.

Robinson, Kim Stanley. *2312*. New York: Hachette, 2013.

Rosenblatt, Adam. "Autism, Advocacy Organizations, and Past Injustice." *Disability Studies Quarterly* 38, no. 4 (2018). https://doi.org/10.18061/dsq .v38i4.6222.

Rutter, Lisa. "Remembering Those We Have Lost to Food Allergies." Not Nuts Moms Group (blog), September 11, 2021. http://nonutsmomsgroup .weebly.com/blog/remembering-those-we-have-lost-to-food-allergies.

Ryan, Sara, and Katherine Runswick-Cole. "Repositioning Mothers: Mothers, Disabled Children and Disability Studies." *Disability and Society* 23, no. 3 (2008): 199–210. https://doi.org/10.1080/09687590801953937.

Sampson, Hugh A., Wence Agbotounou, Claude Thebault, Charles Ruban, Laurent Martin, William H. Yang, et al. "Epicutaneous Immunotherapy (EPIT) Is Effective and Safe to Treat Peanut Allergy: A Multi-national Double-Blind Placebo Controlled Randomized Phase IIb Trial." *Journal of Allergy and Clinical Immunology* 135, no. 2, suppl. S (2015): 201.

Scheper-Hughes, Nancy, and Margaret Lock. "The Mindful Body: A Prolegomenon to Future Work in Medical Anthropology." *Medical Anthropology Quarterly* 1, no. 1 (1987): 6–41. https://doi.org/10.1525/maq.1987.1.1.02a00020.

Schiebinger, Londa. *Nature's Body: Gender in the Making of Modern Science*. Boston: Beacon, 1993.

Schwartz, Maire Jenkins. *Birthing a Slave: Motherhood and Medicine in the Antebellum South*. Cambridge, Mass.: Harvard University Press, 2006.

Scott, Joan W. "The Evidence of Experience." *Critical Inquiry* 17, no. 4 (1991): 773–97.

Senti, Gabriela, Andreas U. Freiburghaus, and Thomas M. Kundig. "Epicutaneous/Transcutaneous Allergen-Specific Immunotherapy: Rationale and Clinical Trials." *Current Opinion in Allergy and Clinical Immunology* 2010, no. 6 (2010): 582–86. https://doi.org/10.1097/ACI.0b013e32833f1419.

Shakespeare, Tom. "Disability, Identity and Difference." In *Exploring the Divide: Illness and Disability*, edited by Colin Barnes and Geof Mercer, 94–113. Leeds: Disability Press, 1996.

Shakespeare, Tom, and Nicholas Watson. "Defending the Social Model."

Disability and Society 12, no. 2 (1997): 293–300. https://doi.org/10.1080 /09687599727380.

Shange, Savannah. *Progressive Dystopia: Abolition, Antiblackness, and Schooling in San Francisco*. Durham, N.C.: Duke University Press, 2019.

Shapin, Steven, and Simon Schaffer. *Leviathan and the Air-Pump: Hobbes, Boyle, and the Experimental Life*. Princeton, N.J.: Princeton University Press, 1985.

Shever, Elana. "Engendering the Company: Corporate Personhood and the 'Face' of an Oil Company in Metropolitan Buenos Aires." *Political and Legal Anthropology Review* 33, no. 1 (2010): 26–46. https://doi.org/10.1111/j.1555 -2934.2010.01091.x.May.

Shotwell, Alexis. *Against Purity: Living Ethically in Compromised Times*. Minneapolis: University of Minnesota Press, 2016.

Sicherer, Scott H., and Hugh A. Sampson. "Food Allergy." *Journal of Allergy and Clinical Immunology* 125, no. 2, suppl. 2 (2010): S116–25. https://doi .org/10.1016/j.jaci.2009.08.028.

Simons, F. Estelle R., Ledit R. F. Ardusso, M. Beatrice Bilò, Victoria Cardona, Motohiro Ebisawa, Yehia M. El-Gamal, et al. "International Consensus on (ICON) Anaphylaxis." *World Allergy Organization Journal* 7, no. 1 (2014): 9. http://dx.doi.org/10.1186/1939-4551-7-9.

Simons, F. Estelle R., Ledit R. F. Ardusso, Vesselin Dimov, Motohiro Ebisawa, Yehia M. El-Gamal, Richard F. Lockey, et al. "World Allergy Organization Anaphylaxis Guidelines: 2013 Update of the Evidence Base." *International Archives of Allergy and Immunology* 162 (2013): 193–204. http://dx.doi .org/10.1159/000354543.

Sismondo, Sergio. "The Scientific Domains of Feminist Standpoints." *Perspectives on Science* 3 (1995): 49–65.

Slayton, Rebecca, and Aaron Clark-Ginsberg. "Beyond Regulatory Capture: Coproducing Expertise for Critical Infrastructure Protection." *Regulation and Governance* 12, no. 1 (2018): 115–30. https://doi.org/10.1111/rego.12168.

Smith, Gwen. "FDA Approves Aimmune's Palforzia OIT, Coming Soon to Allergist Clinics." *Allergic Living*, January 31, 2020. https://www.allergic living.com/2020/01/31/fda-approves-aimmunes-palforzia-oit-coming -soon-to-allergists-clinics/.

Smith, Matthew. *Another Person's Poison: A History of Food Allergy*. New York: Columbia University Press, 2015.

Solomon, Deborah. "Obama Signs Bill to Increase EpiPen Availability in Schools." *Wall Street Journal Blog*, November 13, 2013. https://blogs.wsj .com/washwire/2013/11/13/obama-signs-bill-to-increase-epipen-avail ability-in-schools/.

Sorva, Ritva, and Soili Mikinen-Kiljunen. "Immunodeficiency and Other Clinical Immunology Secretion in Human Milk Varies Widely after Cow's Milk Ingestion in Mothers of Infants with Cow's Milk Allergy." *Journal of Allergy and Clinical Immunology* 93 (1994): 787–92.

Spohr, Heather. "No Sandwich Is More Important than a Child's Life." Huffington Post, September 16, 2015; updated September 16, 2016. https://www.huffpost.com/.

Stein, Michelle M., Cara L. Hrusch, Justyna Gozdz, Catherine Igartua, Vadim Pivniouk, Sean E. Murray, et al. "Innate Immunity and Asthma Risk in Amish and Hutterite Farm Children." *New England Journal of Medicine* 375, no. 5 (2016): 411–21. https://doi.org/10.1056/NEJMoa1508749.

Stevenson, Jennifer L., Bev Harp, and Morton Ann Gernsbacher. "Infantilizing Autism." *Disability Studies Quarterly* 31, no. 3 (2011): 1–17. https://doi.org/10.18061/dsq.v31i3.1675.

Stormer, Nathan. "Addressing the Sublime: Space, Mass Representation, and the Unpresentable." *Critical Studies in Media Communication* 21, no. 3 (2004): 212–40. https://doi.org/10.1080/0739318042000212707.

Strachan, David P. "Family Size, Infection, and Atopy: The First Decade of the 'Hygiene Hypothesis.'" *Thorax* 55, suppl. 1 (2000): S2–10.

Strachan, David P. "Hay Fever, Hygiene, and Household Size." *British Medical Journal* 299 (1989): 1259–60.

Strathern, Marilyn. *Partial Connections*. 2nd ed. Walnut Creek, Calif.: AltaMira, 2004.

Sunder Rajan, Kaushik. *Biocapital: The Constitution of Postgenomic Life*. Durham, N.C.: Duke University Press, 2006.

TallBear, Kim, and Angela Willey. "Introduction: Critical Relationality: Queer, Indigenous, and Multispecies Belonging beyond Settler Sex and Nature." *Imaginations* 10, no. 1 (2019): 4–15. https://doi.org/10.17742/image.cr.10.1.1.

Thomas, Katie. "Clinical Trials of Coronavirus Drugs Are Taking Longer than Expected." *New York Times*, August 14, 2020. https://www.nytimes.com/.

Timmermans, Stefan. *Sudden Death and the Myth of CPR*. Philadelphia: Temple University Press, 1999.

Tomes, Nancy. *The Gospel of Germs: Men, Women, and the Microbe in American Life*. Cambridge, Mass.: Harvard University Press, 1998.

Tomes, Nancy. "The Making of a Germ Panic, Then and Now." *American Journal of Public Health* 90, no. 2 (2000): 191–98.

Trnka, Susanna, and Catherine Trundle. "Competing Responsibilities: Moving beyond Neoliberal Responsibilisation." *Anthropological Forum* 24, no. 2 (2014): 136–53. https://doi.org/10.1080/00664677.2013.879051.

U.S. Food and Drug Administration. "January 31, 2020 Approval Letter—PALFORZIA." Biologics license application approval. https://fda.report/media/134857/January+31-2020-Approval-Letter-+PALFORZIA.pdf/.

Vadas, Peter, Yvonne Wai, Wesley Burks, and Boris Perelman. "Detection of Peanut Allergens in Breast Milk and Saliva." *JAMA* 285, no. 13 (2001): 1746–48.

Valenčius, Conevery Bolton. *The Health of the Country: How American Settlers Understood Themselves and Their Land*. New York: Basic, 2002.

Van Evra, J. "Kitchens that Cook." *Allergic Living*, Fall 2014.

Waggoner, Miranda R. "Parsing the Peanut Panic: The Social Life of a Contested Food Allergy Epidemic." *Social Science and Medicine* 90 (2013): 49–55. https://doi.org/10.1016/j.socscimed.2013.04.031.

Welker, Marina A. "'Corporate Security Begins in the Community': Mining, the Corporate Social Responsibility Industry, and Environmental Advocacy in Indonesia." *Cultural Anthropology* 24, no. 1 (2009): 142–79. https://doi.org/10.1111/j.1548-1360.2009.00029.x.

Williamson, Bess. *Accessible America: A History of Disability and Design*. New York: New York University Press, 2019.

Wood, Robert A. "New Horizons in Allergen Immunotherapy." *JAMA* 315, no. 16 (2016): 1711–12. https://doi.org/10.1001/jama.2016.4078.

Woodrum, Homa. "All Auvi-Q Epinephrine Autoinjectors Recalled." Oh Mah Deehness! (blog), October 28, 2015. https://ohmahdeehness.wordpress.com/2015/10/28/102815-all-auvi-q-epinephrine-autoinjectors-recalled/ (locked).

Yancy, George. *Look, a White! Philosophical Essays on Whiteness*. Philadelphia: Temple University Press, 2012.

Zeiger, Robert S. "Food Allergen Avoidance in the Prevention of Food Allergy in Infants and Children." *Pediatrics* 111, no. 6 (2003): 1662–71.

Zigon, Jarrett, and C. Jason Throop. "Moral Experience: Introduction." *Ethos* 42, no. 1 (2014): 1–15. https://doi.org/10.1111/etho.12035.

INDEX

Danya Glabau is industry assistant professor and director of science and technology studies in the Department of Technology, Culture, and Society at NYU Tandon School of Engineering.